Essential Mathematics

David Rayner
David Allman
Laurence Campbell

Book 1i

Elmwood Press

First published 1998 by
Elmwood Press
80 Attimore Road
Welwyn Garden City
Herts. AL8 6LP
Tel. 01707 333232

British Library Cataloguing in Publication Data

Rayner, David

   1. Mathematics – 1961 –
   I. Title

ISBN 0 952 4438 64

Numerical answers are published in a separate book

Artwork by Emma Djonokusumo
          Francis Maynard
          Angela Lumley

Typeset and illustrated by Tech-Set, Gateshead, Tyne and Wear
Printed and bound in Great Britain by Redwood Books, Trowbridge, Wiltshire

PREFACE

Essential Mathematics Books *1i*, *2i* and *3i* are written for pupils in the 'middle' ability range for ages 11 to 14/15. Most classrooms contain children with a range of abilities in mathematics. These books are written to cater for this situation.

The authors believe that children learn mathematics most effectively by *doing* mathematics. Many youngsters who find mathematics difficult derive much more pleasure and enjoyment from the subject when they are doing questions which help them build up their confidence. Pupils feel a greater sense of satisfaction when they work in a systematic way and when they can appreciate the purpose and the power of the mathematics they are studying.

The authors, who are all experienced teachers, emphasise a thorough grounding in the fundamentals of number when working in the lower secondary classroom. In particular the recommendations of the National centre for Numeracy lie behind the approach adopted to mental arithmetic and calculations performed without calculators.

There is no set path through the books and it is anticipated that most teachers will prefer to take sections in the order of their own choice. No text book will have the 'right' amount of material for every class and the authors believe that it is better to have too much material rather than too little. Consequently teachers should judge for themselves which sections or exercises can be studied later. On a practical note, the authors recommend the use of exercise books consisting of 7 mm squares.

Opportunities for work towards the 'Using and Applying Mathematics' attainment target appears throughout the book. Many activities, investigations, games and puzzles are included to provide a healthy variety of learning experiences. The authors are aware of the difficulties of teaching on 'Friday afternoons' or on the last few days of term, when both pupils and teachers are tired, and suitable activities are included.

The authors are indebted to the many students and colleagues who have assisted them in this work. They are particularly grateful to Vicky Campbell, Jacqui Allman and Micheline Rayner for their advice and encouragement.

David Rayner
David Allman
Laurence Campbell

CONTENTS

Part 1

1.1 Place value

- Whole numbers are made up from units, tens, hundreds, thousands and so on. The value of a figure depends on the position it occupies in the number.

thousands	hundreds	tens	units
5	3	8	7

- In the number 5387:

> the digit 5 means 5 thousands
> the digit 3 means 3 hundreds
> the digit 8 means 8 tens
> the digit 7 means 7 units (ones)

In words we write 'five thousand, three hundred and eighty-seven'.

- Each of the figures that make up a number is called a *digit*
  The number 2 is a single digit number.
  The number 792 is a three digit number.

Exercise 1   [Oral]

State the value of the figure underlined.

1. 3<u>5</u>	**2.** 1<u>2</u>6	**3.** <u>1</u>04	**4.** <u>9</u>7	**5.** <u>6</u>9
6. 347<u>8</u>	**7.** <u>1</u>28	**8.** 4<u>6</u>3	**9.** <u>2</u>116	**10.** <u>3</u>00
11. 2<u>1</u>6	**12.** 74<u>3</u>11	**13.** <u>8</u>5 109	**14.** 29<u>3</u>	**15.** 4<u>1</u>2 405
16. <u>3</u>5 714	**17.** <u>6</u> 500 000	**18.** <u>4</u>09	**19.** <u>9</u> 491 111	**20.** 6 <u>5</u>10 123

Exercise 2

In Questions **1** to **10** write down the number which goes in each box.

1. $375 = \square + 70 + 5$

2. $418 = 400 + \square + 8$

3. $562 = \square + 60 + 2$

4. $4329 = 4000 + \square + 20 + 9$

5. $37\,413 = \square + 7000 + 400 + 10 + 3$

6. $48\,607 = 40\,000 + \square + 600 + 7$

7. $5117 = 5000 + 100 + \square + 7$

8. $65\,409 = \square + 5000 + 400 + 9$

9. $207\,425 = 200\,000 + 7000 + 400 + 20 + \square$

10. $99\,999 = \square + 9000 + 900 + 90 + 9$

In Questions **11** to **28** write the numbers in figures.

11. Eight hundred and ten.
12. One thousand two hundred and sixty-four.
13. One thousand five hundred.
14. Two thousand six hundred and ten.
15. Three thousand and twenty.
16. Four thousand and six.
17. Six thousand and fifty-eight.
18. Seven thousand and eighty-nine.
19. Eight thousand five hundred and twenty-six.
20. Nine thousand and ninety-nine.
21. Ten thousand, four hundred and eighty.
22. One hundred and one thousand, three hundred and sixteen.
23. One million and seventeen.
24. One million, six hundred thousand, one hundred and seventy-four.
25. Sixteen million, two thousand and four.
26. Eight thousand million.
27. Three and a half million.
28. Seven and a half thousand.

When you write a cheque to pay for something you have to write the amount in figures *and* in words.

Here is a cheque to pay 'Grange Motors' for a car.

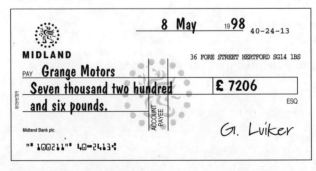

Exercise 3

1. Draw a picture of a cheque like the one shown. Pay yourself £10 304 and write the amount in figures and in words. Ask your teacher to sign the cheque! (But don't be too surprised if he/she declines.)

Write the following numbers in words

2. 101	**3.** 123	**4.** 150	**5.** 1200	**6.** 3270
7. 4031	**8.** 5009	**9.** 1356	**10.** 67300	**11.** 107 326
12. 970 001	**13.** 1 000 001	**14.** 180 000 000	**15.** 7 654 321	**16.** 900 019

17. Here are three number cards

One number that can be made with the three cards is 583.
(a) Use the three cards to make a number which is more than 583.
(b) Use the three cards to make a number which is less than 583.
(c) Use the three cards to make an even number.

18. Here are four number cards

(a) Use all the cards to make the largest possible number.
(b) Use all the cards to make the smallest possible number.

19. You are looking for a mystery number.
Use the clues to find it.

- the sum of the digits is 10
- the number reads the same forwards as backwards
- the number is less than 2000
- the number has no zeros
- the number has four digits

20. Here are three number cards

Make a list of all the different three figure numbers you can make.

21. Write down the number that is ten more than
(a) 3645   (b) 471   (c) 53 408   (d) 5005

22. Write down the number that is one hundred more than
    (a) 5341   (b) 8094   (c) 2941   (d) 6666

23. Write down the number that is one thousand *less* than
    (a) 56 985   (b) 2389   (c) 62 540   (d) 50 458

24. Write down the numbers in order, from the smallest to the largest

(a) 2010,	2645,	2045,	2654	
(b) 5124,	5099,	5322,	5119,	5085
(c) 63 414,	62 495,	63 411,	62 455,	63 407

And finally . . .

A taxi driver who spent six years writing out every number from one to a million in an attempt to win a place in the Guinness Book of records has been told he may have to start again.

The compilers have a rule that the numbers should be in words rather than digits!

1.2 Addition

- Method 1: Using 'carrying'

    (a) 54 + 281 + 3052   (b) 40514 + 24 + 3216
       line up the units digits

```
        54                    40514
       281                       24
     + 3052                  + 3216
      ─────                   ─────
      3387                    43754
        1                        1
```

- Method 2: Work from the left [i.e. Add the most significant digits first.]

(a)	374	(b)	432	(c)	5327	(d)	6529
	+ 27		+ 265		+ 824		+ 3782
	300		600		5000		9000
	90		90		1100		1200
	11		7		40		100
	401		697		11		11
					6151		10 311

Notes: A. In (c) 300 + 800 = 1100 and 7 + 4 = 11. Work 'in your head'.
       B. Many people prefer this method. Give it a try!

Exercise 1

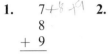

Copy and complete the following addition problems.

1. $7 + 8 + 9$ **2.** 17 **3.** 9 **4.** 47
   8    $+\ 14$ $+\ 13$ $+\ 34$
$+\ 9$

5.   6 **6.** 19 **7.** 67 **8.** 32
   38   27   44   49
$+\ 44$ $+\ 3$ $+\ 5$ $+\ 51$

9. 126 **10.** 48 **11.**   9 **12.** 28
$+\ 37$ $+\ 173$ 17   63
            $+\ 193$ $+\ 205$

13. 355 **14.** 573 **15.** 301 **16.** 114
$+\ 278$ $+\ 209$ 99   9
                $+\ 257$ $+\ 867$

17. 501 **18.** 634 **19.** 389 **20.** 371
   397   769   193   567
$+\ 124$ $+\ 127$ $+\ 624$ $+\ 462$

In Questions **21** to **40** set the problems out correctly in columns.

21. $3 + 12 + 109$ **22.** $27 + 260$ **23.** $584 + 617$
24. $39 + 357$ **25.** $3 + 109 + 61$ **26.** $5034 + 69$
27. $201 + 76 + 40$ **28.** $679 + 63 + 4$ **29.** $54 + 507 + 2704$
30. $2030 + 69 + 5$ **31.** $6006 + 708 + 99$ **32.** $842 + 67 + 2011$
33. $1089 + 891 + 19 + 9$ **34.** $5867 + 321 + 45 + 9$ **35.** $8647 + 198$
36. $873 + 2316 + 473$ **37.** $2644 + 55685$ **38.** $26\,514 + 749$
39. $45\,609 + 20\,047$ **40.** $67\,508 + 95\,607 + 436$

41. Find the missing digits.

$5\ \boxed{} + \boxed{}\ 4 = 78$

$4\ \boxed{} + \boxed{}\ 8 = 110$

$3\ \boxed{} + \boxed{}\ 5 = 82$

42. Write the numbers 1 to 9 in the circles so that each side of the square adds up to 12.

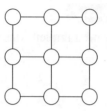

43. Here are three eggs. Arrange the numbers 1, 2, 3, ... 9 so that the numbers in each egg add up to 15.
Try to find different ways of doing it.

44. Choose 3 digits from 2, 3, 5, 7.   ☐☐ + ☐ = 32

Put them in the boxes to make a true statement.

Addition – Keywords

The following words are all associated with addition.

'Add'   Two *add* two?
'Plus'   Two *plus* two?
'Greater than'   What number is two *greater than* two?
'Count on'   *Count on* two from two, where are you?

'And'   What is two *and* two?
'Sum'   What is the *sum* of two and two?
'More than'   What is two *more than* two?
'Total'   What is the *total* of two and two?
'Altogether'   What is two and two *altogether*?

All these statements are saying ... $2 + 2 = 4$

2 GOOD
2 BE
‾‾‾‾‾‾‾‾
4 GOTTEN

What is the *sum of* nine hundred and eighty-one and one hundred and eighty-nine?

$$\begin{array}{r} 981 \\ + 189 \\ \hline 1170 \\ \hline \end{array}$$

The answer is ...

Exercise 2

Do these questions without a calculator.

1. Sixteen add twenty-seven.

2. What is the sum of forty-eight and ninety-seven?

3. What is seventy-five plus sixty-nine?

4. What number is sixty-six greater than fifty-nine?

5. What number is thirty-nine more than eighty-seven?

6. What is the total of one hundred and twenty-four and two hundred and seventy-eight?

7. If you count on thirty-seven from sixty-five, what number will you reach?

8. How much do seventy-seven and eighty-nine make altogether?

9. What is sixty-eight and forty-seven?

10. What is the sum of one hundred and sixty four and eight hundred and thirty seven?

11. Jack was playing cricket, he scored 124 in his first innings and 38 in his second innings. What was the total number of runs he scored?

12. There are 30 days in September, 31 in October, 30 in November and 31 in December. How many days altogether in these four months?

13. Kathy and Jenny were playing darts. Jenny scored 59. Kathy scored 28 more than Jenny. What did Kathy score?

14. Tina scored 55 marks in her maths test. Mary scored 18 more. What was Mary's mark in the test?

15. Eddie had 27 pence, Jim had 34 pence and Joe had 49 pence. How much money did they have altogether?

16. Add together 142 and 759.

17. Karen has three dogs. 'Amy' is aged 12, 'Jody' is 15 and 'Foxy' is 9. What is the total of their combined ages?

18. Roy has 148 conkers and Dave has 79. How many conkers do they have altogether?

19. Billy needs to add together 327 and 609. What answer should he get?

20. Find the sum of the three numbers: two and a half million, eighty-eight thousand and three and a half thousand.

Cross number puzzles 1

Copy the following cross number puzzles onto squared paper. Complete the puzzles.

1.

Clues across		Clues down	
1.	37 + 38	1.	57 + 15
3.	55 + 49	2.	20 + 27
5.	71 + 6	3.	24 + 86
6.	89 + 20	4.	29 + 11
7.	39 + 11	5.	33 + 46
8.	34 + 51	6.	49 + 62
9.	17 + 24	7.	17 + 38
10.	23 + 95	8.	12 + 68
12.	41 + 15	9.	15 + 31
13.	13 + 56	10.	27 + 88
15.	69 + 9	11.	53 + 33
17.	49 + 9	12.	16 + 42
18.	86 + 80	14.	20 + 71
19.	46 + 46	15.	65 + 11
		16.	15 + 17

2.

Clues across		Clues down	
1.	19 + 38	1.	163 + 419
3.	871 + 105	2.	36 + 34
5.	67 + 24	4.	257 + 387
6.	261 + 548	5.	822 + 92
7.	356 + 55	8.	518 + 67
8.	314 + 250	10.	746 + 201
9.	17 + 26	11.	354 + 579
12.	288 + 471	12.	703 + 66
14.	143 + 274	13.	899 + 79
16.	213 + 504	15.	162 + 567
17.	210 + 109		
18.	62 + 27		

Magic squares

Look at this numbered square ...

8	1	6
3	5	7
4	9	2

Add the numbers across in rows ←——→

$8 + 1 + 6 = 15$
$3 + 5 + 7 = 15$
$4 + 9 + 2 = 15$

Add the numbers in the columns ↕

$8 + 3 + 4 = 15$
$1 + 5 + 9 = 15$
$6 + 7 + 2 = 15$

Add the numbers diagonally ↘ ↗

$8 + 5 + 2 = 15$
$4 + 5 + 6 = 15$

All the answers are the same. In this case 15.

When a set of numbers is arranged to do this it is called a 'magic square'.

Here is another magic square ...

6	13	8
11	9	7
11	5	12

Exercise 3

Copy and complete the following magic squares

1.

4	3	
	5	
		6

2.

		3
	6	
9		4

3.

	10	8
	7	
	4	

4.

		11
5	12	7

5.

6		2
	5	
8		

6.

6	7	
13	8	
	9	

7.

	6	10	15
16		5	4
	12	8	
		11	

8.

9	14		
		16	7
12	3	15	8
6			

9.

11			10
2	13	16	
		4	
7	12		6

10.

10		7	13
5			
17		4	
6		11	9

11.

	13	10		24
23	17		19	
2	16	14	12	26
			11	7
4		18	25	8

12.

	22	1	20	19
24	8		16	
	21	13		
14	10		18	12
7	4		6	23

13. Try to make your own magic square using a 3 × 3 grid.

14. Try to make your own magic square using a 4 × 4 grid.

1.3 Two dimensional shapes

Lines and angles

- Lines that meet at a point . . .

    . . . or cross each other . . .

    . . . create angles.

- Lines which are at right angles are *perpendicular* to each other.

- Lines like these which never meet are called *parallel*. To show that lines are parallel we draw arrows.

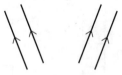

- A *horizontal* line is parallel to the horizon.

- A *vertical* line is perpendicular to the surface of the earth.

Look around the classroom. Where can you see parallel lines? Where can you see *perpendicular* lines?

Can you see anything which is *vertical*? Is there anything which is *horizontal*?

Builders sometimes use a plumb line or a spirit level.
What is a plumb line?
What is a spirit level?

For each of the letters of the word 'LINES' use the following 'key' to indicate ...

1. perpendicular lines $\longrightarrow$

2. parallel vertical lines $\longrightarrow$ V for vertical

3. parallel horizontal lines $\longrightarrow$ H for horizontal

4. angles $\longrightarrow$

... like this:-

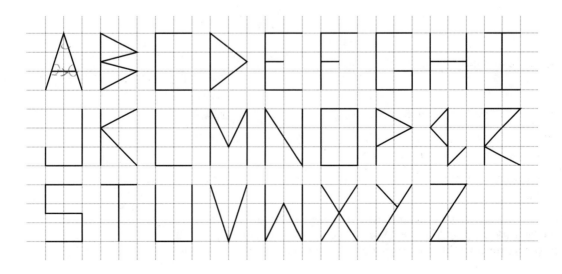

Exercise 1

Copy out the key given in the above example and the stencil of the alphabet below onto squared paper. Use the key to show on all the letters any:
(a) perpendicular lines (b) parallel vertical lines   (c) parallel horizontal lines   (d) angles.

Exercise 2

In Questions **1** to **3** write the sentence choosing the correct word.

1. 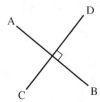 AB is (parallel/perpendicular) to CD.

2.   LM is (parallel/perpendicular) to MN.
ON is (parallel/perpendicular) to LM.
OL is (parallel/perpendicular) to MN.

3. CD is _____ to EF.

AB is _____ to CD.

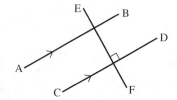

4. In the rectangle PQRS, RQ is perpendicular to SR.
(a) Which other line is perpendicular to PQ?
(b) Which line is parallel to PQ?

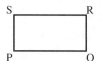

5. Find out which lines are perpendicular.

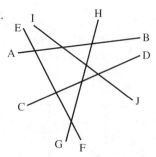

6. Can you see any parallel lines in the diagram?

7. Copy the diagram on the right.
(a) Draw a line through C which is perpendicular to AB
(b) Draw a line through D which is parallel to AB
(c) Draw a line through D which is perpendicular to the line AB.

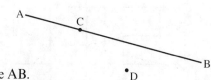

8.

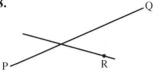

Copy the diagram on the left.
(a) Draw a line through R which is parallel to PQ.
(b) Draw a line through R which is perpendicular to PQ.

9.* Answer true or false (Think carefully).
(a) Two vertical lines are always parallel.
(b) Two horizontal lines are always parallel.

Triangles

- A plane figure with three sides and angles is a triangle.

- A triangle with three different sides and three different angles is a *scalene* triangle.

- A triangle with two sides the same length and two angles the same is an *isosceles* triangle.

- A triangle with three sides the same length and three equal angles is an *equilateral* triangle.

- A triangle which contains a right angle is a *right angled* triangle.

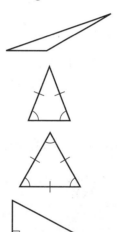

<table><tr><td>**Exercise 3**</td></tr></table>

For each of the following triangles state whether it is scalene, isosceles, equilateral or right angled. (Lines of the same length are indicated by dashes and equal angles are marked.)

1. 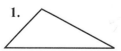 **2.** 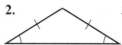 **3.**  **4.**   **5.**

6. 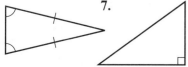 **7.** **8.**   **9.**   **10.**

Quadrilaterals

● A plane figure with four sides and angles is a *quadrilateral*

Here are some special types of quadrilaterals:

1. A *square* has all its sides equal in length and all its angles are right angles.

2. A *rectangle* has pairs of opposite sides equal in length and all its angles are right angles.

3. A *parallelogram* has its opposite sides equal in length and parallel. Its opposite angles are equal.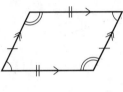

4. A *rhombus* is a parallelogram with all its sides equal.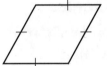

5. A *trapezium* has one pair of opposite sides parallel.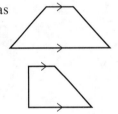

6. A *kite* is a quadrilateral with two pairs of adjacent sides equal in length. (Adjacent means 'next to'.)

Polygons

A polygon is a plane figure with straight sides. A polygon can have any number of sides from 3 upwards.

Here is a five-sided polygon or pentagon.

If a polygon is described as *regular*, then all its sides and angles are equal. Here is a regular pentagon.

Here are the names of other common polygons:
Hexagon = 6 sides; Heptagon = 7 sides; Octagon = 8 sides;
Nonagon = 9 sides; Decagon = 10 sides.

Exercise 4

Write down the name for each shape. If the shape has a special name like 'parallelogram' or 'kite' write that name. Otherwise write 'quadrilateral', 'hexagon', 'regular pentagon' and so on.

1.

2.

3.

4.

5.

6.

7.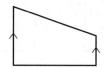

8.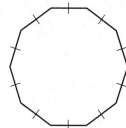

9.

10.

11.

12.

13.

14.

15.

16.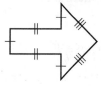

17.

18.

19.

20.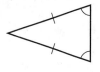

21. Draw any rectangle. Make a statement about the diagonals of a rectangle.

22. Draw any rhombus. Make a statement, with as many facts as possible, about the diagonals of a rhombus.

Shapes investigation

On a square grid of 9 dots it is possible to draw several different triangles with vertices on dots. A vertex (plural vertices) is where two lines meet. Look at the three examples below:

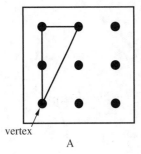 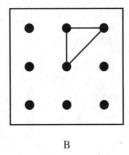 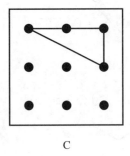

vertex

A

B

C

A and B are different triangles but C is the same as A. If a triangle could be cut out and placed exactly over another triangle then the two triangles are the same. The two triangles are called *congruent*.

1. Copy A and B above and then draw as many different triangles as you can. Check carefully that you have not repeated the same triangle.

2. On a grid of 9 dots it is also possible to draw several different *quadrilaterals*.

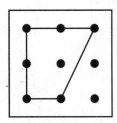 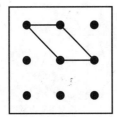 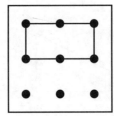

Copy the three shapes above and then draw as many other different quadrilaterals as possible. You are doing well if you can find 12 shapes but there are a few more!

Check carefully that you have not repeated the same quadrilateral. (Congruent shapes are not allowed.)

1.4 Subtraction

- Method 1: 'Exchanging'

(a)
```
   5 8 3
 −1 4 7
```

(b)
```
   6 7 4 3
 −3 9 2 7
```

Exchange ten from 80 to make 13

```
  5 ⁷8̷ ¹3
 −1 4  7
  4 3  6
```

Exchange in two places.

```
  ⁵6̷ ¹7 ³4̷ ¹3
 − 3  9  2  7
   2  8  1  6
```

- Method 2: 'Look at the numbers.'

The calculation 205 − 97 can be done by exchanging but there is
an easier way.
From 97 to 200 = 103
From 205 to 200 = 5
So the answer is 108

Do these subtractions using this method

(a) 302 − 84

(b) 5005 − 4997

Exercise 1

Copy each of the following problems and perform the calculation.
(No calculators.)

1.
```
   49
 − 15
```

2.
```
   76
 −  7
```

3.
```
   83
 − 67
```

4.
```
   92
 −17
```

5.
```
   50
 − 26
```

6.
```
   421
 −  59
```

7.
```
   368
 − 274
```

8.
```
   573
 −  94
```

9.
```
   900
 − 487
```

10.
```
   1001
 −  697
```

In Questions **11** to **30** write the numbers in columns and then
subtract.

11. 33 − 16   **12.** 24 − 7   **13.** 57 − 19   **14.** 40 − 13   **15.** 167 − 78
16. 319 − 234   **17.** 743 − 517   **18.** 800 − 342   **19.** 965 − 877   **20.** 2001 − 416

21. Two hundred and four take away forty-eight.
22. Five hundred and thirteen take away one hundred and twenty-five.
23. Two hundred and eight take away thirty-one.
24. Six hundred and nineteen take away two hundred and twenty-seven.
25. Seven hundred and fifty take away three hundred and ninety-one.
26. One thousand take away six hundred and sixty-one.
27. Nine hundred and twelve take away four hundred and fifty.
28. Five hundred and one take away one hundred and eighty.
29. One hundred and eleven take away eighty-nine.
30. One thousand take away one hundred and eleven.

Subtraction – Keywords

The following words are all associated with subtraction.

'Subtract' Three *subtract* two equals?
'Take away' Three *take away* two equals?
'Difference between' What is the *difference between* three and two?
'Minus' What is three *minus* two?
'Less than' What is two *less than* three?

'Fewer than' What number is two *fewer than* three?
'Count back' If you *count* two *back* from three, what number do you reach?
'From' What is two *from* three?
'Left over' What is *left over* if you take two from three?

All these statements are saying $3 - 2 = 1$

Exercise 2

1. What is seventeen subtract nine?

2. Thirty-four take away nineteen equals?

3. What is the difference between ninety-three and sixty-seven?

4. What is one hundred and seven minus twenty-nine?

5. What is sixty-eight less than two hundred and four?

6. What number is eighty-three fewer than three hundred?

7. If you count sixty-nine back from one hundred and thirty-eight, what number do you reach?

8. What is seventy-five from one hundred and sixty-four?

9. There were one hundred and eighty-six crisps in a bag. Forty-nine were eaten. How many crisps were left over?

10. There are eight hundred and one pupils in a school. If there are three hundred and eighty three boys, how many girls are in the school?

11. There are 365 days in a year, 176 days have passed. How many days are left in the year?

12. What is the difference between £431 and £134?

13. There were 100 biscuits in a tin. Jackie ate 29, how many biscuits were left?

14. An apple tree had 189 apples growing on it. After a windy night, 93 apples had fallen off the tree. How many apples were still on the tree?

15. Bob needs to work out 743 minus 529. What answer should he get?

16. Julie needs to take £123 from £321. What answer should she get?

17. Dawn's tennis racket cost £78. Mark's cricket bat cost £127. What is the difference in the two costs?

18. Vicky's book was 900 pages long. She had read 529 pages. How many pages does she still have to read to finish the book?

19. What is 303 subtracted from 3001?

20. A monster bouncy castle can hold a maximum of 1000 children. There are 223 children bouncing around inside. How many fewer than the maximum is this?

21. John says '26 + 39 = 65'   Graham says   'So I know three facts:
$$39 + 26 = 65$$
$$65 - 26 = 39$$
$$65 - 39 = 26$$

In each question write down the number fact given and then write down the three related number facts.

(a) $24 + 7 = 31$, $\square + \square = 31$

   $31 - \square = \square$, $31 - \square = \square$

(b) $47 + 19 = 66$, $\square + \square = \square$,

   $66 - \square = \square$, $\square - \square = \square$

(c) $85 + 47 = 132$, $\square + \square = \square$

   $\square - \square = \square$, $\square - \square = \square$

(d) $429 + 85 = 514$, $\square + \square = \square$,

   $\square - \square = \square$, $\square - \square = \square$

22. Work out the calculation stated and then write down the three other related facts

   (a) $14 + 39$ (b) $44 + 72$ (c) $115 - 81$

Cross number puzzles 2

Copy the following cross number puzzles onto squared paper. Complete the puzzles using the clues given.

1.

Clues across

1. $501 - 26$
3. $231 - 147$
4. $189 - 68$
6. $70 - 40$
7. $471 - 190$
8. $83 - 47$
11. $425 - 350$
12. $200 - 143$

Clues down

1. $501 - 78$
2. $118 - 67$
3. $1000 - 182$
5. $301 - 75$
8. $613 - 286$
9. $31 - 19$
10. $42 - 28$

2. **Clues across**

1. $586 - 330$
4. $231 - 152$
5. $1154 - 789$
6. $2010 - 921$
8. $420 - 359$
10. $918 - 397$
11. $821 - 648$
12. $615 - 574$

Clues down

1. $2503 - 187$
2. $101 - 45$
3. $1000 - 349$
4. $811 - 23$
7. $9999 - 978$
9. $580 - 423$

1.5 Coordinates 1

- To get to the point P on this grid we go **across** 1 and **up** 3 from the bottom corner.
  The position of P is (1, 3).
  The numbers 1 and 3 are called the **coordinates** of P.
  The coordinates of Q are (4, 2).
  The *origin* is at (0, 0).

- The *across* coordinate is always *first* and the *up* coordinate is *second*.
  Remember: 'Along the corridor and up the stairs'.

- Notice also that the *lines* are numbered, *not* the squares.

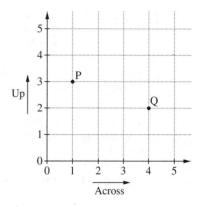

1. Write down the coordinates of all the points marked like this: A(5, 1) B(1,4)

   Don't forget the brackets.

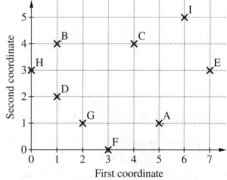

2. The map below shows a remote Scottish island used for training by the S.A.S.

   Write down the coordinates of the following places:
   (a) Rocket launcher
   (b) H.Q.
   (c) Hospital A
   (d) Rifle range
   (e) Officers' mess
   (f) Radar control

3. Make a list of the places which are at the following points:
   (a) (2, 8)   (b) (7, 8)
   (c) (3, 3)   (d) (6, 4)
   (e) (2, 6)   (f) (6, 2)
   (g) (2, 4)   (h) (9, 1)

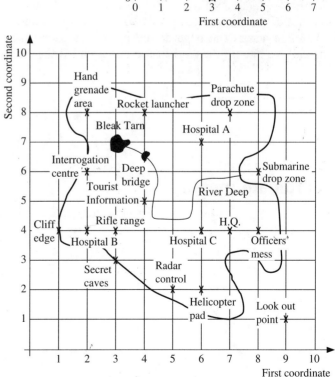

4. The map below shows the first two holes on a rather hazardous golf course. What is at the following points?

(a) (6, 3)   (b) (4, 2)   (c) (2, 6)
(d) (6, 4)   (e) (3, 3)   (f) (7, 3)

5. (a) Write down the positions in which the ball might land if *you* played the first hole.
(b) Where would you like the ball to go if your maths teacher was playing the hole?

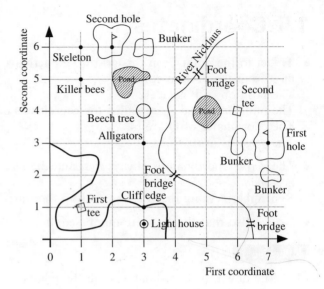

6. Make up your own map. Mark some interesting points and make a list, giving the coordinates of eight points.

x and *y* coordinates (*x*, *y*)

We call the first coordinate of a point the *x*-coordinate and the second coordinate the *y*-coordinate. So for the point (1, 4) the *x*-coordinate is 1 and the *y*-coordinate is 4.

The line across the page at the bottom is called the *x* axis and the line up the page at the side is called the *y* axis.

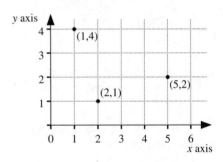

Coordinate messages

Example:- Write down the letters situated at these coordinates:-

(3, 2), (0, 0), (0, 3), (2, 1), (1, 2)
   ↓   ↓   ↓   ↓   ↓
   M   A   T   H   S

Note 'T' is at (0, 3) meaning zero across, three up, but 'D' is at (3, 0) meaning three across, zero up.

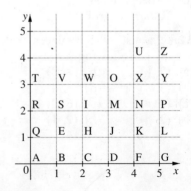

Exercise 2

Use the grid opposite to decode these messages:-

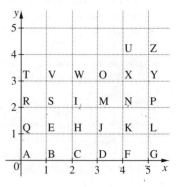

1. (5, 2), (5, 1), (3, 3), (0, 3), (0, 3), (0, 3), (2, 2), (4, 2), (5, 0),
   (5, 2), (3, 3), (2, 2), (4, 2), (0, 3), (1, 2). (two words).

2. (3, 0), (0, 2), (0, 0), (2, 3),
   (0, 0)
   (5, 0), (0, 2), (2, 2), (3, 0). (three words).

3. (4, 2), (4, 4), (3, 2), (1, 0), (1, 1), 0, 2).
   (5, 1), (2, 2), (4, 2), (1, 1), (1, 2).
   (4, 2), (3, 3), (0, 3).
   (1, 2), (0, 1), (4, 4), (0, 0), (0, 2), (1, 1), (1, 2). (four words).

4. (5, 0), (3, 3).
   (0, 0), (2, 0), (0, 2), (3, 3), (1, 2), (1, 2).
   (1, 0), (1, 1), (4, 0), (3, 3), (0, 2), (1, 1).
   (5, 0), (3, 3), (2, 2), (4, 2), (5, 0).
   (4, 4), (5, 2). (five words).

5. Write your own coded message from the grid.

Coordinate pictures

Plot the points below and join them up in order.
(a) (2, 4), (8, 1), (6, 3), (4, 4),
    (2, 6), (2, 4), (0, 3), (6, 2).
(b) (5, 3½), (4, 5), (3¼, 4⅔).

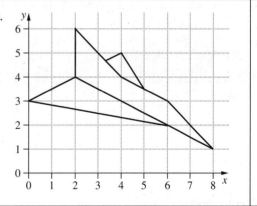

Exercise 3

Plot the points given and join them up in order.
Write on the grid what the picture is.

1. Draw x and y axes with values from 0 to 14.
   (a) (6, 13), (1, 3), (2, 1), (12, 1), (8, 9), (6, 5),
       (4, 5), (8, 13), (6, 13), (8, 13), (13, 3), (12, 1).

   (b) (1, 3), (9, 3), (7, 7), (6, 5), (8, 5).
       Now colour in the shape.

2. Draw x and y axes with values from 0 to 10.
   (a) (3, 2), (4, 2), (5, 3), (3, 5), (3, 6), (2, 7), (1, 6),
       (1, 8), (2, 9), (3, 9), (5, 7), (4, 6), (4, 5), (6, 4)
       (8, 4), (8, 5), (6, 7), (5, 7).
   (b) (7, 4), (9, 2), (8, 1), (7, 3), (5, 3).
   (c) (1, 6), (2, 8), (2, 9), (2, 7).
   (d) Draw a dot at (3, 8).
       Colour in the shape.

3. Draw x and y axes with values from 0 to 16
   (a) (4, 9), (1, 11), (3, 8), (1, 5), (4, 7), (6, 5), (7, 5), (8, 3),
       (9, 5), (11, 5), (12, 7), (15, 9), (15, 10), (12, 11), (9, 11),
       (8, 14), (7, 11), (6, 11), (4, 9).
   (b) (15, 12), (16, 12), (16, 13), (15, 13), (15, 12).
   (c) (14, 14), (13, 14), (13, 15), (14, 15), (14, 14).
   (d) (12, 8), (13, 8).
   (e) Draw a dot at (13, 10).
       Colour in the shape.

4. Draw axes with both x and y from 0 to 17.
   (a) (5, 1), (6, 6), (6, 3), (7, 2), (6, 2), (5, 1).
   (b) (8, 11), (8, 8), (10, 10), (11, 12), (11, 15).
   (c) (2, 14), (1, 14), (1, 15), (2, 15).
   (d) (12, 1), (11, 2), (10, 2), (10, 4), (9, 6), (8, 7), (7, 10),
       (8, 11), (9, 13), (11, 15), (10, 17), (8, 17), (7, 16), (4, 16),
       (2, 15), (2, 14), (3, 13), (5, 13), (6, 12), (4, 7), (4, 2),
       (3, 2), (2, 1), (12, 1).
   (e) (7, 16), (7, 15).
   (f) (5, 13), (6, 13).

5. Draw axes with both x and y from 0 to 11.
   (a) (7, 1), (3, 1), (1, 10), (2, 11), (3, 10), (4, 11), (5, 10),
       (6, 11), (7, 10), (8, 6), (8, 5), (9, $4\frac{1}{2}$), (9, 4), (8, 4), (9, 3),
       (5, 3), (5, 2), (7, 1).
   (b) (5, 5), (4, 6), (5, 7), (6, 6), (7, 7), (8, 6), (7, 5), (6, 6), (5, 5).
   (c) (5, 2), (6, 2), (6, $1\frac{1}{2}$).
   (d) (7, 5), (8, 5).
   (e) (7, 4), (8, 4).
   (f) (3, 7), (2, $6\frac{1}{2}$), (3, 6).
   (g) Put dots at (5, 6) and (7, 6).

6. Draw axes with both x and y from 0 to 18.
   (a) (0, 3), (1, 4), (2, 6), (4, 8), (6, 8), (8, 9), (12, 9), (13, 11),
       (12, 12), (12, 14), (14, 12), (15, 12), (17, 14), (17, 12),
       (16, 11), (17, 10), (17, 9), (16, 9), (15, 8), (14, 9), (13, 9).
   (b) (16, 9), (16, 7), (14, 5), (14, 1), (15, 1), (15, 6), (13, 4),
       (13, 1), (12, 1), (12, 4), (11, 5), (9, 5), (9, $6\frac{1}{2}$), (9, 4), (8, 3),
       (8, 1), (7, 1), (7, 4), (6, 6), (6, 4), (5, 3), (5, 1), (6, 1), (6, 3),
       (7, 4), (6, 6), (6, 7), (3, 2), (1, 2), (0, 3).

7. Design your own coordinates picture.

Complete the shape

Two sides of a rectangle are drawn.

Find   (a) the coordinates of the fourth vertex of the
            rectangle
        (b) the coordinates of the centre of the rectangle.

- A *vertex* (plural-*vertices*) is where two straight lines
  meet. It is the mathematical name for a '*corner*'.

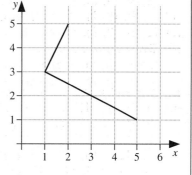

The complete rectangle is shown.
(a) Fourth vertex is at (6, 3)
(b) Centre of rectangle is at $(3\frac{1}{2}, 3)$

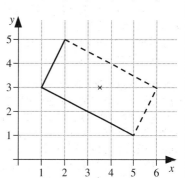

Exercise 4

1. The graph shows several
   incomplete quadrilaterals.
   Copy the diagram and
   complete the shapes.
   (a) Write down the
       coordinates of the fourth
       vertex of each shape.
   (b) Write down the
       coordinates of the centre
       of each shape.

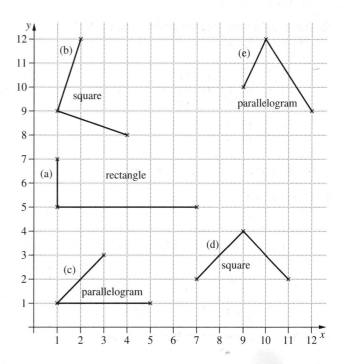

2. Copy the graph shown.
   (a) A, B and F are three corners of a square.
       Write down the coordinates of the other
       corner.
   (b) B, C and D are three corners of another
       square. Write down the coordinates of the
       other corner.
   (c) D, E and F are three corners of a
       rectangle. Write down the coordinates of
       the other corner.

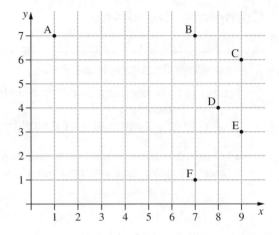

3. Draw a grid with values from 0 to 10. Plot the three points given
   and then find the coordinates of the point which makes a square
   when the points are joined up.
   (a) (1, 2) (1, 5) (4, 5)
   (b) (5, 6) (7, 3) (10, 5)
   (c) (0, 9) (1, 6) (4, 7)

4. You are given the vertices but not
   the sides of two parallelograms P
   and Q.

   For each parallelogram find *three*
   possible positions for the fourth
   vertex.

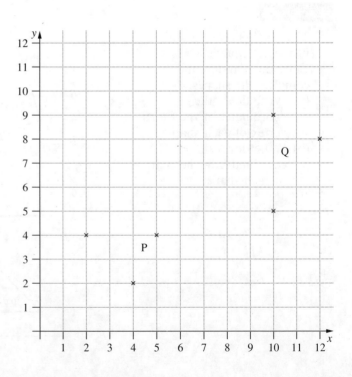

5.

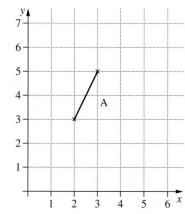

The crosses mark two vertices of an isosceles triangle A.

Find *four* possible points, with whole number coordinates, for the third vertex of the triangle. [There are, in fact, *more* than four points for the third vertex. Find as many as you can.]

6. The diagram shows one side of an isosceles triangle B.
   (a) Find *six* possible points, with whole number coordinates, for the third vertex of the triangle.
   (b) Explain how you could find the coordinates of several more positions for the third vertex.

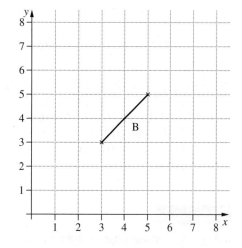

Part 2

2.1 Multiplication

- Multiplication is a quick method of adding together the same number ...
  $7 + 7 + 7 + 7 + 7 + 7 + 7 + 7 + 7$ is the same as 9×7 and $9 \times 7 = 63$.

- Your ability to solve multiplication problems will be greatly improved if you learn your multiplication tables up to 12×12 thoroughly.

Exercise 1

Copy each multiplication and insert the correct answer.

1. $12 \times 5 = ?$	**2.** $6 \times 6 = ?$	**3.** $9 \times 5 = ?$	**4.** $7 \times 6 = ?$
5. $8 \times 5 = ?$	**6.** $8 \times 6 = ?$	**7.** $7 \times 5 = ?$	**8.** $9 \times 6 = ?$
9. $6 \times 5 = ?$	**10.** $12 \times 6 = ?$	**11.** $5 \times 5 = ?$	**12.** $7 \times 7 = ?$
13. $12 \times 4 = ?$	**14.** $8 \times 7 = ?$	**15.** $9 \times 4 = ?$	**16.** $9 \times 7 = ?$
17. $8 \times 4 = ?$	**18.** $12 \times 7 = ?$	**19.** $7 \times 4 = ?$	**20.** $8 \times 8 = ?$
21. $6 \times 4 = ?$	**22.** $9 \times 8 = ?$	**23.** $5 \times 4 = ?$	**24.** $12 \times 8 = ?$
25. $4 \times 4 = ?$	**26.** $9 \times 9 = ?$	**27.** $12 \times 3 = ?$	**28.** $12 \times 9 = ?$
29. $9 \times 3 = ?$	**30.** $12 \times 10 = ?$	**31.** $8 \times 3 = ?$	**32.** $11 \times 11 = ?$
33. $7 \times 3 = ?$	**34.** $12 \times 11 = ?$	**35.** $6 \times 3 = ?$	**36.** $12 \times 12 = ?$
37. $5 \times 3 = ?$	**38.** $3 \times 3 = ?$	**39.** $10 \times 10 = ?$	**40.** $4 \times 3 = ?$

Exercise 2

Speed Test 1.
Copy and complete the grids opposite. Time yourself on grid 1. Try to improve your time on grid 2.

×	7	2	12	8	6	3	11	9	4	5
7	49									
2										
12										
8										
6				48						
3						9				
11										
9										
4										
5										

×	2	9	6	3	5	11	12	8	7	4
2										
9										
6										
3										
5										
11										
12										
8										
7										
4										

Multiplication by 10, 100 and 1000

$2 \times 10 = 20$
$6 \times 10 = 60$
$13 \times 10 = 130$

- When multiplying whole numbers by 10, just add a zero to the number being multiplied.

$3 \times 100 = 300$
$12 \times 100 = 1200$
$40 \times 100 = 4000$

- When multiplying whole numbers by 100, just add on two zeros to the number being multiplied.

$4 \times 1000 = 4000$
$10 \times 1000 = 10\,000$
$39 \times 1000 = 39\,000$

- When multiplying whole numbers by 1000, just add on three zeros to the number being multiplied.

Exercise 3

Copy and complete the following multiplications.

1. $5 \times 10 = ?$ **2.** $7 \times 100 = ?$ **3.** $3 \times 1000 = ?$ **4.** $12 \times 10 = ?$
5. $40 \times 10 = ?$ **6.** $137 \times 100 = ?$ **7.** $19 \times 100 = ?$ **8.** $30 \times 100 = ?$
9. $314 \times 100 = ?$ **10.** $13 \times 1000 = ?$ **11.** $67 \times 1000 = ?$ **12.** $80 \times 1000 = ?$

13. $601 \times 10 = ?$ **14.** $302 \times 100 = ?$ **15.** $901 \times 100 = ?$ **16.** $300 \times 10 = ?$
17. $21 \times 1000 = ?$ **18.** $100 \times 61 = ?$ **19.** $2170 \times 10 = ?$ **20.** $1000 \times 43 = ?$
21. $10 \times 27 = ?$ **22.** $304 \times 100 = ?$ **23.** $1000 \times 50 = ?$ **24.** $0 \times 10 = ?$
25. $10 \times 10 = ?$ **26.** $10 \times 100 = ?$ **27.** $100 \times 1000 = ?$ **28.** $10 \times 1000 = ?$
29. $100 \times 100 = ?$ **30.** $1000 \times 1000 = ?$ **31.** $21 \times 10 \times 100 = ?$ **32.** $7 \times 1000 \times 100 = ?$

33. How many £10 notes are in (a) £1000, (b) £2500, (c) £140 000?

34. How many £100 notes are in (a) £1800, (b) £200 000, (c) £5 million?

35. How many 1p coins are in (a) £10, (b) £500, (c) £2700?

36. Copy and complete these two sentences:
  (a) Multiplying by 100 is the same as multiplying by ☐ and
    again by ☐ .

  (b) Multiplying by 1000 is the same as multiplying by ☐ ,
    again by ☐ and again by ☐

37. Cans of coke at 55p each are put in packs of 10.
  Ten packs are put in a box.
  One hundred boxes are put in a container.
  Find the cost of:
  (a) 1 pack
  (b) 1 box
  (c) 1 container
  (d) 100 containers.

38. Magazines costing £2 each are wrapped in packs of 10.
  Ten packs are put in a box.
  Ten boxes are put in a van.
  Find the cost of:
  (a) 1 pack
  (b) 1 box
  (c) 1 van load
  (d) 1000 van loads.

An investigation into multiplication by 11

Multiplying single digit numbers by eleven is easy …

$1 \times 11 = 11$
$2 \times 11 = 22$
$3 \times 11 = 33$
$4 \times 11 = 44$
$5 \times 11 = 55$ etc.

Here is a method for multiplying two digit numbers by eleven:

Example 1. $11 \times 53 = ?$

space
↓

Step 1.   Separate 53 into 5 __ 3
Step 2.   Add the digits of 53, $5 + 3 = 8$
Step 3.   Place the total of the digits in the space ... 5 8 3
$11 \times 53 = 583$.

Example 2. $11 \times 89 = ?$

space
↓

Step 1.   Separate 89 into 8 __ 9
Step 2.   Add the digits of 89, $8 + 9 = 17$
Step 3.   Place the last digit of 17 in the   879
          space, but add the ten of 17 to the $+1$
          first digit of the answer $11 \times 89 = 979$

Use the method of multiplication by eleven to answer these problems.

1. 11×14 **2.** 11×23 **3.** 11×35 **4.** 11×52 **5.** 11×57

6. 11×61 **7.** 11×75 **8.** 11×81 **9.** 11×99 **10.** 11×50

11. Investigate multiplying by eleven three digit numbers, four digit numbers and so on. Can you discover any patterns? ... Look at the examples below.

$11 \times 427 = 4697$
$11 \times 324 = 3564$
$11 \times 516 = 5676$

Short multiplication

- The order in which you multiply numbers is not important. For example 7×35 is the same as 35×7.
- Here is a 'pencil and paper' method using carrying.

(a)   52
      $\times\ 3$
      156

(b)   49
      $\times\ 8$
      392
       7

(c)   231
      $\times\ 6$
      1386
       1

Exercise 4

Work out

1.	$\begin{array}{r} 32 \\ \times\ 5 \\ \hline \end{array}$	**2.**	$\begin{array}{r} 61 \\ \times\ 4 \\ \hline \end{array}$	**3.**	$\begin{array}{r} 35 \\ \times\ 3 \\ \hline \end{array}$	**4.**	$\begin{array}{r} 48 \\ \times\ 2 \\ \hline \end{array}$

5.	$\begin{array}{r} 26 \\ \times\ 6 \\ \hline \end{array}$	**6.**	$\begin{array}{r} 51 \\ \times\ 8 \\ \hline \end{array}$	**7.**	$\begin{array}{r} 62 \\ \times\ 9 \\ \hline \end{array}$	**8.**	$\begin{array}{r} 89 \\ \times\ 7 \\ \hline \end{array}$

9.	$\begin{array}{r} 241 \\ \times\ 2 \\ \hline \end{array}$	**10.**	$\begin{array}{r} 416 \\ \times\ 4 \\ \hline \end{array}$	**11.**	$\begin{array}{r} 513 \\ \times\ 3 \\ \hline \end{array}$	**12.**	$\begin{array}{r} 505 \\ \times\ 5 \\ \hline \end{array}$

13.	$\begin{array}{r} 267 \\ \times\ 8 \\ \hline \end{array}$	**14.**	$\begin{array}{r} 216 \\ \times\ 6 \\ \hline \end{array}$	**15.**	$\begin{array}{r} 307 \\ \times\ 7 \\ \hline \end{array}$	**16.**	$\begin{array}{r} 199 \\ \times\ 9 \\ \hline \end{array}$

17. 7×345 **18.** 208×5 **19.** 6×3143 **20.** 6082×7

Work out

(a) $\quad 42 \times 20$
$\quad = 42 \times 2 \times 10$
$\quad = 84 \times 10$
$\quad = 840$

(b) $\quad 213 \times 300$
$\quad = 213 \times 3 \times 100$
$\quad = 639 \times 100$
$\quad = 63\,900$

(c) $\quad 13 \times 5000$
$\quad = 13 \times 5 \times 1000$
$\quad = 65 \times 1000$
$\quad = 65\,000$

---

21. 43×20 **22.** 31×30 **23.** 24×50 **24.** 35×300
25. 52×400 **26.** 63×500 **27.** 600×211 **28.** 7000×21
29. 407×70 **30.** 312×600 **31.** 162×4000 **32.** $521 \times 30\,000$

Multiplication Keywords

The following words are all associated with multiplication.

"Multiplied by"   Two *multiplied by* three equals?
"Lots of"   Two *lots of* three equals?
"Times"   Two *times* three equals?
"Product"   What is the *product* of two and three?

All these statements are saying $2 \times 3 = 6$

Exercise 5

Write down the calculation and then work out the answer.

1. What is 7 multiplied by 12?

2. What are 11 lots of 5?

3. What is 7 times 6?

4. What is the product of 4 and 8?

5. What is three multiplied by eight?

6. What is the product of three and nine?

7. What is twelve times eleven?

8. What is ten times itself?

9. What are five lots of twelve?

10. What is the product of nine and seven?

11. A bus has 42 seats. How many passengers can be carried by a fleet of 6 buses?

12. A solid fuel stove uses 23 kilograms of coal per day. How much does it use in seven days?

13. Suppose you save 5 pence for every day you attend school (190 days). How much money will you have saved?

14. There are 52 playing cards in a 'deck'. How many playing cards are there altogether in six decks?

15. There are 80 tea bags per packet of tea. How many tea bags are there altogether in 12 packets?

16. Geoff grows peas with exactly eleven peas per pod. Geoff picks 77 pods. How many peas will Geoff have to eat?

17. Copy and complete this multiplication square.

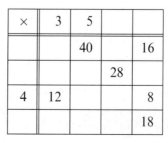

×	3	5		
		40		16
			28	
4	12			8
				18

18. If you have 6 video tapes each of 360 minutes duration, how many minutes of taping can you do?

19.* Mike knows that $221 \times 31 = 6851$. Explain how he can use this information to work out 222×31.

20.* Given that $357 \times 101 = 36\,057$, work out 358×101 without multiplying.

Number Investigation – Russian Multiplication

If you can multiply by two and divide by two, then multiplying large numbers is easy in Russia!

Example:- Work out 11×19 using Russian multiplication.

		First column	Second column
Step 1	Write the numbers in two columns.	11	19

Step 2   Always divide the number in the first column by two and *ignore any remainders*. Always *double* the number in the second column.

$$
\begin{array}{ll}
11 \; (\div 2) & 19^* \; (\times 2) \\
5 \; (\div 2) & 38^* \; (\times 2) \\
2 \; (\div 2) & 76 \; (\times 2) \\
\quad (\div 2) &
\end{array}
$$

Step 3   Continue this process until you obtain one in the first column.

$$1 \qquad 152^*$$

Step 4   Now list all the numbers in the second column that are on the same line as an *odd* number in the first column.

$$
\begin{array}{ll}
\text{List} & 19 \\
& 38 \\
& 152
\end{array}
$$

(Indicated by an asterisk*.)

Step 5   Add together these numbers

$$
\begin{array}{r}
19 \\
38 \\
+152 \\
\hline
209
\end{array}
$$

Answer $11 \times 19 = 209$

Work out these problems using Russian multiplication:-

1. 17×21	**2.** 19×25	**3.** 68×15	**4.** 16×13	**5.** 15×111
6. 31×22	**7.** 99×101	**8.** 232×25	**9.** 42×32	**10.** 461×121

2.2 Turning

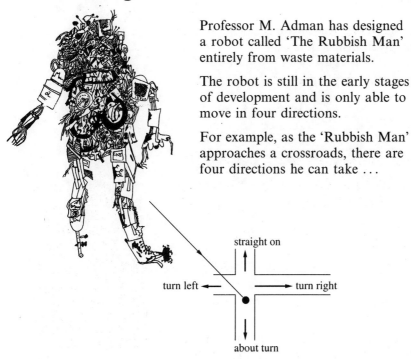

Professor M. Adman has designed a robot called 'The Rubbish Man' entirely from waste materials.

The robot is still in the early stages of development and is only able to move in four directions.

For example, as the 'Rubbish Man' approaches a crossroads, there are four directions he can take ...

The 'Rubbish Man's' options are:-

1. Turn left (causing a change in direction of 90°).
2. Turn right (causing a change in direction of 90°).
3. Go straight on (meaning no change in direction).
4. About turn (causing a change in direction of 180°).

Three of the four options programmed into the 'Rubbish Man' cause a change in his direction. To change direction he needs to *turn* through an *angle*.

A *quarter turn* is a turn of **90°**, called *1 right angle*.
A *half turn* is a turn of **180°**, called *2 right angles*.
A *three-quarter* turn is a turn of **270°**, called *3 right angles*.
A *full turn* is a turn of **360°**, called *4 right angles*.

- A right angle is an angle of 90° and is always indicated by the following symbol.

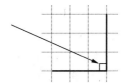

- When turning through right angles we have two options, we can turn clockwise (⤺) or anti-clockwise (⤸).
- Example:

Draw the new direction of travel of 'Rubbish Man' after Professor Adman inputs the given instruction:

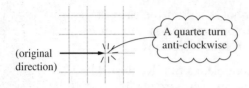

Solution:

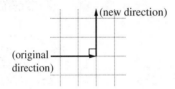

 Exercise 1

For each question you are given an arrow giving the original direction 'Rubbish man' is travelling. Copy each diagram and show his new direction of travel after each given instruction.

1.

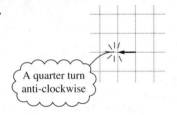

2.

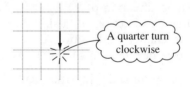

3.

4.

5.

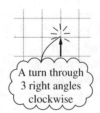

6.

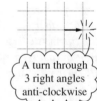

7.

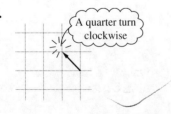

8.

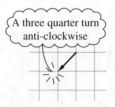

9.

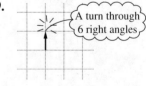

10. These pictures have been hung incorrectly. Give instructions to turn them the right way round. Remember to give both the angle and the direction.

(a)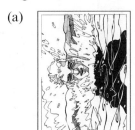

(b)

(c)

(d)

(e)

(f)

In Questions **11** to **19** copy each diagram and then draw its new position after it has been turned. You can use tracing paper if you wish.

11.
A quarter turn
anti-clockwise

12.
A half turn

13.
A quarter turn
clockwise

14.
A three quarter
turn clockwise

15.
A right angle
turn anti-clockwise

16.
A turn through
2 right angles

17.
A 90° turn
anti-clockwise

18.
A 90° turn
clockwise

19.
One and a half
turns clockwise

In Questions **20** to **25** describe the turn.

20.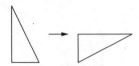

21.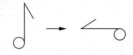

22.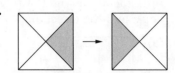

23.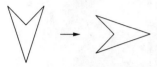

24.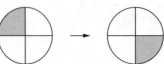

25.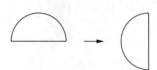

26. (a) This shape is going
to be turned 90°
clockwise around
the point A

Here is
the result.

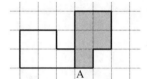

(b) Turn this shape
90° clockwise around
the point B

Shade in the new
position of the shape

In Questions **27** to **29** copy the shape on squared paper and then
draw and shade its new position.

27.

Half turn around
the point C

28.

Quarter turn clockwise
around the point D

29.

Turn 90° anti-clockwise
around the point E

LOGO

LOGO is used to give commands to move a turtle on a computer.
Here is a list of the main commands.

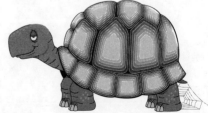

FD 20   Go **ForwarD** 20 spaces
BK 30   Go **BacK** 30 spaces

RT 90   **R**ight **T**urn 90 degrees
RT 45   **R**ight **T**urn 45 degrees
LT 90   **L**eft **T**urn 90 degrees

PU   **P**en **U**p   } These are used to move across the
PD   **P**en **D**own } screen without drawing a line.

Here are two examples in which the turtle goes from A to B.

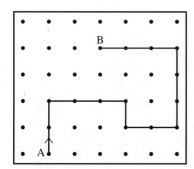

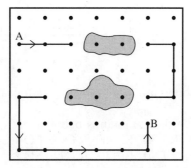

FD 20, RT 90, FD 30, RT 90,
FD 10, LT 90, FD 20, LT 90,
FD 30, LT 90, FD 30

In this one the turtle has to
'fly over' the obstacles shown.
FD 20, PU, FD 30, PD, FD 10,
RT 90, FD 20, RT 90, FD 10,
PU, FD 40, PD, FD 10, LT 90,
FD 20, LT 90, FD 50, LT 90,
FD 10

Exercise 2

1. Write down the commands that would move the turtle from A to B. The dots are 10 spaces apart

(a)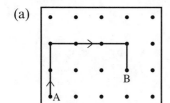

(b)

2. Write the commands that would move the turtle from A to B. In this question the turtle has to 'jump over' the obstacles shown by shaded areas.

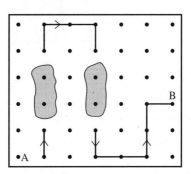

3. Write the commands that would move the turtle along the route given.
   (a) A → E → D → C → F → A
   (b) A → B → D → H → G → I → J → A
   (c) A → B → A → F → C

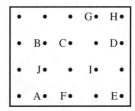

4. Leslie Smith wants to write her
   initials. Write down the LOGO
   commands.

5. Write down the LOGO commands for *your* own initials.

6. Draw the patterns given by the commands below.
   (a) FD 50, RT 90, FD 50, RT 90, FD 40, RT 90, FD 40, RT 90,
       FD 30, RT 90, FD 30, RT 90, FD 20, RT 90, FD 20, RT 90,
       FD 10, RT 90, FD 10.
   (b) FD 40, RT 90, FD 20, RT 90, FD 20, RT 90, FD 20, LT 90,
       FD 20, LT 90, PU, FD 30, PD, FD 20, LT 90, FD 20, LT 90,
       FD 20, BK 20, RT 90, FD 20, LT 90, FD 20.

Compass directions

Another way of describing a direction is provided by the *points* of
the *compass*.

There are four major directions (called cardinal points) on a
compass:

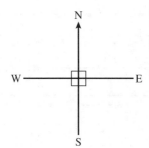

N represents north.
E represents east.
S represents south.
W represents west.

You can remember this easily by thinking in a clockwise order that
Naughty Elephants Squirt Water!

The directions between the four cardinal points are:

NE representing North-East.
SE representing South-East.
SW representing South-West.
NW representing North-West.

(a) You are facing north and then make a quarter turn anti-clockwise. In which direction are you now facing?

You must now be facing west.

(b) You are facing south-east and then make a half-turn. In which direction are you now facing?

You must now be facing north-west.

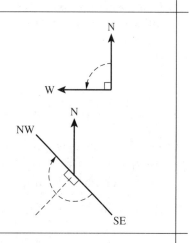

Exercise 3

Copy and complete this table.

	You are facing	Movement (Angle and Direction)	Direction you are now facing
1.	N	180°	?
2.	E	360°	?
3.	S	90° clockwise	?
4.	W	90° clockwise	?
5.	NW	180°	?
6.	SE	90° anti-clockwise	?
7.	NE	270° clockwise	?
8.	SW	270° anti-clockwise	?
9.	S	90° anti-clockwise	?
10.	E	?	W
11.	NW	?	SW
12.	NE	?	E
13.	W	?	S
14.	?	90° clockwise	W
15.	?	90° anti-clockwise	S
16.	?	180°	NE
17.	?	90° clockwise	E
18.	SW	?	S
19.	N	?	SW
20.	S	?	NE

21. A ship is sailing around an island. Copy and complete the missing compass directions of the ship's journey.

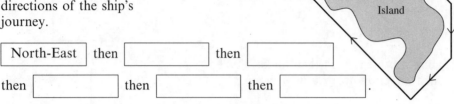

North-East	then		then	

then [ ] then [ ] then [ ] .

22. The points A, B, C, D, E, F, G, H, I are places on a map. Work out where I am in the following:

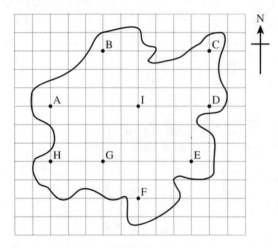

(a) I am North of G and West of C
(b) I am South of A and West of E
(c) I am West of D and North of F
(d) I am East of H and South of B
(e) I am South-East of G and South of I
(f) I am East of A and South of C
(g) I am South-West of C and East of H
(h) I am North-West of G and South-West of B.

Finding North

By Day: using the sun and your non-digital watch.

Step 1. Hold your arm in front of your stomach so that you can read your watch.
Step 2. Turn your body so that the *hour* hand of your watch points to the sun.
Step 3. Halve the angle between the hands on your watch. This is the *north to south line*.
Step 4. In the morning as you look north the sun is on your right (the east). As you look north in the afternoon the sun is on your left.

Examples

(a)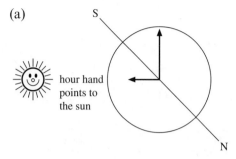

Time: 9.00 a.m.
Morning, so sun is on the right (eastward)

(b)

Time: 4.00 p.m.
Afternoon, so sun is on the left (westward)

2.3 Division

- Division is the reverse process of multiplication.

"Two fives are ten"
$2 \times 5 = 10$
The numbers 2, 5 and 10 form a *number bond*

Question: How many 2's in 10?
Solution: Put your fingers over the 2 and 10, the answer is 5.
(It's the only number left you can see!)
Question: How many 5's in 10?
Solution: Put your fingers over the 5 and 10, the answer is 2.

- Example: Number Bond 7, 9, 63

(a) $63 \div 7 = ?$ The answer is 9.
(b) $63 \div 9 = ?$ The answer is 7.

- GOVERNMENT NUMERACY WARNING:
  Knowing your multiplication tables will seriously improve your performance in division.

Exercise 1

Copy and complete the questions below. The number bonds are given if you need them.

1.

$18 \div 3 = ?$

2.

$24 \div 6 = ?$

3.

$36 \div 4 = ?$

4.

$30 \div 6 = ?$

5.

$48 \div 8 = ?$

6.

$35 \div 5 = ?$

7.

$32 \div 8 = ?$

8.

$15 \div 3 = ?$

9.

$90 \div 10 = ?$

10.

$49 \div 7 = ?$

11.

$108 \div 9 = ?$

12.

$132 \div 11 = ?$

In questions **13** to **36** you are given three numbers, for example, 3, 6 and 18. There are four statements you can write connecting these numbers using the symbols $\times$, $\div$ and $=$.

They are ... $3 \times 6 = 18$
$6 \times 3 = 18$
$18 \div 6 = 3$
$18 \div 3 = 6$

Write the four correct statements using $\times$, $\div$ and $=$ for the numbers given below.

13. 3, 4, 12   **14.** 5, 12, 60   **15.** 3, 8, 24
16. 5, 9, 45   **17.** 3, 7, 21   **18.** 7, 9, 63
19. 6, 9, 54   **20.** 3, 9, 27   **21.** 4, 9, 36
22. 4, 8, 32   **23.** 6, 7, 42   **24.** 5, 7, 35
25. 4, 7, 28   **26.** 8, 9, 72   **27.** 4, 12, 48
28. 5, 8, 40   **29.** 7, 12, 84   **30.** 5, 6, 30
31. 7, 8, 56   **32.** 4, 5, 20   **33.** 6, 8, 48
34. 10, 12, 120   **35.** 3, 12, 36   **36.** 9, 12, 108

Exercise 2

Copy and complete the following division problems.

1. $6 \div 3 = ?$
2. $8 \div 4 = ?$
3. $48 \div 8 = ?$
4. $88 \div 11 = ?$
5. $16 \div 2 = ?$
6. $10 \div 2 = ?$
7. $49 \div 7 = ?$
8. $90 \div 9 = ?$
9. $20 \div 5 = ?$
10. $99 \div 11 = ?$
11. $50 \div 5 = ?$
12. $96 \div 12 = ?$
13. $24 \div 6 = ?$
14. $14 \div 7 = ?$
15. $54 \div 6 = ?$
16. $100 \div 10 = ?$
17. $28 \div 4 = ?$
18. $15 \div 3 = ?$
19. $55 \div 5 = ?$
20. $108 \div 9 = ?$
21. $48 \div 6 = ?$
22. $16 \div 4 = ?$
23. $56 \div 7 = ?$
24. $110 \div 10 = ?$
25. $72 \div 9 = ?$
26. $18 \div 6 = ?$
27. $60 \div 5 = ?$
28. $120 \div 10 = ?$
29. $60 \div 12 = ?$
30. $20 \div 4 = ?$
31. $63 \div 7 = ?$
32. $121 \div 11 = ?$
33. $70 \div 7 = ?$
34. $22 \div 11 = ?$
35. $64 \div 8 = ?$
36. $132 \div 11 = ?$
37. $84 \div 7 = ?$
38. $24 \div 4 = ?$
39. $55 \div 11 = ?$
40. $144 \div 12 = ?$
41. $88 \div 11 = ?$
42. $27 \div 3 = ?$
43. $66 \div 6 = ?$
44. $33 \div 11 = ?$
45. $96 \div 8 = ?$
46. $28 \div 7 = ?$
47. $70 \div 10 = ?$
48. $66 \div 11 = ?$
49. $5 \div 1 = ?$
50. $45 \div 9 = ?$
51. $0 \div 7 = ?$
52. $5\frac{1}{2} \div 5\frac{1}{2} = ?$

Dividing larger numbers

- The order in which you divide numbers *is* important. For example $12 \div 3$ is *not* the same as $3 \div 12$.

- Here is a 'pencil and paper' method for dividing.

  (a) $625 \div 5$

  $$5 \overline{)6^12^25} \quad 125$$

  (b) $936 \div 4$

  $$4 \overline{)9^13^16} \quad 234$$

  (c) $3073 \div 7$

  $$7 \overline{)3^30^27^63} \quad 0439$$

Exercise 3

Work out

1. $3 \overline{)99}$
2. $2 \overline{)42}$
3. $4 \overline{)48}$
4. $7 \overline{)84}$
5. $5 \overline{)65}$
6. $6 \overline{)72}$
7. $7 \overline{)847}$
8. $9 \overline{)558}$
9. $8 \overline{)128}$
10. $9 \overline{)729}$
11. $2 \overline{)678}$
12. $6 \overline{)3372}$
13. $3 \overline{)729}$
14. $5 \overline{)725}$
15. $4 \overline{)1028}$
16. $8 \overline{)1856}$
17. $6 \overline{)1296}$
18. $7 \overline{)343}$
19. $9 \overline{)6561}$
20. $6 \overline{)2796}$
21. $8 \overline{)2056}$
22. $5 \overline{)1025}$
23. $6 \overline{)7776}$
24. $7 \overline{)5082}$
25. $3050 \div 10$
26. $1387 \div 1$
27. $38\,199 \div 7$
28. $14\,032 \div 8$
29. $31\,386 \div 6$
30. $3490 \div 5$
31. $28\,926 \div 9$
32. $15\,638 \div 7$

Division keywords

The following words are all associated with division.

'Divided by'   Six *divided by* three equals?
'Shared between'   Six *shared between* three is equal to?
'Goes into'   Three *goes into* six, how many times?
'Lots of'   How many *lots of* three are there in six?

All these statements are saying ... 6 ÷ 3 = 2

Exercise 4

1. What is twenty-four divided by three?

2. What is fifty-six divided by seven?

3. How many nines go into sixty-three?

4. How many lots of six are there in seventy-two?

5. What is 120 divided by 10?

6. What is 108 shared between 9?

7. How many times does 4 go into 64?

8. How many lots of 3 are there in 78?

9. Woody has 240 matchsticks which he must divide into groups of 3. How many groups will he have?

10. Four dinosaurs each laid the same number of eggs. Altogether there are 104 eggs. How many eggs did each dinosaur lay?

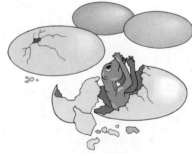

11. Davy, Dozy, Beaky, Mick and Tich are 5 dogs sharing a large tin of 'Muttmeat' which contains 215 delicious chunks. How many chunks does each dog get if it is shared out equally?

12. 'Guzzintas' fizzy drink, comes in six-can packets. Ellen has to pack them into a box which holds 216 cans. How many six-packs of 'Guzzintas' will the box hold?

13. Jake has to share his 'Megamunch' crisps with Max and Joe. He has 243 crisps in his packet. How many will Jake, Max and Joe get each if they are shared out equally?

14. (a) What is £132 divided between eleven?
    (b) What is £512 shared between 8 people?

15. Divide 87 acorns equally between 3 squirrels?
How many does each squirrel get?

16. How many years are there in 156 months?

17. Twelve pencils cost £1·80. How much does one pencil cost?

Remainders

- Suppose you need to share 267 cakes between 5 people.

Work out 267 ÷ 5:

$$\begin{array}{r} 5\,3 \\ 5\overline{)2\,6\,^17} \end{array} \text{ remainder } 2$$

Each person gets 53 cakes and there are 2 left over.

Sometimes it is better to write the remainder as a fraction.
In the calculation above the answer is $53\frac{2}{5}$.
So each person could get $53\frac{2}{5}$ cakes.

- Work out 432 ÷ 7:

$$\begin{array}{r} 6\,1 \\ 7\overline{)4\,3\,^12} \end{array} \text{ remainder } 5$$

The answer is '61 remainder 5' or $61\frac{5}{7}$.

Exercise 5

Write the answer: (a) with a remainder,   (b) as a mixed fraction.

1. $5\overline{)432}$ **2.** $4\overline{)715}$ **3.** $6\overline{)895}$ **4.** $3\overline{)164}$

5. $8\overline{)514}$ **6.** $9\overline{)375}$ **7.** $5\overline{)2642}$ **8.** $2\overline{)7141}$

9. 4079 ÷ 7   **10.** 2132 ÷ 5   **11.** 4013 ÷ 8   **12.** 235 ÷ 6

13. 657 ÷ 10   **14.** 8327 ÷ 10   **15.** 85 714 ÷ 6   **16.** 4826 ÷ 9

17. 2007 ÷ 7   **18.** 9998 ÷ 9   **19.** 6732 ÷ 11   **20.** 84 563 ÷ 7

Think about the remainder

- How many teams of 5 can you make from 113 people?

Work out 113 ÷ 5.

$$\begin{array}{r} 2\,2 \\ 5\overline{)1\,1\,^13} \end{array} \text{ remainder } 3$$

Here we round *down*. You can make 22 teams and there will be 3 people left over.

- An egg box holds 6 eggs. How many boxes do you need for 231 eggs?

Work out 231 ÷ 6.

$$\begin{array}{r} 3\,8 \\ 6\overline{)2\,3\,^51} \end{array} \text{ remainder } 3$$

Here we round *up* because you must use complete boxes. You need 39 boxes altogether.

Exercise 6

In these questions you will get a remainder. Decide whether it is more sensible to round *up* or to round *down*.

1. Tins of spaghetti are packed 8 to a box. How many boxes are needed for 913 tins?

2. A prize consists of 10 000 one pound coins. The prize is shared between 7 people. How many pound coins will each person receive?

3. There are 23 children in a class. How many teams of 4 can be made?

4. Eggs are packed six in a box. How many boxes do I need for 33 eggs?

5. Tickets cost £6 each and I have £38. How many tickets can I buy?

6. I have 204 plants and one tray takes 8 plants. How many trays do I need?

7. There are 51 children in the dining room and a table seats 6. How many tables are needed to seat all the children?

8. I have 100 cans of drink. One box holds 8 cans. How many boxes can I fill?

9. Five people can travel in one car and there are altogether 93 people to transport. How many cars are needed?

10. There are 332 children in a school. One coach holds 50 children. How many coaches are needed for a whole school trip?

11. I have 300 packets of crisps. One box holds 42 packets. How many boxes can I fill? (You can do this without 'long division'.)

12. How many 9 p stamps can I buy with a £5 note?

Divisibility tests: an investigation

Whole numbers are divisible by:

2 if the number is even
3 if the sum of the digits is divisible by 3
4 if the last *two* digits are divisible by 4
5 if the last digit is 0 or 5
6 if the number is even and also divisible by 3
8 if half of it is divisible by 4
9 if the sum of the digits is divisible by 9
10 if _____ (fill in the space)

A Copy and complete the table below, using $\sqrt{}$'s and ×'s.

Number	Divisible by						
	2	3	4	5	6	8	9
363	×	√					
224							
459							
155							
168							
865							
360							
2601							

B You will notice that there is no test above for divisibility by 7. *Investigate* the following test for four-, five- or six-digit numbers:

Test 18 228

Find the difference between the last 3 digits and the digits at the front. $228 - 18 = 210$

If this difference is divisible by 7, then the original number is divisible by 7.

Try the test on these numbers:

37 177, 8498, 431 781, 42 329, 39 579, 910 987.

Now choose some numbers of your own.

C *Investigate* to find out whether or not a similar test works for divisibility by 11.

Crossnumber Puzzle 3

Copy the grid below. Fill in the grid using the clues.

1		2		3	4				5
		6	7						
8	9		10	11			12	13	
							14		
15			16		17	18			
		19			20				21
22	23						24		
			25	26		27			
28		29		30					
		31					32		

Clues across

1. $536 + 219$
3. $2511 - 699$
6. 5×15
8. $637 \div 7$
10. $591 \div 3$
12. 64×8
14. $11 \times 11 \times 4$
15. $101 - 39 + 7$
16. $2000 - 238$
19. 3×14
20. $180 - 135$
22. 809×7
24. $96 + 79$
25. $182 - 139$
27. $3 \times 3 \times 3$
28. $1000 - 599$
30. $4657 + 2732$
31. $15 \times 5 \times 3$
32. 2×30

Clues down

1. $9 \times 9 \times 9$
2. 3×19
4. $1001 - 114$
5. 8×128
7. $100 - 49$
9. 13×13
11. $1000 - 83$
12. 3×18
13. 4×45
15. 5×127
16. $9999 - 8765$
17. 8×80
18. $1000 \div 40$
19. $19 + 17 + 10$
21. $3 \times 50 \times 10$
23. $6100 \div 10$
24. $2000 - 204$
26. $750 - 375$
27. $112 \div 4$
28. 7×7
29. $132 \div 11$

Number messages

Instructions:-

1. Start in the box marked X.
2. Work out the answer to the question at the bottom of the box.
3. Find the box which has the answer in the top right hand corner.
4. Write down the letter in this box. Now work out the answer to the question in that box.
5. Look for the answer as in (3.) Don't forget to record the letter!
6. Continue this process until you arrive back at box X.
7. Read the message.

1.

100	61	40	62	71
X	A	U	D	F
8 + 17	77 + 12	21 + 35	27 + 33	37 + 22
25	4	70	89	23
O	G	N	N	S
63 + 8	49 + 51	2 + 2	45 + 17	14 + 17
91	60	88	22	56
N	R	P	O	R
38 + 25	12 + 19	16 + 75	16 + 24	17 + 8
27	52	31	99	85
H	I	U	B	J
27 + 24	21 + 49	82 + 9	48 + 33	65 + 33
20	3	59	63	17
Y	W	F	N	A
13 + 9	12 + 80	28 + 33	37 + 15	27 + 11

2.

100	48	26	29	22
X	B	W	A	O
27 − 19	25 − 16	19 − 8	51 − 17	81 − 40
16	31	17	43	5
A	R	T	S	U
47 − 29	50 − 30	65 − 43	80 − 17	27 − 11
39	46	1	28	15
N	O	A	E	H
42 − 13	13 − 8	101 − 1	98 − 81	60 − 19
41	40	70	38	77
P	L	G	M	N
75 − 27	71 − 70	43 − 24	16 − 7	71 − 42
99	9	18	34	8
Q	A	R	N	Y
43 − 29	94 − 17	41 − 13	2 − 1	66 − 20

3.

100	41	24	42	27
X	B	O	A	C
3 × 5	3 × 2	2 × 9	7 × 8	7 × 7
81	32	51	83	21
C	A	S	T	K
6 × 7	2 × 8	7 × 4	6 × 8	7 × 9
20	14	56	7	45
E	R	L	E	O
3 × 10	3 × 8	3 × 9	2 × 7	1 × 1
15	49	18	16	1
L	U	O	T	R
6 × 4	10 × 5	3 × 7	5 × 9	10 × 10
64	72	90	50	63
O	P	H	L	N
9 × 9	10 × 9	9 × 8	4 × 8	8 × 8

4.

100	20	5	21	14
X	E	T	H	A
20 ÷ 5	9 ÷ 3	49 ÷ 7	8 ÷ 4	39 ÷ 3
12	16	3	18	11
A	M	H	C	B
99 ÷ 9	21 ÷ 3	15 ÷ 15	51 ÷ 17	20 ÷ 10
9	13	15	8	7
G	S	T	R	O
3 ÷ 1	60 ÷ 5	30 ÷ 6	12 ÷ 2	70 ÷ 7
10	4	19	20	21
N	B	P	E	D
100 ÷ 1	24 ÷ 3	81 ÷ 3	57 ÷ 3	30 ÷ 5
1	25	17	2	6
T	Y	S	U	I
28 ÷ 2	100 ÷ 50	99 ÷ 3	30 ÷ 2	90 ÷ 10

5.

100	19	96	6	81
X	I	E	P	S
12 × 7	9 × 9	18 ÷ 3	12 × 8	7 × 8
95	144	121	61	116
S	D	F	R	T
54 + 7	10 × 10	84 ÷ 7	7 × 5	43 − 17
84	91	29	0	22
O	R	Y	C	L
20 ÷ 4	71 − 49	0 × 7	32 − 7	12 × 12
12	35	26	9	8
T	A	O	O	H
38 + 47	2 ÷ 1	11 × 11	49 + 42	16 ÷ 4
56	37	5	10	85
W	U	U	I	H
72 ÷ 8	22 + 7	67 + 49	8 × 5	58 − 39

2.4 Angles 1

Estimating angles

When angles are measured accurately they
are usually in *degrees*.
We write degrees as a number followed by
the degree symbol °.

   A full turn = 360°
   A half turn = 180°
   A quarter turn = 90°

An angle of 90° is called a *right angle*.

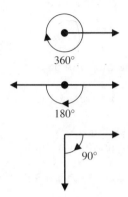

Exercise 1

State whether these angles are correctly or incorrectly labelled. Do
not measure the angles, estimate!

1.

2.

3.

4.

5.

6.

7.

8.

9.

10.

11.

12.

13.

14.

15.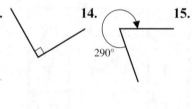

16.

17.

18.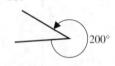

- Any angle between 0° and 90° is
  called an *acute* angle.

- Any angle between 90° and 180°
  is called an *obtuse* angle.
- Any angle bigger than 180° is
  called a *reflex* angle.

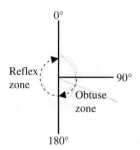

Exercise 2

State whether the following angles are acute, obtuse or reflex.

1. **2.**  **3.** **4.** **5.**

6. **7.** **8.** **9.** **10.**

11. **12.** **13.** **14.** **15.**

16. Estimate the size of each of the angles above.

Labelling angles

- The angle shown is $\hat{ABC}$ (or $\hat{CBA}$).
- This angle is $\hat{POR}$ (or $\hat{ROP}$).

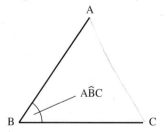 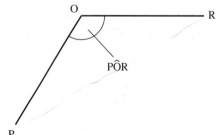

The 'B' must be in the middle.   The 'O' must be in the middle.

- Angles are labelled with capital letters and the middle letter wears
  a 'hat' to indicate an angle.

Exercise 3

Copy each diagram and write down the size of each angle requested.

1.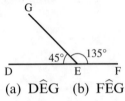

(a) DÊG   (b) FÊG

2.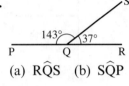

(a) RQ̂S   (b) SQ̂P

3.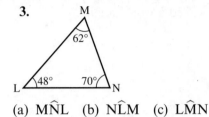

(a) MN̂L   (b) NL̂M   (c) LM̂N

4.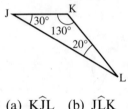

(a) KĴL   (b) JL̂K   (c) JK̂L

5.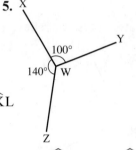

(a) ZŴX   (b) XŴY

6.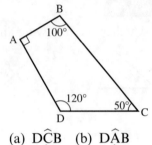

(a) DĈB   (b) DÂB
(c) CD̂A   (d) AB̂C

Using a protractor

A *protractor* is an instrument used to measure angles accurately. Most protractors are manufactured with two scales. One scale reads clockwise, the other anti-clockwise.

It is important to read the correct scale on any protractor in order to measure or draw an angle accurately.

Example:

Measure angle AÔB.

Step 1.   AÔB is acute (less than 90°).

Step 2.   Starting at 0° (along AO) you are moving clockwise. Read the clockwise scale. AÔB = 40°.

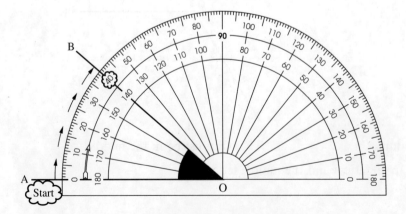

Exercise 4

Give the measurement of each angle listed below.
Remember to read the correct scale. Some questions are done for you, to remind you of this.

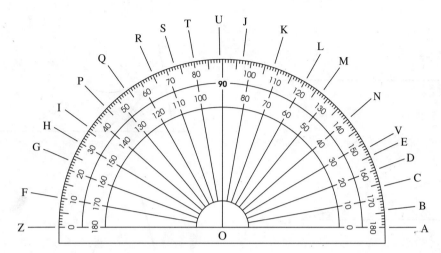

1. AÔD = 20°	**2.** AÔN =	**3.** AÔL = 60°	**4.** AÔK =
5. ZÔF =	**6.** ZÔP = 45°	**7.** ZÔR =	**8.** ZÔT = 80°
9. ZÔI =	**10.** ZÔG =	**11.** AÔC =	**12.** AÔV =
13. AÔQ = 126°	**14.** AÔP =	**15.** AÔF =	**16.** AÔB =
17. ZÔH =	**18.** ZÔB =	**19.** ZÔC =	**20.** ZÔD =
21. AÔG =	**22.** AÔH =	**23.** AÔI =	**24.** AÔM =
25. AÔR =	**26.** ZÔE =	**27.** ZÔJ =	**28.** ZÔK =
29. ZÔL =	**30.** ZÔM =	**31.** AÔE =	**32.** AÔJ =
33. AÔU =	**34.** AÔS =	**35.** ZÔN =	**36.** ZÔQ =
37. ZÔS =	**38.** ZÔU =	**39.** ZÔV =	**40.** AÔT =

Exercise 5

Measure these angles.

1.

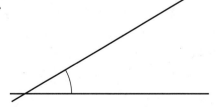

2.

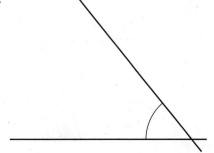

3.

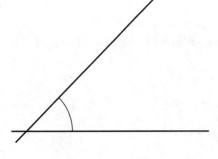

4.

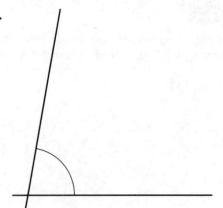

5.

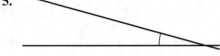

6.

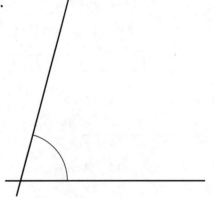

7.

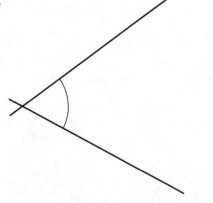

8.

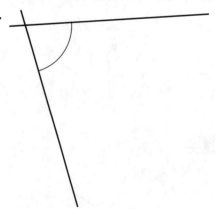

9.

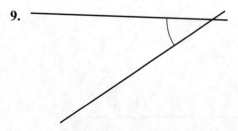

10.

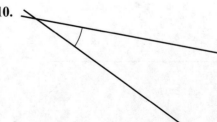

11.

12.

13.

14.

15.

16.

17.

18.

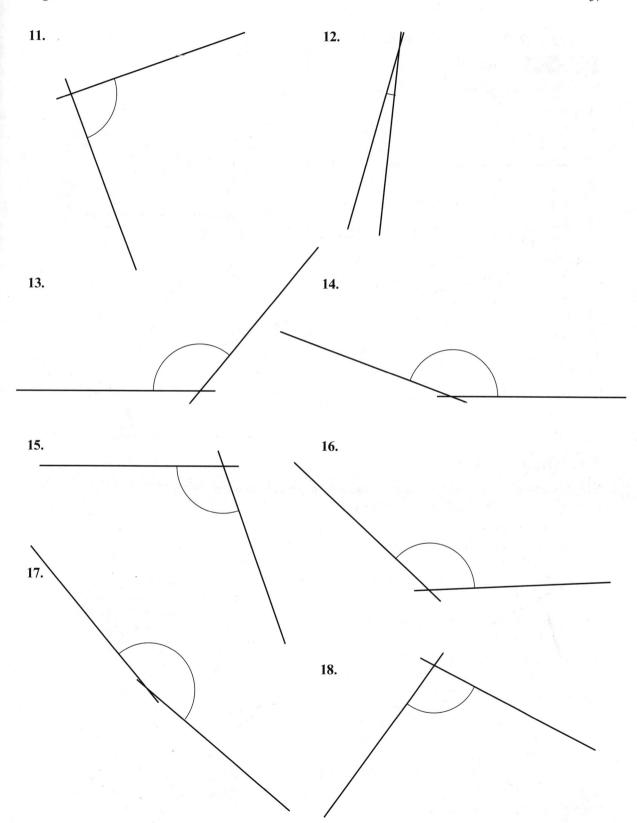

Using a protractor review

Exercise 6   (More difficult)

Measure the following angles.

1. BÂC
2. RĈD
3. DÊR
4. EÂB
5. DR̂C
6. BÊA
7. SR̂B
8. AĈB (reflex)
9. DT̂B
10. CP̂E
11. CD̂E
12. DŜC
13. DĈB
14. ED̂S
15. UD̂Q
16. EĈB (reflex)

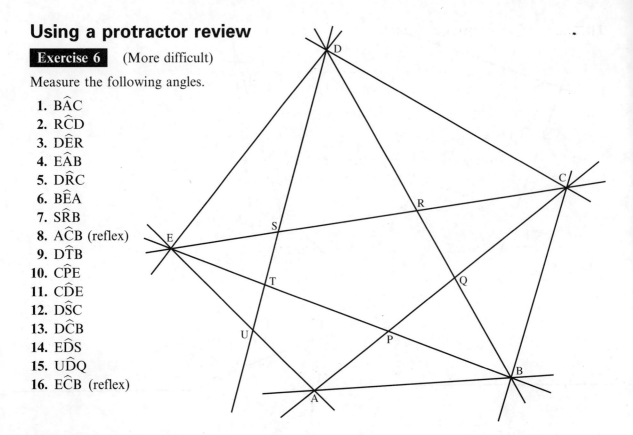

The 'Mystic Rose'

For this activity you need a circular protractor, a pencil and ruler.
(You *could* use a semi-circular protractor)

Step 1.   On a sheet of unlined paper, place a circular protractor with the zero pointing up the paper (↑).

Step 2.   With a sharp pencil draw around your protractor.

Step 3.   Mark where zero is, then mark 30°, 60°, 90°, 120° ... 330°.

Step 4.   Remove the protractor. Using a ruler and pencil join the 0° mark to all the marks made around the outside of the circle with straight lines. Next join the 30° mark to all other marks with straight lines. Repeat this for the 60°, 90° mark and so on up to the 330° mark so that each point is joined to every other point around the circle. This is the 'Mystic Rose'.

Step 5.   Colour in your Rose.

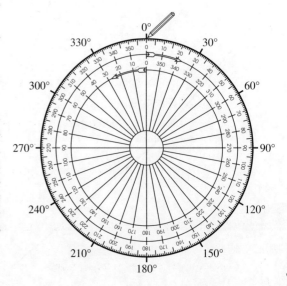

Curves from straight lines

Curve 1

Step 1. On a sheet of unlined paper, place a circular protractor with the zero pointing up the paper (↑).

Step 2. With a sharp pencil draw around your protractor.

Step 3. Mark 0° and then mark every 10° until you return to zero.

Step 4. Label zero degrees with a nought, label 10° the number one, 20° the number 2 and so on until you reach 350° which is number 35.

Step 5. Write the number 36 above your nought and continue numbering around the protractor for the second time. Your last number should be 71 (see the diagram below).

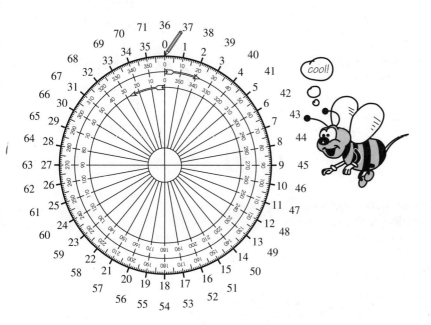

Step 6. Remove the protractor. You can obtain two different patterns as follows, but use a separate diagram for each.

   (i) Join 0 → 10, 1 → 11, ↔ 12, 3 → 13, 4 → 14 and so on with straight lines (join each number to ten more than its value).

   (ii) Join 1 → 2, 2 → 4, 3 → 6, 4 → 8, 5 → 10 and so on with straight lines (join each number to its double).

Curve 2

The third pattern is strictly for the enthusiast!

Step 1. Set the protractor out as you have done before, draw around it, but you must mark every 5°, starting at zero.

Step 2.   Label zero with a nought but this time you must do three
          circuits of labelling numbers until you reach 215!

          Here is a section of the circle to show
          the numbers.

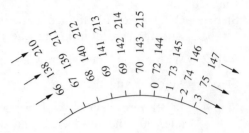

Step 3.   Join 1 → 3, 2 → 6, 3 → 9, 4 → 12, 5 → 15 and so on with
          straight lines (join each number to its treble). You may
          need a calculator with this one ... Good Luck!

2.5 Decimals 1

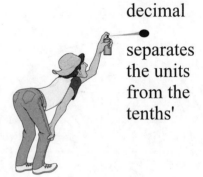

'The decimal separates the units from the tenths'

● Decimals are used with money and with
  measurements of lengths, weights, times.

● The diagram below shows numbers we would see if we could
  'zoom in' on an imaginary ruler.

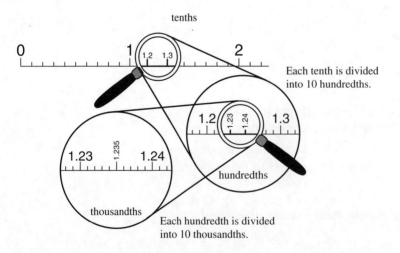

The numbers between 1·2 and 1·3 go up by 0·01 at a time:
   1·21, 1·22, 1·23, 1·24 ...
The numbers between 1·23 and 1·24 go up by 0·001 at a time:
   1·231, 1·232, 1·233, 1·234, 1·235 ...

- Here are some decimal numbers.

Number	Hundreds H	Tens T	Units U	•	Tenths $\frac{1}{10}$	Hundredths $\frac{1}{100}$	Thousandths $\frac{1}{1000}$
538·1	5	3	8	•	1		
42·63		4	2	•	6	3	
0·04			0	•	0	4	
7·125			7	•	1	2	5

- £5·29 means £5 and $\frac{29}{100}$ ths of a pound, or £5 and 29 pence.

  9·6s means 9 seconds and $\frac{6}{10}$ ths of a second.

  18·29 metres means 18 metres and $\frac{29}{100}$ ths of a metre or 18 m and 29 cm.

  1·725 kilograms means 1 kilogram and $\frac{725}{1000}$ ths of a kilogram or 1 kilogram and 725 grams.

Exercise 1

Copy and complete the table below putting each digit in its correct place.

Question number	Number	Hundreds	Tens	Units	•	Tenths	Hundredths	Thousandths
1	56·7				•			
2	83·94				•			
3	137·071				•			
4	40·503				•			
5	179·03				•			
6	25·019				•			
7	3·142				•			
8	0·037				•			
9	2·004				•			
10	0·001				•			

In Questions **11** to **30** give the value of the underlined digit.

11. 4·5̲3	**12.** 3·8̲2	**13.** 7·5̲3	**14.** 9·1̲2	**15.** 15·0̲2
16. 5·0̲4	**17.** 6̲·07	**18.** 3·4̲	**19.** 4̲1·6	**20.** 5·36̲2
21. 4·8̲57	**22.** 3·2̲12	**23.** 2·52̲2	**24.** 7·1̲64	**25.** 1·73̲5
26. 4·8̲07	**27.** 5·73̲1	**28.** 0·1̲01	**29.** 3̲·142	**30.** 2·71̲8

Ordering decimals

Consider these three decimals ...

0·09, 0·101, 0·1.

Which is the correct order from lowest to highest?

- When ordering decimals it is always helpful to write them with the same number of figures after the decimal point.

0·09 $\longrightarrow$ 0·090   Empty spaces can be
0·101 $\longrightarrow$ 0·101   filled with zeros.
0·1 $\longrightarrow$ 0·100

Now we can clearly see the correct order of these decimals from lowest to highest ... 0·090, 0·1, 0·101.

Exercise /

In Questions **1** to **16** answer True (T) or False (F).

1. 0·7 is less than 0·71

2. 0·61 is more than 0·16.

3. 0·08 is more than 0·008

4. 0·5 is equal to 0·500

5. 0·613 is less than 0·631

6. 7·0 is equal to 0·7.

7. 6·2 is less than 6·02

8. 0·09 is more than 0·1.

9. 2·42 is equal to 2·420

10. 0·63 is less than 0·36

11. 0·01 is more than 0·001

12. 0·78 is less than 0·793

13. 8 is equal to 8·00

14. 0·4 is more than 0·35

15. 0·07 is less than 0·1

16. 0·1 is equal to $\frac{1}{10}$.

17. Here is a pattern of numbers based on 3. $\longrightarrow$

Write a similar pattern based on 7 and extend it from 70 000 000 down to 0·0007. Write the numbers in figures and in words

three thousand	3000
three hundred	300
thirty	30
three	3
nought point three	0·3
nought point nought three	0·03

18. What does the digit 7 in 3·271 represent? And the 2? And the 1?

19. What does the digit 3 in 5·386 represent? And the 6? And the 8?

20. Write the decimal fraction equivalent to:
   (a) three tenths
   (b) seven hundredths
   (c) eleven hundredths
   (d) four thousandths
   (e) sixteen hundredths
   (f) sixteen thousandths.

21. Write down the single operation needed [+, −, × or ÷] when you change:
(a) 5·32 to 5·72
(b) 11·042 to 11·047
(c) 0·592 to 0·392
(d) 0·683 to 0·623.

Exercise 2

In Questions **1** to **20** arrange the numbers in order of size, smallest first.

1. 0·21, 0·31, 0·12.

2. 0·04, 0·4, 0·35.

3. 0·67, 0·672, 0·7.

4. 0·05, 0·045, 0·07.

5. 0·1, 0·09, 0·089.

6. 0·75, 0·57, 0·705.

7. 0·41, 0·041, 0·14.

8. 0·809, 0·81, 0·8.

9. 0·006, 0·6, 0·059.

10. 0·15, 0·143, 0·2.

11. 0·04, 0·14, 0·2, 0·53.

12. 1·2, 0·12, 0·21, 1·12.

13. 2·3, 2·03, 0·75, 0·08.

14. 0·62, 0·26, 0·602, 0·3.

15. 0·5, 1·3, 1·03, 1·003.

16. 0·79, 0·792, 0·709, 0·97.

17. 1·23, 0·321, 0·312, 1·04.

18. 0·008, 0·09, 0·091, 0·075.

19. 2·05, 2·5, 2, 2·046.

20. 1·95, 9·51, 5·19, 5·1.

21. Here are numbers with letters
(a) Put the numbers in order, smallest first. Write down just the letters.
(b) Finish the sentence using letters and numbers of your own. The numbers must increase from left to right.

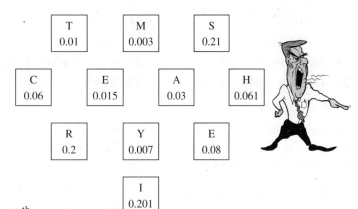

22. Increase the following numbers by $\frac{1}{10}^{th}$:
(a) 3·27
(b) 14·8
(c) 0·841

23. Increase the following numbers by $\frac{1}{100}^{th}$:
(a) 11·25
(b) 1·294
(c) 0·382

24. Increase the following numbers by $\frac{1}{1000}^{th}$:
(a) 3·142
(b) 2·718
(c) 1·414

25. Write the following amounts in pounds:
(a) 11 pence.
(b) 2 pence.
(c) 5 pence.
(d) 10 pence.
(e) 20 pence.
(f) 50 pence.

Adding and subtracting decimals

Remember: Line up the decimal points

(a) 2·4 + 3·23   (b) 7 − 2·3   (c) 0·31 + 4 + 11·6

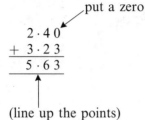

put a zero

```
    2 · 4 0
  + 3 · 2 3
    5 · 6 3
```

(line up the points)

```
   6 7 · 1 0
  −   2 · 3
      4 · 7
```

(write 7 as 7·0)

```
    0 · 31
    4 · 00
 + 11 · 60
   15 · 91
```

(write 4 as 4·00)

Exercise 1

1. 1·2 + 3·4	**2.** 2·7 + 5·1	**3.** 9·4 + 0·2
4. 5·6 + 2·7	**5.** 4·9 + 0·8	**6.** 6·3 + 2·9
7. 7·4 + 9·6	**8.** 14·3 + 9·8	**9.** 46·7 + 8·0
10. 5 + 0·26	**11.** 2·9 + 4·37	**12.** 8·62 + 7·99
13. 0·078 + 2·05	**14.** 10·04 + 3·005	**15.** 13·47 + 27·084
16. 1·97 + 19·7	**17.** 4·56 + 7·890	**18.** 456·7 + 8·901
19. 16·374 + 0·947 + 27	**20.** 3·142 + 2·71 + 8	

Now do these.

21. 3·8 − 2·4	**22.** 8·7 − 6·5	**23.** 4·8 − 6·5
24. 4·8 − 0·7	**25.** 7·1 − 4·6	**26.** 5 − 3·8
27. 13·8 − 6·5	**28.** 11·2 − 7·4	**29.** 19·9 − 8·1
30. 29·6 − 14	**31.** 59·2 − 34·8	**32.** 81·8 − 29·9
33. 8 − 2·7	**34.** 6·7 − 4·29	**35.** 47·2 − 27·42
36. 94·63 − 5·9	**37.** 2·97 − 1·414	**38.** 25·52 − 1·436
39. 3·142 − 1·414	**40.** 2·718 − 1·732	

Exercise 2

Work out

1. £1·45 + 75 p	**2.** £1·00 + £0·75 + 19 p
3. £2·60 + £4·05 + £0·59	**4.** 35 p + 85 p + £1·65
5. £5·00 − £1·50	**6.** £3 − 25 p
7. £10 − 75 p	**8.** £20 − £3·99

9. Geri bought her local team's replica football kit, shirt costing £10·75, shorts costing £3·99 and socks for £2·59. How much did she spend?

10. Winona spent £5·15 in the supermarket and £10·99 in the music shop. How much change did she get from £20?

11. What must be added to £5·63 to make £18?

12. Which five different coins make a total of £1·37?

13. David has £3·20 and wants to buy articles costing £1·10, 66 p, £1·99 and 45 p. How much more money does he need?

14. Which six different coins make £1·78?

15. Jane went to a shop and bought a book for £2·95 and a compact disc for £10·95. She paid with a £50 note. What change did she receive?

Top Banana!   The Banana man of Tesco's.

The following article is a true story. Read the article (which deliberately contains blanks) and then answer the questions below.

He is called the Banana man of Tesco. In a special offer Phil Calcott bought almost half a ton of bananas. He then gave it all away and still made a profit on the deal. In a way Mr Calcott made his local store pay him to take away its own fruit.

The offer said that if you bought a 3 lb bunch of bananas at £1.17, you would gain 25 Tesco 'Club Card' points. These points could be used to buy goods worth £1.25.

Mr Calcott asked the store to load up his Peugeot 205 with bananas.

'I took a car load at a time because even with the back seat down and the boot full I could only fit in 460 lbs of bananas,' he said.

He returned for another load the next day and altogether spent £ ____ buying 942 lbs of the fruit. This earned him almost ____ ,000 Tesco 'Club Card' points.

1. How much would it cost to buy ten 3 lb bunches of bananas?

2. How many Tesco Club Card points would you get?

3. How much would the points be worth?

4. How much profit would you make on this deal?

5. Do you like bananas?

6. Write down the paragraph, which starts 'He returned ...' and fill in the missing numbers.

Part 3

3.1 Accurate drawing

When an architect designs a house he has to draw accurate plans for a builder to follow. In this section you will use a protractor and a pair of compasses to construct accurate diagrams involving triangles and quadrilaterals. Later you will also construct nets from which three dimensional shapes can be made.

Drawing angles

Example: To draw an angle of 70°.

Step 1. Draw a horizontal line.

right hand end of line.

Step 2. Put your protractor on one end of the line. (In this case we shall use the right hand end of the line.)

Step 3. Starting from zero, move around the scale clockwise and mark 70°.

Step 4. Remove the protractor and join the right hand end of the line to your 70° mark.

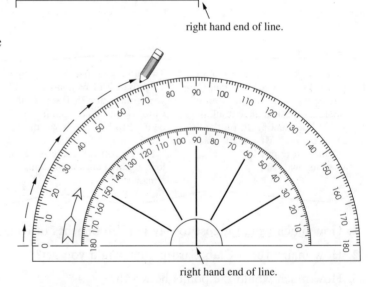

right hand end of line.

Exercise 1

Use your protractor to draw the following angles.

1. 60°	**2.** 20°	**3.** 45°	**4.** 79°	**5.** 9°
6. 115°	**7.** 90°	**8.** 51°	**9.** 18°	**10.** 130°
11. 47°	**12.** 170°	**13.** 94°	**14.** 135°	**15.** 87°

Constructing triangles

A triangle is an extremely rigid structure. It is used extensively in the real world to support many objects. These objects can range from large structures, such as the roof on your house, to smaller structures, such as the brackets holding up your bookshelf.

Draw the triangle ABC full size and measure the length *x*.
(a) Draw a base line *longer than* 8·5 *cm*
(b) Put the centre of the protractor on A and measure an angle 64°. Draw line AP.
(c) Similarly draw line BQ at an angle 40° to AB.
(d) The triangle is formed.
    Measure *x* = 5·6 cm.

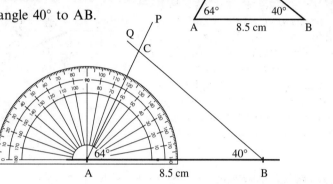

Exercise 2

Construct the triangles and measure the lengths of the sides marked *x*.

1.

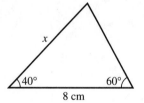

2.

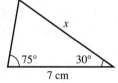

3.

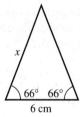

4.

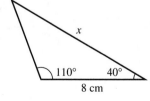

5.

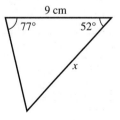

6.

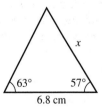

7.

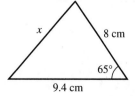

8.

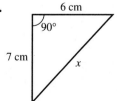

9.

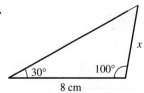

Questions **10**, **11**, **12** are more difficult.

10.
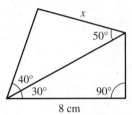

11.
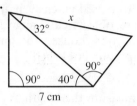

12.
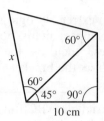

Constructing a triangle given three sides

Draw triangle XYZ and measure XẐY.

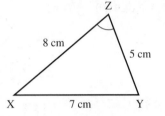

(a) Draw a base line longer than 7 cm and mark X and Y exactly 7 cm apart.

(b) Put the point of a pair of compasses on X and draw an arc of radius 8 cm.

(c) Put the point of the pair of compasses on Y and draw an arc of radius 5 cm.

(d) The arcs cross at the point Z so the triangle is formed.

Measure XẐY = 60°

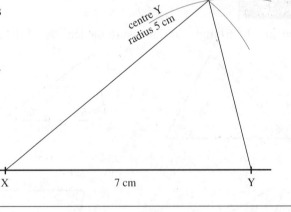

Exercise 3

In Questions **1** to **6** use a pair of compasses and measure the angle x.

1.
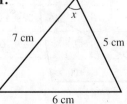

2.
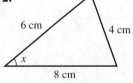

3.
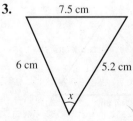

4.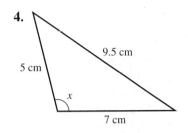

5.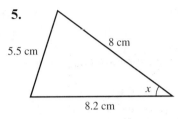

6.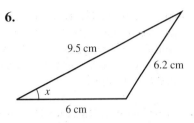

Questions **7**, **8**, and **9** are more difficult.

7.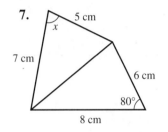

8.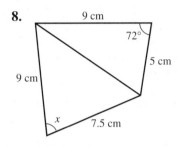

9.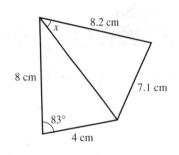

3.2 Number patterns

Prime numbers

A *prime* number is divisible by only two different numbers: by itself and by one. The first six prime numbers are 2, 3, 5, 7, 11, 13. Note that one is *not* a prime number.

1. Draw a number square like the one shown.
   (a) Cross out in pencil the number 1.
   (b) Cross out in pencil all the even numbers, but leave the number 2.
   (c) Draw a red circle around all the numbers divisible by 3, but leave the number 3.
   (d) Cross out in pencil all the numbers divisible by 5, but leave the number 5.
   (e) Draw a green circle around all the numbers divisible by 7, but leave the number 7.
   (f) Cross out in red all the numbers divisible by 11, but leave the number 11.

   You should be able to see several patterns in the table.

   (g) The numbers divisible by 3 form diagonals across the table.
   (h) The numbers divisible by 11 form one diagonal across the table.
   (i) The numbers divisible by 7 form a pattern which is not so obvious. Can you describe it?

1	2	3	4	5	6	7	8	9	10
11	12	13	14	15	16	17	18	19	20
21	22	23	24	25	26	27	28	29	30
31	32	33	34	35	36	37	38	39	40
41	42	43	44	45	46	47	48	49	50
51	52	53	54	55	56	57	58	59	60
61	62	63	64	65	66	67	68	69	70
71	72	73	74	75	76	77	78	79	80
81	82	83	84	85	86	87	88	89	90
91	92	93	94	95	96	97	98	99	100

The numbers which have been left blank are all the prime numbers between 1 and 100. You have drawn a square for finding prime numbers known as the 'sieve of Eratosthenes'. Eratosthenes was a famous Greek mathematician working over 2000 years ago.

2. How many prime numbers are there between 1 and 100?

3. Write down two prime numbers which add up to another prime number.

4. How many of the prime numbers are even?

5. How many of the prime numbers are odd?

6. Find three prime numbers which add up to another prime number.

7. (Harder) Use a calculator to find which of the following are prime numbers.

(a) 103   (b) 145   (c) 151   (d) 188
(e) 143   (f) 108   (g) 221   (h) 293
(i) 493   (j) 323   (k) 1999   (l) 2639

Factors

- The number 12 can be written as two numbers multiplied together in three different ways

$$\boxed{1 \times 12} \qquad \boxed{2 \times 6} \qquad \boxed{3 \times 4}$$

The numbers 1, 12, 2, 6, 3, 4 are all the *factors* of 12.

- $\boxed{1 \times 8} = 8 \qquad \boxed{2 \times 4} = 8$

The factors of 8 are 1, 2, 4, 8.

Exercise 2

Write down all the factors of the following numbers

1. 6	**2.** 4	**3.** 10	**4.** 7	**5.** 15
6. 18	**7.** 24	**8.** 21	**9.** 36	**10.** 40
11. 32	**12.** 31	**13.** 60	**14.** 63	**15.** 85

16. Factors of a number which are also prime numbers are called prime factors. We can find these prime factors using a 'factor tree'

(a) Here is a factor tree for 60   (b) Here is a factor tree for 24

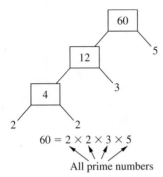

$60 = 2 \times 2 \times 3 \times 5$

All prime numbers

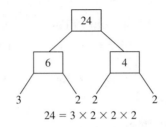

$24 = 3 \times 2 \times 2 \times 2$

(c) You can turn the diagram upside down and then draw a trunk around the number and branches to give a real 'tree shape'. Some people like to draw the prime factors inside apples, pears, bananas and so on.

(d) Draw a factor tree for 36.

In Questions **17** to **28** draw a factor tree for each number.

17. 28	**18.** 32	**19.** 34	**20.** 81
21. 84	**22.** 216	**23.** 294	**24.** 200
25. 1500	**26.** 2464	**27.** 4620	**28.** 98 175

29. The number 345 has 3 and 5 as factors.
Write another three-digit number which has 3 and 5 as factors.

30. The number 432 has 2 and 9 as factors.
Write another three-digit number which has 2 and 9 as factors.

31.* Which number less than 100 has the most prime factors?

32.* Which number less than 1000 has the most *different* prime factors? (You cannot repeat a factor.)

Multiples

The *multiples* of 5 divide by 5 with no remainder.
The first four multiples of 5 are 5, 10, 15, 20.
The first four multiples of 6 are 6, 12, 18, 24.

Exercise 3

Write down the first four multiples of:

1. 3	**2.** 4	**3.** 2	**4.** 7	**5.** 10

Write down the first six multiples of:

6. 5	**7.** 8	**8.** 9	**9.** 11	**10.** 20

11. Find which numbers the following sets are multiples of
  (a) 8, 12, 20, 28
  (b) 25, 30, 55, 60
  (c) 14, 21, 35, 70

In Questions **12** to **16** find the 'odd one out'. (The number which is not a multiple of the number given.)

12. Multiples of 6: 18, 24, 32, 48, 54.

13. Multiples of 11: 33, 77, 101, 132.

14. Multiples of 10: 5, 10, 20, 30, 60.

15. Multiples of 9: 18, 27, 45, 56, 72.

16. Multiples of 7: 49, 77, 91, 105, 18.

17. Find three numbers that are multiples of 3 and 4.

18. Find three numbers that are multiples of 2 and 5.

19. Find three numbers that are multiples of 2, 3 and 5.

20. Find two numbers that are multiples of 2, 4 and 6.

Square numbers and cube numbers

Exercise 4

1.

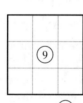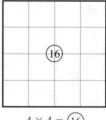

$1 \times 1 = ①$ $2 \times 2 = ④$ $3 \times 3 = ⑨$ $4 \times 4 = ⑯$

  (a) The first four *square* numbers are 1, 4, 9, 16.
  (b) Draw diagrams with labels to show the next three square numbers.

2. A square number is obtained by multiplying a number by itself.
  3×3 is written 3^2 (We say '3 squared...')
  4×4 is written 4^2

  Work out
  (a) 5^2 (b) 8^2 (c) 10^2 (d) 1^2

3. Work out
  (a) $3^2 + 4^2$ (b) $1^2 + 2^2 + 3^2$ (c) $9^2 + 10^2$

4. (a) Write down this sentence and fill in the missing numbers

$$1 \qquad\qquad = 1 \qquad = 1^2$$

$$1 + 3 \qquad\qquad = 4 \qquad = 2^2$$

$$1 + 3 + 5 \qquad = \Box \qquad = \Box^2$$

$$1 + 3 + 5 + 7 \quad = \Box \qquad = \Box^2$$

(b) Write down the next five lines of the sequence.

5. What number when multiplied by itself gives the following
   (a) 49   (b) 81   (c) 144

6. The *square root* of a number is the number which is multiplied by itself to give that number. The symbol for square root is $\sqrt{\ }$.
So $\sqrt{9} = 3$, $\sqrt{16} = 4$, $\sqrt{100} = 10$
Work out
   (a) $\sqrt{25}$ (b) $\sqrt{81}$ (c) $\sqrt{49}$ (d) $\sqrt{1}$

7. Copy the following and fill in the spaces

   (a) $7^2 = 49$, $\sqrt{49} = \Box$ (b) $14^2 = 196$, $\sqrt{196} = \Box$

   (c) $21^2 = 441$, $\sqrt{\Box} = 21$ (d) $3 \cdot 3^2 = 10 \cdot 89$, $\sqrt{\Box} = 3 \cdot 3$

8. *Lagrange's theorem.* A famous mathematician called Lagrange proved that every whole number could be written as the sum of four or fewer square numbers.

For example: $21 = 16 + 4 + 1$
$$19 = 16 + 1 + 1 + 1$$
$$35 = 25 + 9 + 1$$

Check that the theorem applies to the following numbers.

   (a)   10   (b)   24   (c)   47
   (d)   66   (e)   98   (f)   63
   (g)   120   (h)   141   (i)   423

If you can find a number which needs more than four squares you will have disproved Lagrange's theorem and a new theorem will be named after you.

9. The numbers 1, 8, 27 are the first three *cube* numbers.

$1 \times 1 \times 1 = 1^3 = 1$ (we say '1 cubed')
$2 \times 2 \times 2 = 2^3 = 8$ (we say '2 cubed')
$3 \times 3 \times 3 = 3^3 = 27$ (we say '3 cubed')

The odd numbers can be added in groups to give an interesting sequence:

$$1 \qquad\qquad = 1 \qquad = 1^3$$
$$3 + 5 \qquad\quad = 8 \qquad = 2^3$$
$$7 + 9 + 11 \quad = 27 \qquad = 3^3$$

Write down the next three rows of the sequence to see if the sum of each row always gives a cube number.

Happy numbers

- (a) Take any number, say 23.
  (b) Square the digits and add: $2^2 + 3^2 = 4 + 9 = 13$
  (c) Repeat (b) for the answer: $1^2 + 3^2 = 1 + 9 = 10$
  (d) Repeat (b) for the answer: $1^2 + 0^2 = 1$

  23 is a so-called 'happy' number because it ends in one.

- Take another number, say 7.

  Write 7 as 07 to maintain the pattern of squaring and adding the digits.
  Here is the sequence:

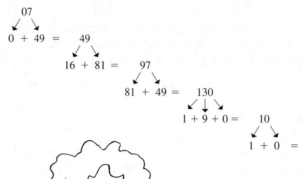

So 7 is a happy number also.

With practice you may be able to do the arithmetic in your head and write: $07 \rightarrow 49 \rightarrow 97 \rightarrow 130 \rightarrow 10 \rightarrow 1$.

You may find it helpful to make a list of the square numbers 1^2, 2^2, $3^2, \ldots 9^2$.

- Your task is to find all the happy numbers from 1 to 100 and to circle them on a grid like the one shown.
  This may appear to be a very time-consuming and rather tedious task!
  But remember: Good mathematicians always look for short cuts and for ways of reducing the working.

So think about what you are doing and good luck!
As a final check you should find that there are 20 happy numbers from 1 to 100.

1	2	3	4	5	6	7	8	9	10
11	12	13	14	15	16	17	18	19	20
21	22	23	24	25	26	27	28	29	30
31	32	33	34	35	36	37	38	39	40
41	42	43	44	45	46	47	48	49	50
51	52	53	54	55	56	57	58	59	60
61	62	63	64	65	66	67	68	69	70
71	72	73	74	75	76	77	78	79	80
81	82	83	84	85	86	87	88	89	90
91	92	93	94	95	96	97	98	99	100

Satisfied numbers

The number 4 is an even number *and* a square number. It *satisfies* both categories.

1. Copy the grid below and use a pencil for your answers (so that you can rub out mistakes.)
Write the numbers from 1 to 9, one in each box, so that all the numbers satisfy the conditions for both the row and the column.

	Number between 5 and 9	Square number	Prime number
Factor of 6	6	?	?
Even number	?	?	?
Odd number	?	?	?

2. Copy the grid and write the numbers from 1 to 9, one in each box.

	Prime number	Multiple of 3	Factor of 16
Number greater than 5			
Odd number			
Even number			

3. This one is more difficult. Write the numbers from 1 to 16, one in each box.

	Prime number	Odd number	Multiple of two	Even number
Numbers less than 7				
Factor of 36				
Numbers less than 12				
Numbers between 11–17				

4. Design a grid with categories of your own and ask a friend to solve it.

3.3 Three dimensional objects

Three dimensional objects have three dimensions ... length, width
and depth.
Three dimensional is abbreviated to '3D'.
3D objects are often referred to as 'solids' or 'solid objects'.
Below are some familiar 3D objects.

Special Names are given to certain 3D solid objects ...

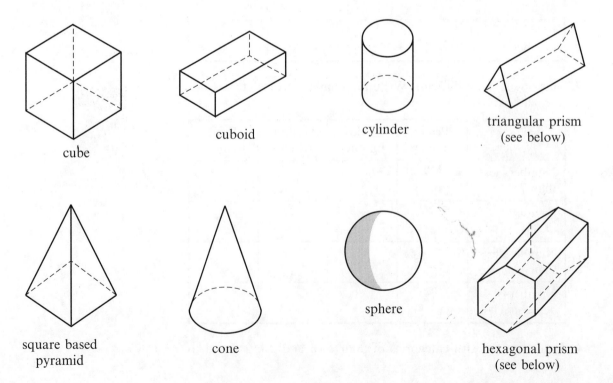

cube

cuboid

cylinder

triangular prism
(see below)

square based
pyramid

cone

sphere

hexagonal prism
(see below)

- A *prism* has the same cross section throughout its length. Here is a triangular prism.

  If you cut through the prism parallel to its end, (the face marked A in the diagram) you produce a congruent shape (marked A').

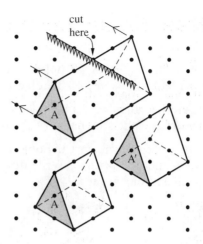

Exercise 1

Copy the following diagrams and complete the accompanying sentence using words from the page opposite.

1.

A dice is a _____

2.

A filing cabinet is a _____

3.

A tin of soup is a _____

4.

White light is changed by directing it through a _____

5.

The tepee is in the shape of a _____

6.

A snooker ball is a _____

7.

The ice hockey puck is a _____

8.

The roof of this bell tower is a _____

9.

A pencil is a _____ with a _____ at one end

Exercise 2

Below are drawn ten 3D objects labelled A to J.

1. Write down the letters of all objects that are prisms and write
   next to the letter the name of the object.

2. Write down the letters of all the objects that are non-prisms and
   write next to the letter the name of the object.

3. For the 10 objects given, sort the objects into two groups (other
   than prisms and non-prisms). Write down your two groups and
   how you chose your groups.

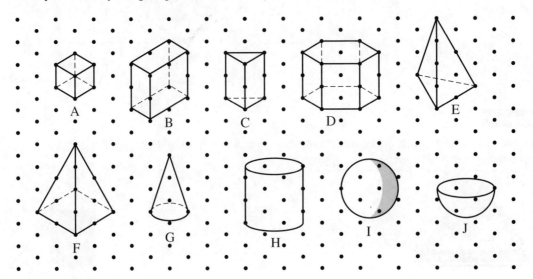

Faces, edges and vertices

Many three-dimensional shapes have
faces, *edges* and *vertices* (plural of
vertex). The diagram opposite shows
a cuboid.

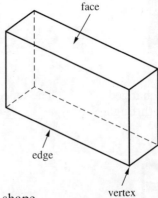

The *faces* of the cuboid are the flat surfaces on the shape.
There are 6 faces on a cuboid.
The *edges* of the cuboid are the lines that make up the shape.
There are 12 edges on a cuboid.
The vertices of the cuboid are where the edges meet at a point.
There are 8 vertices on a cuboid.

In Questions **1** to **8** you are given the diagrams of different three-dimensional objects. Copy and complete the table below the diagrams. The details for the cuboid above have been done for you.

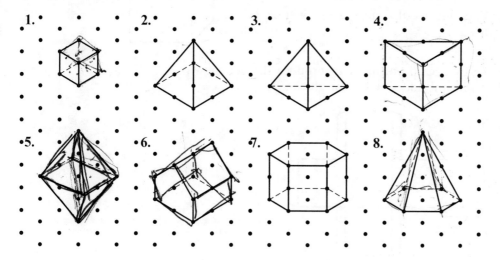

No	Shape	Faces	Edges	Vertices
Example	cuboid	6	12	8
1.	cube			
2.	square based pyramid			
3.	tetrahedron			
4.	triangular based prism			
5.	octahedron			
6.	pentagonal based prism			
7.	hexagonal based prism			
8.	hexagonal based pyramid			

9. Examine carefully the results of your table.
   (a) Try to find a connection between the number of faces, edges and vertices of the three-dimensional objects given.
   (b) A certain shape has 9 faces and 6 vertices. How many edges does it have?

Nets for making shapes

- If the cube shown was made of cardboard, and you cut along some of the edges and laid it out flat, you would have a *net* of the cube.

  There is more than one net of a cube as you will see in the exercise below.

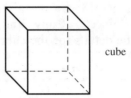

cube

- To make a cube from card you need to produce the net shown below complete with the added 'tabs' for glueing purposes.

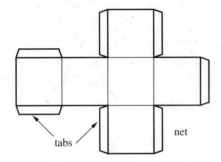

tabs

net

- In this section you will make several interesting 3D objects. You will need a pencil, ruler, scissors and either glue (Pritt Stick) or Sellotape.

  Score all lines before cutting out the net. This makes assembly of the object easier. Don't forget the tabs!

Exercise 4

1. Here are several nets which may or may not make cubes. Draw the nets on squared paper, cut them out and fold them to see which ones do make cubes.

(a)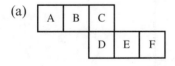

(b)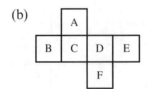

(c)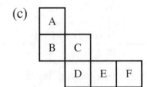

(d)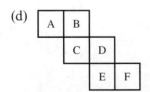

(e)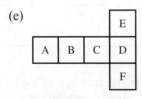

2. For the nets which *did* make cubes in Question **1**, state which of the faces B, C, D, E or F was opposite face A on the cube.

In Questions **3** and **4** draw the net and cut it out to make the object shown.

3.

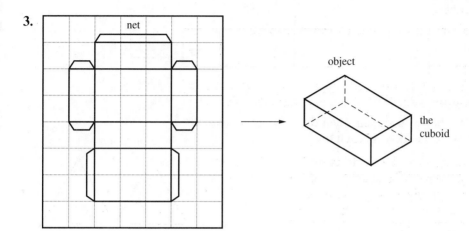

4.

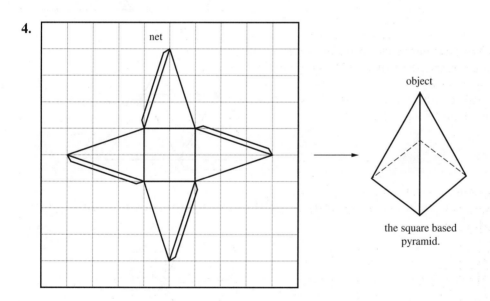

5. Draw a net which could be used to make the closed box shown.
Use squared paper.

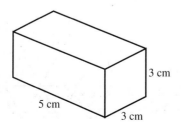

6. Each diagram below shows *part* of the net of a cube. Each net needs one more square to complete the net.

(a) 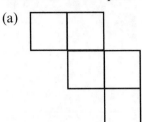   (b)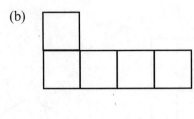

Cut out each of the shapes given and then draw the four possible nets which would make a cube with each one.

7. Some interesting objects can be made using triangle dotty paper. The basic shape for the nets is an equilateral triangle. With the paper as shown the triangles are easy to draw.

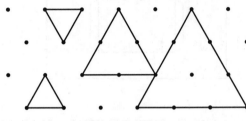

Make the sides of the triangles 3 cm or 4 cm long so that the objects are easy to make.
Here is the net of a tetrahedron.
Draw it and then cut it out.

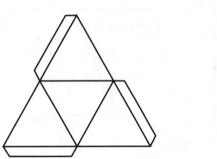

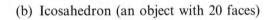

8. Here are two more.
(a) Octahedron (octa: eight; hedron: faces)   (b) Icosahedron (an object with 20 faces)

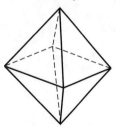   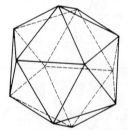

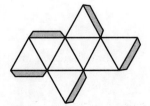   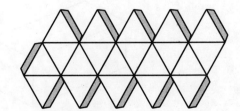

3.4 Time

Analogue – 12 hour watch

Digital – 24 hour watch

The 24 hour clock

The times which most people use in their everyday lives are times measured from midnight or from mid-day (noon). In the morning 9 o'clock is 9 hours after midnight and is written 9.00 a.m. In the afternoon 4 o'clock is 4 hours after mid-day (noon) and is written 4.00 p.m.

Using the 24 hour clock all times are measured from midnight. This means 9.00 a.m. is written 09.00 and 4.00 p.m. is written 16.00.

Here are three times converted from the 12 hour clock to the 24 hour clock

(a) 8.00 a.m. = 08.00
(b) 9.30 p.m. = 21.30
(c) 3.15 p.m. = 15.15

Remember   a.m. is an abbreviation of ante meridiem and means before mid-day,

p.m. is an abbreviation of post meridiem and means after mid-day

Exercise 1

Write the following in the 24-hour system.

1. 8.00 a.m.	**2.** 9.30 p.m.	**3.** 6.00 p.m.
4. 5.30 a.m.	**5.** 7.40 p.m.	**6.** 10.00 p.m.
7. 7.15 p.m.	**8.** 10.45 p.m.	**9.** 8.30 a.m.
10. 4.15 a.m.	**11.** 2.25 a.m.	**12.** 1.30 p.m.
13. 7.20 p.m.	**14.** 6.50 a.m.	**15.** 7.10 a.m.

16. Two minutes before midnight.
17. Two and a half hours before midnight.
18. Five minutes before noon.
19. Three and a half hours after noon.
20. One hour after midnight.
21. One and a half hours before noon.
22. Twenty minutes after midnight.
23. Five hours before midnight.
24. Six minutes after noon.
25. Fifty minutes after midnight.

Write the following in the 12-hour system.

26. 07.00	**27.** 19.30	**28.** 11.20	**29.** 04.45
30. 20.30	**31.** 21.15	**32.** 09.10	**33.** 11.45
34. 23.10	**35.** 20.00	**36.** 12.00	**37.** 01.40
38. 04.00	**39.** 07.07	**40.** 13.13	**41.** 12.15
42. 12.30	**43.** 15.45	**44.** 16.20	**45.** 05.16

Time intervals

● Find the time interval between 15.40 and 18.05.

From 15.40 to 16.00 : 20 minutes   (count on to the next hour)
From 16.00 to 18.05 : 2 hours 5 minutes   (count on from 16.00)
Altogether there is 2 hours 25 minutes

Exercise 2

Find the number of hours and minutes between the following.

1. 20.10 and 21.20	**2.** 21.40 and 23.50
3. 22.15 and 23.10	**4.** 19.30 and 20.05
5. 20.16 and 23.36	**6.** 11.25 and 13.10
7. 09.40 and 12.00	**8.** 21.17 and 23.10
9. 23.04 and 23.57	**10.** 17.45 and 23.10
11. 05.15 and 07.05	**12.** 11.26 and 14.40
13. 9.50 a.m. and 11.05 a.m.	**14.** 9.30 a.m. and 2.05 p.m.
15. 11.10 a.m. and 1.30 p.m.	**16.** 7.30 a.m. and 7.30 p.m.
17. 10.40 a.m. and 12.40 p.m.	**18.** 5.40 a.m. and 1.00 p.m.
19. 11.55 a.m. and 3.10 p.m.	**20.** 1.35 a.m. and 8.40 a.m.

21. 22.30 on Monday to 03.30 on Tuesday
22. 21.00 on Thursday to 01.40 on Friday
23. 17.30 on Monday to 02.00 on Tuesday
24. 23.45 on Saturday to 02.10 on Sunday
25. 22.50 on Thursday to 07.00 on Friday
26. 07.00 on Friday to 02.00 on Saturday
27. 09.30 on Monday to 04.30 on Tuesday
28. 09.15 on Wednesday to 02.45 on Thursday
29. 22.10 on Friday to 07.35 on Saturday
30. 06.30 on Friday to 16.30 on Saturday

3.5 Mental arithmetic

Mental calculation strategies

In this section we will look at strategies for adding and subtracting numbers mentally. The introduction is followed by 12 questions to practise the new techniques.

Later in the book there are mental arithmetic tests which contain a wider variety of questions.

A. 'Easy-to-add' numbers

When numbers are added the order of the numbers does not matter:

$23 + 17 \qquad = 17 + 23$
$41 + 9 + 110 = 110 + 9 + 41$

Many pairs of numbers are easy to add together mentally

e.g. $17 + 23 = 40, \qquad 18 + 32 = 50, \qquad 33 + 7 = 40$

Practice questions

Look for 'easy-to-add' pairs of numbers in the following. If necessary change the order of the numbers in your head and then write down the answer without working.

1. $5 + 17 + 15$ **2.** $8 + 27 + 12$ **3.** $17 + 13 + 16$
4. $22 + 48 + 11$ **5.** $9 + 87 + 11$ **6.** $19 + 41 + 37$
7. $17 + 15 + 25$ **8.** $18 + 2 + 57$ **9.** $16 + 3 + 24$
10. $90 + 110 + 58$ **11.** $75 + 37 + 25$ **12.** $215 + 49 + 51$

B. Splitting the numbers

- $23 + 48 :$ $20 + 40 = 60$ and $3 + 8 = 11$
  So $23 + 48 = 60 + 11 = 71$

- $255 + 38 :$ $250 + 30 = 280$ and $5 + 8 = 13$
  So $225 + 38 = 280 + 13 = 293$

- Other way
  $23 + 48 = 23 + 40 + 8 = 63 + 8 = 71$
  $255 + 38 = 255 + 30 + 8 = 285 + 8 = 293$

  $576 - 43 = 576 - 40 - 3 = 536 - 3 = 533$
  $95 - 48 = 95 - 40 - 8 = 55 - 8 = 47$

Practice questions

1. $34 + 47$ **2.** $65 + 28$ **3.** $78 + 23$ **4.** $57 + 24$
5. $88 - 31$ **6.** $97 - 42$ **7.** $84 + 17$ **8.** $82 - 35$
9. $66 + 37$ **10.** $58 + 34$ **11.** $62 - 44$ **12.** $206 + 105$

C. Add/subtract

$9, 19, 29 \ldots 11, 21, 31, \ldots$, adjusting by one.

- $54 + 19 = 54 + 20 - 1 = 63$

- $77 + 41 = 77 + 40 + 1 = 118$

- $63 + 59 = 63 + 60 - 1 = 122$

- $54 - 31 = 54 - 30 - 1 = 23$

- $77 - 39 = 77 - 40 + 1 = 38$

- $95 - 29 = 95 - 30 + 1 = 66$

Practice questions

1. $67 + 21$ 2. $37 + 51$ 3. $36 + 39$ 4. $76 + 29$
5. $45 + 29$ 6. $70 - 21$ 7. $80 - 41$ 8. $44 + 58$
9. $33 + 96$ 10. $91 - 37$ 11. $53 + 41$ 12. $48 - 23$

Mental arithmetic tests

There are several sets of mental arithmetic questions in this section.
It is intended that a teacher will read out each question twice, with
all pupils' books closed. The answers are written down without any
written working. Each test of 20 questions should take about 20
minutes.

Mental Arithmetic Test 1

1. Write the number six thousand and thirty-one in figures.

2. What number should you subtract from fifty-one to get the answer twenty-four?

3. What is twenty multiplied by ten?

4. What is thirty-five divided by seven?

5. Add together nine, three and eighteen.

6. Write nought point five as a fraction.

7. How many centimetres are there in ninety millimetres?

8. What is two point three multiplied by ten?

9. How many quarters make up two whole ones?

10. The side of a square is four metres. What is the area of the square?

11. If sixty per cent of teachers in a school are female what percentage of teachers are male?

12. A bus journey starts at seven twenty. It lasts fifty-five minutes. At what time does it end?

13. In the morning the temperature is minus three degrees celsius. What will be the temperature after it rises eleven degrees?

14. Write a factor of twenty-four which is greater than one.

15. What is three squared?

16. Write down any multiple of nine.

17. How much change from ten pounds would you get after spending eight pounds and fifty pence?

18. Write down the number that is halfway between fourteen and twenty?

19. Fifty per cent of a number is thirty-two. What is the number?

20. What is the reflex angle between clock hands showing three o'clock?

Mental Arithmetic Test 2

1. Add together seven, three and twelve.

2. Write the number that is thirteen less than one hundred.

3. What is nine multiplied by seven?

4. Write the number two thousand and thirty-seven in figures.

5. Write nought point two five as a fraction.

6. What is two hundred and ten divided by one hundred?

7. Change thirteen centimetres into millimetres.

8. What is double seventeen?

9. How many ten pence coins make three pounds and seventy pence?

10. What is four hundred and fifty-eight to the nearest ten?

11. What number is half way between six and thirteen?

12. A television programme starts at five minutes to seven and lasts thirty-five minutes. At what time does the programme finish?

13. One third of a number is six. What is the number?

14. How many twenty pence coins would you get for ten pounds?

15. What number is eight squared?

16. What is three quarters of one hundred?

17. If seventy-seven per cent of pupils in a school are right-handed, what percentage are left-handed?

18. Write seven tenths as a decimal number.

19. The temperature in Weston-super-Mare was minus two degrees, the temperature in Benidorm was eleven degrees warmer. What was the temperature in Benidorm?

20. David ate one hundred and twenty degrees of a circular wedding cake. Jacqui ate sixty degrees. How many degrees of cake were left?

Mental Arithmetic Test 3

1. Write the number two thousand one hundred and four in figures

2. What number is eight more than thirty-seven?

3. If oranges cost twelve pence each, how many can I buy for one pound?

4. With three darts I score seven, double five and treble eleven. What is my total score?

5. A film lasting one and half hours starts at seven twenty-five p.m. What time does the film finish?

6. If I buy a pen for twenty-eight pence and a note pad for forty-two pence, how much change do I get from one pound?

7. What number is nine less than forty-six?

8. What is half of half of sixty?

9. How many twenty pence coins make five pounds?

10. What is the perimeter of a rectangular lawn fifteen metres by six metres?

11. I am facing South-West and the wind is hitting me on my back. What direction is the wind coming from?

12. If eight per cent of pupils of a school are absent, what percentage of pupils are present?

13. Write nought point nine as a fraction.

14. What is twenty-fifteen in twelve hour clock time?

15. How many degrees are there in three right angles?

16. A quarter of my wages is taken in tax. What percentage have I got left?

17. How many grams are there in half a kilogram?

18. What four coins make seventy-six pence?

19. One angle in an isosceles triangle is one hundred and ten degrees. How large is each of the other two angles?

20. What number is one hundred times bigger than nought point two?

Mental Arithmetic Test 4

1. What are eight twenties?

2. What number is nineteen more than eighty-seven?

3. Write in figures the number six-thousand and eleven.

4. What is one quarter of twenty-eight?

5. What is the sum of sixty-three and twenty-nine?

6. How many sevens are there in eighty-four?

7. A pair of shorts costs £8·99, how much change do you get from a £10 note?

8. Subtract forty-five centimetres from two metres giving your answer in metres as a decimal number.

9. If you have three thousand and eleven pennies, how much do you have in pounds and pence?

10. The perimeter of a square is sixteen centimetres. What is the length of the side of the square?

11. How many metres are there in 1·5 kilometres?

12. What is fifty per cent of fifty pounds?

13. How many sides has a heptagon?

14. I think of a number, double it and the answer is five. What was the number I thought of?

15. What is three thousand four hundred and sixty-nine to the nearest hundred?

16. What is nought point two squared?

17. Two angles of a triangle add up to one hundred and fifty-five degrees. What size is the third angle?

18. Write noon in twenty-four hour clock time.

19. You are facing south and turn through three right angles anti-clockwise, what direction are you now facing?

20. A thermometer in a freezer compartment shows minus five degrees. The temperature outside the freezer is thirteen degrees celsius. What is the difference in temperature between inside and outside?

Mental Arithmetic Test 5

1. What is nought point one as a percentage?

2. How many edges has a triangular based pyramid?

3. What is three quarters of sixty pounds?

4. Change nineteen forty-five into twelve hour clock time.

5. I am facing north-west and turn through one and a half right-angles in a clockwise turn. In which direction am I now facing?

6. What is the product of ten and twenty-five?

7. What is the sum of the numbers 1, 2, 3, 4, 5?

8. How much change from a ten pound note will I receive if I spend three pounds and ninety-nine pence?

9. How many 2p coins are worth the same as twenty 5p coins?

10. How many centimetres are there in one hundred and five millimetres?

11. Two angles in a triangle are forty-five and sixty-five degrees. What is the third angle?

12. A 'pools' prize of six million pounds is shared equally between one hundred people. How much does each person receive?

13. What is the probability I roll an even number on a fair dice?

14. What is the next prime number after thirteen?

15. How many seconds are there in one hour?

16. I bought a magazine for 79p and paid with a £1 coin. My change consisted of five coins. What were they?

17. What is the perimeter of a square whose area is nine centimetres squared?

18. What is the name given to a triangle which has two sides the same length and a pair of equal triangles?

19. Write down the number that is halfway between twenty-seven and eighty-three.

20. Answer true or false: 1 km is longer than 1 mile.

Mental Arithmetic Test 6

1. Write ten million pence in pounds.

2. Write down a sensible estimate for eleven multiplied by ninety-nine.

3. Write the number two thousand one hundred and seven in figures.

4. What is nine hundred and fifty-eight to the nearest hundred?

5. In a survey three quarters of people like football. What percentage of people like football?

6. What decimal number is twenty-three divided by one hundred?

7. How many twenty pence coins make three pounds?

8. How many twelve pence pencils can you buy for one pound?

9. One third of a number is eight. What is the number?

10. Write nine tenths as a decimal number.

11. What is the name of the quadrilateral which has only one pair of parallel sides?

12. What number is 10 less than ninety thousand?

13. A sphere is a prism. True or false?

14. What is the probability of scoring less than six on a fair dice?

15. I think of a number, divide it by three and the answer is seven. What number did I think of?

16. What is the area of a rectangle nine metres by seven metres.

17. How many quarters are there in one and a half?

18. How many millimetres are there in one metre?

19. How many hours of recording time are there on a two hundred and forty minute video tape?

20. What number is squared to produce eighty-one?

3.6 Mid book review

This section contains six review exercises
Review exercises 1 and 2 cover material in part 1
Review exercises 3 and 4 cover material in part 2
Review exercises 5 and 6 cover material in part 3.

Review exercise 1

Work out

1.	81	2.	682	3.	599	4.	235
	-45		$+\ 74$		-315		$+409$

5. $566 + 278$ 6. $657 - 340$ 7. $171 + 681$ 8. $963 - 148$

9. $534 - 208$ 10. $589 - 99$.

11. There were 122 peaches in a box. 63 were sold. How many peaches were left?

12. There are 763 books in a library. A further 128 books are put on the shelves. How many books does the library now have altogether?

13. There are exactly 135 worms in a garden. A
    hungry Robin ate 49 of them for breakfast.
    How many worms are left?

14.   This is a number triangle. The numbers
                            along each edge add up to 9.

                            Copy and complete the triangle.

                            The six numbers are 1, 2, 3, 4, 5, 6.

15. A box has a mass of 230 g when empty.
    When it is full of sugar the total mass is 650 g.
    What is its mass when it is half full?

16. In a school 316 of the pupils have lunch at the
    school and 97 go home to lunch. How many
    pupils have lunch altogether?

17. This is a number ring.
    Start with any number and multiply the units digit
    by 4 and then add the tens digit.

    For example $(15) \rightarrow 5 \times 4 + 1 \rightarrow (21)$

    The rule is then repeated on 21 and so on.

    Use the same rule to complete this number ring.

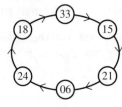

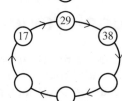

18. Write down the co-ordinates of the points which
    make up the 'S'. You must give the points in the
    correct order starting at the bottom left.

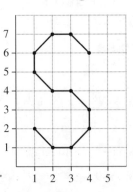

19. Draw a grid with values from 0 to 10. Plot the points below and
    join them up in order. You should obtain two letters of the
    alphabet
    (a) (1, 5)   (3, 1)   (4, 3)   (5, 1)   (7, 5)
    (b) (8, 5)   (8, 1)   (8, 3)   (10, 3) (10, 5) (10, 1)

20. Here are three number cards.
One number that can be made with the three cards is 617.

(a) Use the three cards to make a number which is *more* than 617.
(b) Use the three cards to make a number which is *less* than 617.
(c) Use the three cards to make an even number.

21. Here are four number cards.

Use *all four* cards for the following
(a) An add. The answer must be less than 100.

(b) A take away.
The answer must be less than 20.

22. Make a copy of the cross number pattern and complete the puzzle using the clues given.

Clues across	Clues down
1. $63 + 79$	1. $527 - 418$
3. $71 - 37$	2. $136 + 89$
4. $965 - 668$	3. $241 + 134$
5. $839 + 126$	6. $840 - 211$
7. $100 - 49$	8. $1001 - 815$
9. $17 - 9$	10. $924 - 867$
10. $329 + 267$	11. $25 + 38$
12. $604 - 528$	12. $100 - 27$
13. $1036 - 643$	

Review exercise 2

Mastermaths – Two dimensional objects
How many can you score out of twenty?

1. Name the triangle with three equal sides and angles.

2. What is the name of the triangle with two equal angles?

3. A triangle has sides of three different lengths. What type of triangle is it?

4. What four sided shape has all sides the same length and all angles equal?

5. What quadrilateral has two pairs of sides the same length and all angles equal?

6. Which quadrilateral has all four sides the same length but only opposite angles equal?

7. Which quadrilateral has two pairs of sides the same length but only opposite angles equal?

8. Which quadrilateral has two pairs of equal sides but only one pair of opposite angles equal?

9. Which quadrilateral has only one pair of parallel sides?

10. What is the name of a five-sided shape?

11. What is the name of a six-sided shape?

12. What is the name of an eight-sided shape?

13. What is the name of a regular four-sided shape?

14. How many sides has a decagon?

15. True or false: All squares are rectangular.

16. What is the general name of a many sided shape?

17. A regular hexagon can be made from 6 equilateral triangles. True or False?

18. What is the name given to all four-sided shapes?

19. Any quadrilateral can be cut into two triangles. True or false?

20. What is the correct mathematical name for an 'oblong'?

Review exercise 3

'Bonzo' the dog likes to bury food in the garden so he can have a 'snack' between meals.

On the right is a bird's-eye view of Bonzo's garden and where he has hidden his snacks. Bonzo's position is indicated.

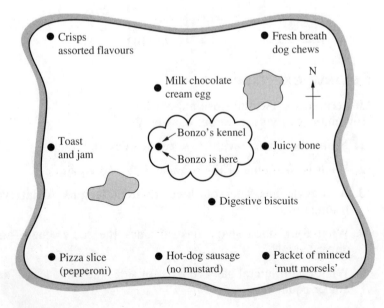

State the direction in which 'Bonzo' must travel from his kennel in order to eat the following:

1. Pizza slice (pepperoni).
2. Digestive biscuits.
3. Crisps (assorted flavours).
4. Milk chocolate cream egg.
5. Toast and jam.
6. Juicy bone.
7. Hot-dog sausage (no mustard).
8. Packet of minced 'mutt morsels'.

'Bonzo' decides to stock-take on his well hidden snacks. He starts from his kennel and tours the garden. State the direction he must take on each stage of his journey in the following questions.

9. Kennel to crisps.
10. Crisps to fresh breath dog chews.
11. Fresh breath dog chews to pizza slice (pepperoni).
12. Pizza slice to toast and jam.
13. Toast and jam to Hot-dog sausage.
14. Hot-dog sausage to packet of 'mutt morcels'.
15. 'Mutt morcels' to digestive biscuits.
16. Digestive biscuits to juicy bone.
17. Juicy bone to kennel.
18. Kennel to milk chocolate cream egg.

Review exercise 4

In Questions **1** to **12** state whether the angle marked is acute, obtuse, reflex or otherwise and give an estimate of its size in degrees.

1.
2.
3.
4.

5.
6.
7.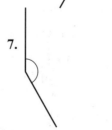
8.

9.
10.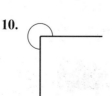
11.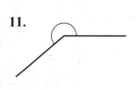
12.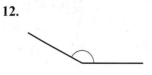

In Questions **13** to **16** write down the line which is correct.

13. (a) 0·07 is equal to 0·7
     (b) 0·07 is greater than 0·7
     (c) 0·07 is less than 0·7

14. (a) 0·23 is equal to 0·32
     (b) 0·23 is greater than 0·32
     (c) 0·23 is less than 0·32

15. (a) 0·03 is equal to 0·030
     (b) 0·03 is greater than 0·030
     (c) 0·03 is less than 0·030

16. (a) 0·09 is equal to 0·01
     (b) 0·09 is greater than 0·1
     (c) 0·09 is less than 0·1

In Questions **17** to **22** arrange the numbers in order of size, smallest first.

17. 0·79, 0·791, 0·709, 0·97

18. 0·3, 0·33, 0·303, 0·033

19. 1, 0·99, 0·989, 0·09

20. 1·2, 0·12, 0·21, 1·12

21. 0·08, 0·096, 1, 0·4

22. 0·008, 0·09, 0·091, 0·0075

23. Which list is arranged in ascending order?

   A   0·14, 0·05, 0·062, 0·09
   B   0·14, 0·09, 0·062, 0·05
   C   0·050, 0·062, 0·09, 0·14
   D   0·050, 0·090, 0·14, 0·062

24. Lucy puts 4 pegs in a board. She turns the board through one right angle.
Draw a picture to show how the board looks now.

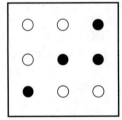

25. There are 5 tyres to each new car. How many tyres are there on 27 new cars?

26. If Jenny has 40 flowers and she puts 8 flowers in each bunch. How many bunches will she have?

27. If your school holiday is for 42 days and there are 7 days to a week, how many weeks holiday is this?

28. Work out the missing digits in each division.

    (a) $\boxed{}\boxed{}2$
       $4\overline{)\,7\;\;2\,\boxed{}}$

    (b) $2\;\;9$
       $3\overline{)\,\boxed{}\;\;7}$

29. A teacher marked 2000 questions. There were 25 pupils in the class. If each pupil did the same number of questions, how many questions did each pupil do?

30. How many hundreds make a million?

Review exercise 5

1. Name the shape whose faces are all squares.

2. Name the shape whose faces are either square or rectangular.

3. What is the name of the family of shapes which have the same cross-section throughout their length?

4. What is the name of the shape formed entirely by triangular faces?

5. What is the name of the shape which has one square face and four triangular faces?

6. Which shape has a circular face at one end and a point at the other?

7. What is the mathematical name for a 'tin can'?

8. What is the mathematical name for a snooker ball?

9. What is the mathematical name for a snooker ball that has been cut in half?

10. A sphere is a prism. True or false?

11. Here is the net for a cube.
    (a) When the net is folded up, which edge will be stuck to the edge JI?
    (b) Which edge will be stuck to the edge AB?
    (c) Which corner will meet corner D?

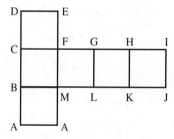

12. Find the number of hours and minutes between:
    (a) 15.30 and 18.00
    (b) 05.35 and 09.10
    (c) 9.30 a.m. and 1.40 p.m.

13. Choose the correct answer: The number of seconds in a day is *about*:

    A 9000   **B** 90 000   **C** 30 000   **D** 300 000

14. Construct the triangles shown and measure the angles marked x.

    (a) 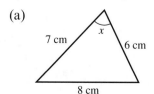   (b)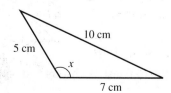

Review exercise 6

1. Copy and continue this pattern for multiples of 7.
   7, 14, 21, ?, ?, ? ...

2. List all the factors of each of these numbers
   (a) 18   (b) 27

3. Copy these numbers and circle the numbers that are not prime.
   (a) 7, 19, 13, 27.   (b) 31, 37, 39, 41.

4. Write down the first five multiples of:
   (a) 6   (b) 8

5. There is just one prime number between the numbers given.
   Copy each question and write the prime number in the box.
   (a) 20, ☐, 26   (b) 44, ☐, 52.

6. Draw a copy of the number grid.
   Find and describe as many patterns as
   possible: for example

   • the square numbers

   • the symmetry in the square

   • the multiples of 3

   • the even numbers.

1	2	3	4	5	6	7	8	9	10
11	12	13	14	15	16	17	18	19	20
21	22	23	24	25	26	27	28	29	30
31	32	33	34	35	36	37	38	39	40
41	42	43	44	45	46	47	48	49	50
51	52	53	54	55	56	57	58	59	60
61	62	63	64	65	66	67	68	69	70
71	72	73	74	75	76	77	78	79	80
81	82	83	84	85	86	87	88	89	90
91	92	93	94	95	96	97	98	99	100

7. Copy each line and write 'odd' or 'even' in place of the box.

   (a) The sum of three odd numbers is ☐.

   (b) The difference between the two odd numbers is ☐.

   (c) The product of two even numbers is ☐.

   (d) The product of two odd numbers is ☐.

   (e) The product of one odd number and one even number is ☐.

8. This is a rough sketch of a triangle.
   Draw the triangle accurately and full size.
   Measure the side marked h.

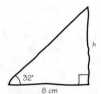

9. I left the cinema at 22.25. The film lasted 2 hours and 35 minutes. At
   what time did it begin?

10. A man's heart beats at 70 beats/min. How many times will his heart beat between 03.30 and 23.30 on the same day?

11. Write the following with the correct signs inside the circles.

(a) $4 \times 3 \times 2 \bigcirc 1 = 25$

(b) $5 \times 2 \times 4 \bigcirc 3 = 37$

(c) $6 + 5 \bigcirc 4 \bigcirc 1 = 8$

12. A lottery payout of £2000 is shared equally between a syndicate of 8 people. How much does each person receive?

13. Ron and Pete were playing a video game. Pete scored 1089 and Ron scored 995. What was the difference in their scores?

14. In one million seconds which of these would you be able to do?

(a) Take a term off school.

(b) Go without sleep for two whole days.

(c) Spend ten days on the beach in France.

(d) Go to Africa for a year.

Explain your working.

Part 4

4.1 Sequences

- Sequences are lists of numbers (and sometimes letters) which have some underlying pattern to them. An important part of any mathematician's job is to search for and explain hidden patterns or structures.

- 2, 9, 4, 7, 6, 41, ... is a list. There is no underlying pattern to the numbers – and so we have no real way of predicting what comes next.

- These are sequences. Their underlying patterns are shown.

Sequence	Structure
3, 5, 7, 9, ...	3 $\;$ (+2) $\;$ 5 $\;$ (+2) $\;$ 7 $\;$ (+2) $\;$ 9 $\;$ (+2)
20, 17, 14, 11, ...	20 $\;$ (−3) $\;$ 17 $\;$ (−3) $\;$ 14 $\;$ (−3) $\;$ 11 $\;$ (−3)
5, 8, 12, 17, ...	5 $\;$ (+3) $\;$ 8 $\;$ (+4) $\;$ 12 $\;$ (+5) $\;$ 17 $\;$ (+6)
2, 2, 4, 12, 48, ...	2 $\;$ (×1) $\;$ 2 $\;$ (×2) $\;$ 4 $\;$ (×3) $\;$ 12 $\;$ (×4) $\;$ 48 $\;$ (×5)
15, 14, 16, 13, 17, ...	15 $\;$ (−1) $\;$ 14 $\;$ (+2) $\;$ 16 $\;$ (−3) $\;$ 13 $\;$ (+4) $\;$ 17 $\;$ (−5)

Exercise 1

1. The numbers in boxes form a sequence. Find the next number.

(a) 10   12   14   16   ☐

(b) 3   8   13   18   ☐

(c) 11   9   7   5   ☐

Winter

In Questions **2** to **17** write down the sequence and find the next number

2. 4, 8, 12, 16,   **3.** 2, 5, 8, 11,
4. 21, 17, 13, 9,   **5.** 2, 4, 8, 16,
6. 1, 2, 4, 7, 11,   **7.** 3, 5, 9, 17,
8. 2, 4, 6, 8,   **9.** 1, 4, 8, 13,
10. 80, 40, 20, 10,   **11.** 5, 8, 12, 17,
12. $\frac{1}{2}$, 1, $1\frac{1}{2}$, 2,   **13.** 2, 20, 200, 2000,
14. 45, 36, 28, 21,   **15.** 1, 3, 9, 27,
16. 56, 28, 14, 7,   **17.** 1, 4, 9, 16,

18. Write down the sequence and find the missing number.

(a) 2   6   ☐   14   18

(b) 3   ☐   12   24   48

(c) $\frac{1}{2}$ 2 $3\frac{1}{2}$ 5   ☐

(d) ☐   8   4   0   −4

19. Copy each sequence and write down the next number
(a) 3·2, 3·4, 3·6, 3·8, ...
(b) 1·76, 1·77, 1·78, 1·79, ...
(c) 0·402, 0·403, 0·404, 0·405, ...
(d) 4·192, 4·194, 4·196, 4·198, ...

20. The rule for the sequences below is *'double and take away 1'*. Find the missing numbers

(a) $3 \to 5 \to 9 \to 17 \to$ ☐

(b) ☐ $\to 7 \to 13 \to 25 \to 49$

(c) ☐ $\to 19 \to$ ☐ $\to 73$

21. The rule for the sequences here is *'multiply by 3 and add 1'*. Find the missing numbers

(a) $1 \to 4 \to 13 \to$ ☐

(b) ☐ $\to 7 \to 22 \to 67$

(c) ☐ $\to 2 \to$ ☐ $\to 22$

22. Copy this pattern and write down the next three lines. Do not use a calculator!

$1 \times 99 = 99$
$2 \times 99 = 198$
$3 \times 99 = 297$
$4 \times 99 = 396$

23. (a) Copy this pattern and write down the next two lines

$$4 \times 8 = 32$$
$$44 \times 8 = 352$$
$$444 \times 8 = 3552$$
$$4444 \times 8 = 35\,552$$

(b) Copy and complete $444\,444\,444 \times 8 =$

Exercise 2

Use your knowledge of sequences to help you answer these questions.

1.

The numbers N1, N2, N3, N4 and M1, M2, M3, M4 form two sequences.
(a) Find M5, M6, N5, N6.
(b) Think of rules and use them to find M15 and N20.

2.

(a) Find C5, D5.
(b) Use a rule to find C10 and D30.

3.

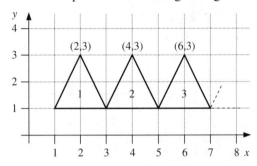

Use a rule to find A10, B20, A35.

4. Here is a sequence of touching triangles.

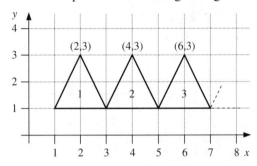

Find the coordinates of:
(a) the top of triangle 5
(b) the top of triangle 50
(c) the bottom right corner of triangle 50
(d) the bottom right corner of triangle 100.

5. Write down the coordinates of the centres of squares 1, 2 and 3.
Find the coordinates of:
(a) the centre of square 4
(b) the centre of square 40
(c) the top right corner of square 4
(d) the top right corner of square 40.

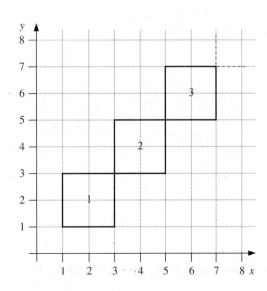

6.

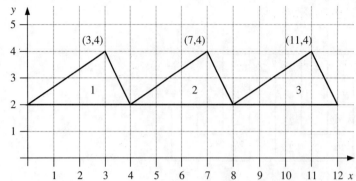

Find the coordinates of the top vertex of:
(a) triangle 4
(b) triangle 20
(c) triangle 2000.

7. Write down the coordinates of the centres of squares 1, 2 and 3.
Find the coordinates of:
(a) the centre of square 4
(b) the centre of square 10
(c) the top vertex of square 70.

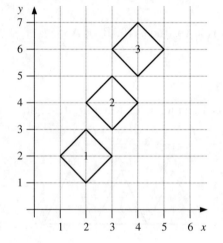

8. Write down the coordinates of the centres of the first six squares.
Find the coordinates of:
(a) the centre of square 60
(b) the centre of square 73
(c) the top left corner of square 90
(d) the top left corner of square 101.

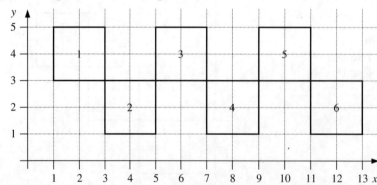

9. Now design some patterns of your own.

Count the crossovers: an investigation

Two straight lines have a maximum of one crossover

Three straight lines have a maximum of three crossovers.

Notice that you can have less than three crossovers if the lines all go through one point. Or the lines could be parallel.
In this work we are interested only in the *maximum* number of crossovers.

Four lines have a maximum of six crossovers.

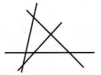

▨ Draw five lines and find the maximum number of crossovers.

▨ Does there appear to be any sort of sequence in your results?
  If you can find a sequence, use it to *predict* the maximum number of crossovers with six lines.

▨ Now draw six lines and count the crossovers to see if your prediction was correct.
  (Remember not to draw three lines through one point.)

▨ Predict the number of crossovers for seven lines and then check if your prediction is correct by drawing a diagram.

▨ Write your results in a table:

Number of lines	Number of crossovers
2	1
3	3
4	6
5	
6	

(a) Predict the number of crossovers for 20 lines.
(b) (Harder) Predict the number of crossovers for 2000 lines.

4.2 Decimals 2

Multiplying decimals by whole numbers

Method 1

- $7.93 \times 4 \approx 8 \times 4 = 32$
  (Estimate first)
  $7.93 \times 4 \quad 7.00 \times 4 = 28.00$
  $ 0.90 \times 4 = 3.60$
  $ 0.03 \times 4 = \underline{0.12} \; +$
  $ 31.72$

- $3.16 \times 6 \approx 3 \times 6 = 18$
  (Estimate first)
  $3.16 \times 6 \quad 3.00 \times 6 = 18.00$
  $ 0.10 \times 6 = 0.60$
  $ 0.06 \times 6 = \underline{0.36} \; +$
  $ 18.96$

Method 2

- $7.24 \times 4 \approx 7 \times 4 = 28$
  (Estimate first)
  $$\begin{array}{r} 7.24 \\ \times 4 \\ \hline 28.96 \\ \hline \scriptstyle 1 \end{array}$$

- $0.096 \times 9 \approx 0.1 \times 9 = 0.9$
  (Estimate first)
  $$\begin{array}{r} 0.096 \\ \times 9 \\ \hline 0.864 \\ \hline \scriptstyle 8\,5 \end{array}$$

> The answer has the same number of figures after the point as there are in the numbers being multiplied.

Exercise 1

Work out

1. $\begin{array}{r}5.1\\ \times2\\\hline\end{array}$	**2.** $\begin{array}{r}2.3\\ \times3\\\hline\end{array}$	**3.** $\begin{array}{r}3.7\\ \times4\\\hline\end{array}$	**4.** $\begin{array}{r}5.6\\ \times5\\\hline\end{array}$
5. $\begin{array}{r}6.13\\ \times6\\\hline\end{array}$	**6.** $\begin{array}{r}10.22\\ \times7\\\hline\end{array}$	**7.** $\begin{array}{r}5.34\\ \times8\\\hline\end{array}$	**8.** $\begin{array}{r}1.29\\ \times9\\\hline\end{array}$

9. 7×0.63 **10.** 1.452×6 **11.** 9×0.074 **12.** 11.3×5

13. 13.6×5 **14.** 0.074×5 **15.** 6×2.22 **16.** 8.4×11

17. Copy and complete with the missing numbers.

  (a) $0.3 \times 4 = \boxed{}$ (b) $0.6 \times \boxed{} = 4.2$

  (c) $\boxed{} \times 5 = 2.0$ (d) $1.5 = 6 \times \boxed{} + 0.3$

  (e) $\boxed{} \times 7 - 2 = 1.5$ (f) $8 \times \boxed{} = 0.16$

18. Find the cost of 4 calculators at £6.95 each.

19. What is the cost of 2 CDs at £10.95 each?

20. If one brick weighs $1.35\,\text{kg}$, how much do 5 weigh?

21. What is the total cost of 6 books at £2·13 each?

22. A new car tyre costs £29·99.
What is the total cost of 4 new tyres?

23. Find the total cost of 8 batteries at £1·19 each.

24. If 1 kg of cheese costs £4·59, find the cost of 3 kg.

25. Ink cartridges cost £1·25 a packet. What is the cost of 10 packets?

26. A sack of coal costs £6·90. Find the total cost of 9 sacks.

27. If 1 litre equals 1·76 pints, how many pints is 8 litres?

In Questions **28** to **31** find the total cost.

28. 2 jars at £1·75 each
4 boxes at £0·40 each
1 bottle at £1·25

29. 3 tins at £0·51 each
5 packets at £1·10 each
2 pints of milk at 22p per pint.

30. 4 litres of oil at 97p per litre
6 bags at £0·33 each
3 lb of meat at £2·12 per lb
1 cauliflower at 42p

31. 18 eggs at 50p per dozen
$\frac{1}{2}$ lb of cheese at £1·30 per lb
3 lb of leeks at 18p per lb
2 packets at £2·30 each

Multiplying by 10, 100, 1000

- Using a calculator, $3·24 \times 10 = 32·4$
$16·17 \times 10 = 161·7$
$0·53 \times 10 = 5·3$
$1·414 \times 10 = 14·14$

'When you multiply by 10 you move the point one place to the right.'

- What do you notice in these calculations?
$4·235 \times 100 = 423·5$
$1·138 \times 100 = 113·8$
$0·258 \times 100 = 25·8$

- Without a calculator, write down the answer to the following:
$1·174 \times 100$
$32·56 \times 10$
$1·2359 \times 1000$

Exercise 2

Do the following calculations

1. $4·23 \times 10$	**2.** $5·63 \times 10$	**3.** $0·427 \times 100$	**4.** $4·63 \times 100$
5. $0·075 \times 10$	**6.** $0·0063 \times 100$	**7.** $1·147 \times 1000$	**8.** $10·7 \times 1000$
9. $6·33 \times 100$	**10.** $0·00714 \times 10000$	**11.** $6·36 \times 100$	**12.** $8·142 \times 10$
13. $0·71 \times 10000$	**14.** $8·9 \times 1000$	**15.** 12×100	**16.** 13×10
17. 7×1000	**18.** $9·2 \times 10000$	**19.** $0·7 \times 100$	**20.** $0·5 \times 100000$

21. 0.01×10 **22.** 5.2×100 **23.** 14×1000

24. 0.1×10 **25.** $0.2 \times 10\,000$ **26.** $8.31 \times 100\,000$

27. 9.2×1 million   **28.** 8.34×1 million   **29.** 0.71×1 million

30. 8.6×100 **31.** 27×1000 **32.** 53×100

33. 0.0084×10 **34.** $0.74 \times 10\,000$ **35.** 91×100

36. 0×1000 **37.** $5.6 \times 10 \times 10$ **38.** $2.14 \times 10 \times 10$

39. $0.0634 \times 10 \times 100$ **40.** $0.1111 \times 100 \times 100$ **41.** $8 \times 100 \times 10$

42. $7.24 \times 100 \times 100$ **43.** $0.12 \times 1000 \times 10$ **44.** $0.1434 \times 100 \times 10$

Division of decimals by whole numbers

(a) $9.6 \div 3$

$$\begin{array}{r} 3.2 \\ 3\overline{)9.6} \end{array}$$

(b) $22.48 \div 4$

$$\begin{array}{r} 5.62 \\ 3\overline{)22.{}^2 48} \end{array}$$

(c) $21.28 \div 7$

$$\begin{array}{r} 3.04 \\ 7\overline{)21.2{}^2 8} \end{array}$$

(d) $3.12 \div 4$

$$\begin{array}{r} 0.78 \\ 4\overline{)3.{}^3 1{}^2 2} \end{array}$$

Exercise 3

1. $8.42 \div 2$ **2.** $205.2 \div 6$ **3.** $18.52 \div 4$

4. $4.984 \div 7$ **5.** $236.0 \div 5$ **6.** $18.93 \div 3$

7. $49.92 \div 8$ **8.** $487.26 \div 9$ **9.** $6.7 \div 5$

10. A father shares £4·56 between his three children. How much does each receive?

11. A length of wood measuring 39·41 cm has to be cut into seven equal lengths. How long is each piece?

12. The total bill for a meal for nine people is £76·23. How much does each person pay if they each paid the same?

13. A pie weighing 2·43 kg is divided into 9 equal pieces. How much does each piece weigh?

14. If 5 bricks weigh 4·64 kg, find the weight of one brick.

15. Five people share the fuel cost of a car journey which amounts to £18·65. How much does each person pay?

16. Six cows produce 33·84 litres of milk each day. What is the average milk production of each cow?

17. How many times will a 9 litre bucket have to be filled and emptied to completely empty a water drum containing 139·5 litres?

18. A telephone call costs £0·10. How many calls can I make if I have £3.50?

19. A steel rod of length 2·86 m is divided into 11 equal pieces. How long is each piece?

20. Ten ball bearings weigh 2·5 kg. What is the weight of one?

Dividing by 10, 100, 1000 etc

The rules for dividing decimals are very similar to the rules for multiplying decimals.

- To divide by 10 move the point one place to the left.
- To divide by 100 move the point two places to the left.
- To divide by 1000 move the point three places to the left.

(a) $56 \div 10 = 5·6$ (b) $6·24 \div 100 = 0·0624$

(c) $3·14 \div 10 = 0·314$ (d) $57 \div 1000 = 0·057$

Exercise 4

Do the following calculations. (They are not all dividing!.)

1. $57·2 \div 10$ **2.** $89·2 \div 10$ **3.** $5·3 \div 10$ **4.** $47·1 \div 100$

5. $141·2 \div 100$ **6.** $19·3 \div 10$ **7.** $1518 \div 100$ **8.** $4·7 \div 100$

9. $25·2 \div 1000$ **10.** $0·63 \div 10$ **11.** $47·2 \div 100$ **12.** $27·9 \div 1000$

13. $6·2 \div 1000$ **14.** $198·7 \div 100$ **15.** $47 \div 10$ **16.** $416 \div 1000$

17. $2400 \div 10\,000$ **18.** $89 \div 100$ **19.** $63 \div 100$ **20.** $7 \div 1000$

21. $0·86 \div 10$ **22.** $516 \div 10\,000$ **23.** $0·077 \div 100$ **24.** $21·9 \div 1000$

25. $500 \div 10\,000$ **26.** $260 \div 100\,000$ **27.** $0·051 \div 100$ **28.** $890·4 \div 10$

29. $4007 \div 100$ **30.** $20 \div 1000$ **31.** $5·14 \times 10$ **32.** $6·26 \times 100$

33. $0·414 \times 100$ **34.** $0·0631 \times 1000$ **35.** $0·005 \times 100$ **36.** $0·0063 \times 10\,000$

37. $47·4 \div 10$ **38.** $8·97 \div 100$ **39.** $54·2 \div 1000$ **40.** 63×100

41. 47×10 **42.** $0·84 \times 10\,000$ **43.** $0·7 \div 100$ **44.** $6·2 \div 10$

45. $4·73 \times 10$ **46.** $0·001 \times 1000$ **47.** $47 \div 100$ **48.** 47×100

49. Here is a table giving some lengths.

distance from train station	10 000 m
distance from home to school	1000 m
length of football pitch	100 m
width of road bridge	10 m
width of door	1 m
length of Pritt Stick	0·1 m
size of a dice	0·01 m
thickness of a 5 p coin	0·001 m

(a) What is ten times the size of a dice?
(b) What is 1000 times the size of a dice?
(c) What is one hundredth of the length of a football pitch?
(d) What is one thousandth of the width of a door?
(e) What is one million times the thickness of a 5 p coin?
(f) How many Pritt Sticks end to end would be the distance from home to school?

50. Make up your own table like the one above and think of distances and objects for lengths from 100 000 m down to 0·001 m.

51. On a calculator $\frac{1}{9} = 0\cdot111\,111\,1$

Without using a calculator, write down $\frac{1}{900}$ as a decimal.

Metric units

Here is a summary of the most important units

Length	Mass	Volume
10 mm = 1 cm	1000 g = 1 kg	1000 ml = 1 litre or 1 *l*
100 cm = 1 m	1000 kg = 1 tonne	
1000 m = 1 km		

Exercise 5

What unit would you use to measure the following:

1. The mass of this book.
2. The length of a pencil.
3. The distance from London to Paris.
4. The length of an ant.
5. The mass of a heavy goods vehicle.
6. The amount of water in a swimming pool.
7. Your height.
8. Your mass.
9. The capacity of a car's petrol tank.
10. The amount of liquid in a cup of tea.

Copy and complete the following:

11. $1.25 \, \text{m} = \underline{\hspace{1cm}} \text{cm}$ **12.** $0.35 \, \text{m} = \underline{\hspace{1cm}} \text{cm}$ **13.** $3 \, \text{m} = \underline{\hspace{1cm}} \text{cm}$

14. $17 \, \text{cm} = \underline{\hspace{1cm}} \text{m}$ **15.** $250 \, \text{cm} = \underline{\hspace{1cm}} \text{m}$ **16.** $5 \, \text{cm} = \underline{\hspace{1cm}} \text{m}$

17. $40 \, \text{mm} = \underline{\hspace{1cm}} \text{cm}$ **18.** $300 \, \text{mm} = \underline{\hspace{1cm}} \text{cm}$ **19.** $5 \, \text{mm} = \underline{\hspace{1cm}} \text{cm}$

20. $1500 \, \text{m} = \underline{\hspace{1cm}} \text{km}$ **21.** $750 \, \text{m} = \underline{\hspace{1cm}} \text{km}$ **22.** $10\,000 \, \text{m} = \underline{\hspace{1cm}} \text{km}$

23. $2 \, \text{kg} = \underline{\hspace{1cm}} \text{g}$ **24.** $8.52 \, \text{kg} = \underline{\hspace{1cm}} \text{g}$ **25.** $0.625 \, \text{kg} = \underline{\hspace{1cm}} \text{g}$

26. $325 \, \text{g} = \underline{\hspace{1cm}} \text{kg}$ **27.** $1627 \, \text{g} = \underline{\hspace{1cm}} \text{kg}$ **28.** $2 \text{ tonnes} = \underline{\hspace{1cm}} \text{kg}$

29. $440 \, \text{ml} = \underline{\hspace{1cm}} l$ **30.** $1976 \, \text{ml} = \underline{\hspace{1cm}} l$ **31.** $2500 \, \text{ml} = \underline{\hspace{1cm}} l$

32. $2.5 \, l = \underline{\hspace{1cm}} \text{ml}$ **33.** $75 \, l = \underline{\hspace{1cm}} \text{ml}$ **34.** $1.76 \, l = \underline{\hspace{1cm}} \text{ml}$

4.3 Rounding off

Here are cuttings from two newspapers:

A. '39748 people paid £511,615 to watch
  Arsenal play ...'

B. '40000 people paid over £500,000 to
  watch Arsenal play ...'

In B the figures have been *rounded off* because the reporter thinks that his readers will not be interested in the exact numbers in the report.

Rules for rounding

- Rounding to the nearest whole number.
  If the first digit after the decimal point is *5 or more* round *up*.
  Otherwise round down.

      57·3 → 57
      89·8 → 90
      5·5 → 6

- Rounding to the nearest 10.
  If the digit in the units column is 5 or more round up.
  Otherwise round down.

      27 → 30
      42 → 40
      265 → 270

- Rounding to the nearest 100.
  If the digit in the tens column is 5 or more round up.
  Otherwise round down.

      593 → 600
      247 → 200
      2643 → 2600

- Rounding to the nearest 1000.
  If the digit in the hundreds column is 5 or more round up.
  Otherwise round down.

      1394 → 1000
      502 → 1000
      11 764 → 12 000

- From the above you will see that when a number is 'right in the middle' we round *up*. This is an internationally accepted rule.

Exercise 1

1. Round off these numbers to the nearest 10.
   (a) 73   (b) 58   (c) 24   (d) 99
   (e) 56   (f) 127   (g) 242   (h) 18
   (i) 29   (j) 589   (k) 37   (l) 51

2. Round off these numbers to the nearest 100.
   (a) 584   (b) 293   (c) 607   (d) 914
   (e) 285   (f) 655   (g) 222   (h) 1486

3. Round off these numbers to the nearest 1000.
   (a) 4555   (b) 757   (c) 850   (d) 2251
   (e) 614   (f) 2874   (g) 25712   (h) 13568

4. Work out these answers on a calculator and then round off the answer to the *nearest whole number*.
   (a) $235 \div 17$ (b) $4714 \div 58$ (c) $2375 \div 11$ (d) $999 \div 17$
   (e) $5 \cdot 62 \times 7 \cdot 04$ (f) $19 \cdot 3 \times 1 \cdot 19$ (g) $53 \cdot 2 \times 2 \cdot 3$ (h) $12 \cdot 6 \times 0 \cdot 93$
   (i) $119 \cdot 6 \div 5 \cdot 1$ (j) $109 \div 0 \cdot 7$ (k) $63 \cdot 4 \div 11$ (l) $1 \cdot 92 \div 0 \cdot 09$

In Questions **5** to **12** rewrite the sentences by rounding off the numbers involved and using the word 'about'. (E.g. Jim swam *about* 300 m.)

5. Mr Sadler drove 3478 miles on his holiday (nearest 100).

6. David saw 5173 cars go past his window (nearest 100).

7. The Sainsbury supermarket took in £49 713·21 last Saturday (nearest 1000).

8. There are 19 763 Junior schools in England and Wales (nearest 1000).

9. The winner of the National Lottery won £6 913 214. (nearest million).

10. There are 15 214 714 cars in the UK (nearest million).

11. Applecroft School raised £2611·26 for charity last year (nearest 100).

12. The population of the USA is 223 516 718 (nearest million).

13. Decide whether you would round these numbers to the nearest 10, 100, 1000, 10 000, 100 000 or 1 000 000.
    (a) The number of children in your school.
    (b) The number of people in Britain.
    (c) The number of people on a full Eurostar.
    (d) The daily circulation of 'The Sun' newspaper.
    (e) The number of miles from London to Birmingham.

In Questions **14** to **16** explain how you would:

14. Estimate how many packets of crisps your
class will eat in a lifetime.

15. Estimate how many bricks there are in one
wall of an ordinary house.

16. Estimate how many entries there are in a
telephone directory.

17. Give an example of a number you would estimate to:
(a) the nearest 1000
(b) the nearest million
(c) the nearest 100.

4.4 Negative numbers

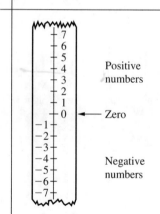

- All numbers above zero are positive numbers.

- Zero is not positive or negative.

- All numbers below zero are negative numbers.

- If a minus symbol appears before a number then it is
a negative number.

- The most common application of negative numbers is in
illustrating temperature.

This is a weather map showing temperatures across
the United Kingdom and Ireland on a day in Winter.

The temperatures are given in degrees Celsius (°C).

Water freezes at 0°C.

The weather map shows lower temperatures in the
north than in the south.

Exercise 1

1. What temperature is shown at each arrow?

   (a) 5°C   (b) 5°C   (c) 5°C   (d) 5°C
        0   0   0   0
        −5   −5   −5   −5
        −10   −10   −10   −10

2.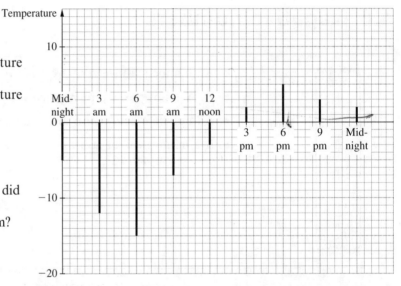

   −2°C   −1°C

   0°C   5°C   −8°C

   (a) Which of these temperatures is the coldest?
   (b) Which of these temperatures is the hottest?
   (c) Which temperatures are below freezing?

3. The graph shows the temperatures for one day in Greenland.

   (a) What was the temperature at 6 pm?
   (b) What was the temperature at 9 am?
   (c) What was the lowest temperature recorded?
   (d) At what time was it −12°C?
   (e) By how many degrees did the temperature go up between 6 am and 6 pm?

4. Find the new temperature in the following problems.
   (a) The temperature is 5°C and falls by 9°C.
   (b) The temperature is −7°C and falls by 4°C.
   (c) The temperature is −6°C and rises by 13°C.
   (d) The temperature is −9°C and rises by 11°C.
   (e) The temperature is 13°C and falls 17°C.

5. State in the following questions whether the temperature has risen or fallen and by how many degrees.
   (a) It was −3°C and it is now −7°C.
   (b) It was 6°C and is now −2°C.
   (c) It was −11°C and is now −5°C.
   (d) It was −9°C and is now 1°C.
   (e) It was 12°C and is now −23°C.

6. Copy and complete the following table:

	Temperature	Change	New temperature
(a)	6°C	+5°C	
(b)	15°C	+8°C	
(c)	18°C	−11°C	
(d)	0°C	−3°C	
(e)	−2°C	−12°C	
(f)		+7°C	12°C
(g)		−8°C	−3°C
(h)	−4°C		−6°C
(i)	−5°C	−4°C	
(j)		−3°C	−7°C

7. Is −2°C warmer or colder than −4°C?

8. Which is colder −7°C or −10°C?

9. Which of these temperatures is the lowest? −3°C, −8°C, −4°C.

10. Is −3°C higher or lower than 2°C?

11. A piece of meat is at a temperature of 15°C before it is put in a freezer.
By how many degrees has its temperature fallen when its temperature is
(a) −1°C   (b) −10°C   (c) −18°C?

Exercise 2

1. The *range* is the difference between the highest and the lowest. The scale shows the highest and lowest temperatures one day in Paris.
The range of the temperatures is 10°C.

Find the range in these temperatures

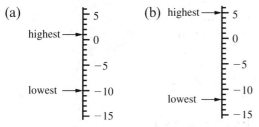 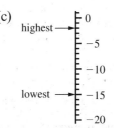

(d) 5°C and −3°C   (e) 0°C and −11°C   (f) 12°C and −10°C.

2. This table shows the highest and lowest temperatures in five places.

	Highest	Lowest
Glasgow	3°C	−11°C
London	12°C	−4°C
Moscow	2°C	−23°C
North Pole	−40°C	−53°C
Rome	15°C	1°C

Find the temperature range for
(a) Glasgow.
(b) Moscow.
(c) Which place had the greatest range in temperature?

3. Here is a number line from −10 to +10

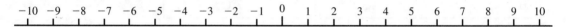

Find the difference between
(a) −7 and 2   (b) −6 and −1   (c) 8 and −3
(d) −5 and 0   (e) −8 and 8   (f) −3 and −10.

4. Write down each sequence and fill in the missing number.

(a)   6   4   2   0   −2   □

(b)   10   6   2   −2   □

(c)   10   7   4   1   −2   □

(d)   9   5   1   □   −7

(e)   −12   −9   −6   −3   □

(f)   □   −1   4   9   14

5. Write down these temperatures in order, coldest first.
(a)   7°,   −2°,   −7°,   0°,   8°,   −5°
(b) −6°,   3°,   −15°,   21°,   −7°   2°
(c) −8°,   11°,   0°,   −5°,   −10°,   2°

6. The heights of places on a map are always measured in relation to sea level. For example a hill marked 510 m is 510 m above sea level.
(a) Think of something which could be at a height of −20 m.
(b) Some places in Holland are at a height of −3 m. What problems does this cause and what do the people do about it?

7. A diver is below the surface of the water at −20 m. She dives a further 8 m, then rises 5 m. At what depth is she now?

4.5 Fractions 1

Action fractions

A fraction such as *one half* is not an object you can just walk over to the mathematics cupboard and take out! To obtain a fraction like *one half* you have to divide a *whole*. A fraction is part of a whole. A whole can be a single object or a collection of objects.

Exercise 1 (For discussion)

This exercise is concerned with what makes a whole and how do you find one third of it. Describe what action you would take to find one third in each of the following situations.

1. One jam tart is to be shared between 3 people. How can you ensure each person will receive an equal share?

2. Two oranges are to be shared by a family of 3. How can you ensure each person has an equal share?

3. You have 12 hot dogs and have invited two friends for a snack with you. How do you divide the hot dogs so that you all have an equal share?

4. You have five sausages to share equally between a family of 3. How do you do this?

5. How long is a third of a half-metre length of wood?

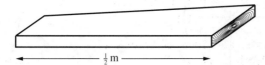
$\frac{1}{2}$ m

Fractions of a whole

- Express the shaded part of the diagram as a fraction of the whole.

3 out of 8 sections are shaded.
The fraction shaded $= \frac{3}{8}$.

- It is not possible to express the shaded part in this diagram as a fraction of the whole. This is because the shape has not been divided equally.

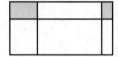

Exercise 2

In each of the following diagrams, express the shaded part of the diagram as a fraction of the whole where possible.

1.

2.

3.

4.

5.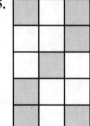

6.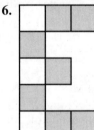

7.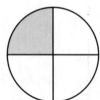

8.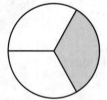

9.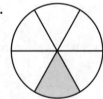

10.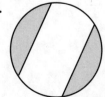

11.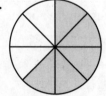

12.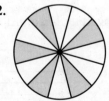

Writing fractions in their simplest form

A fraction is composed of two numbers:

The top number is called the $\longrightarrow$ Numerator

The bottom number is called the $\longrightarrow$ Denominator

The method of changing a fraction into a simpler form is known as 'cancelling down'.

The fraction $\frac{15}{20}$ cancels down to $\frac{3}{4}$.

To do this, use the following method ...

> Find the **highest** possible number that divides exactly into **both** the numerator and denominator

$$\frac{15 \div 5}{20 \div 5} = \frac{3}{4}$$

The highest possible number that divides exactly into 15 and 20 is 5.

Here are three more examples of cancelling down fractions ...

Fraction	Method of cancelling down	Simplest form of fraction
$\frac{8}{12}$	4 goes into 8, 2 times 4 goes into 12, 3 times	$\frac{2}{3}$
$\frac{12}{15}$	3 goes into 12, 4 times 3 goes into 15, 5 times	$\frac{4}{5}$
$\frac{32}{40}$	8 goes into 32, 4 times 8 goes into 40, 5 times	$\frac{4}{5}$

Exercise 3

Copy and complete the table below to cancel down each fraction into its simplest form:

No.	Fraction	Method of cancelling down	Simplest form of fraction
1.	$\frac{9}{12}$	3 goes into 9: ___ times 3 goes into 12: ___ times	____
2.	$\frac{6}{24}$	6 goes into 6: ___ time 6 goes into 24: ___ times	____
3.	$\frac{8}{10}$	2 goes into 8: ___ times 2 goes into 10: ___ times	____

Express each fraction in its simplest form:

4. $\frac{8}{20}$ 5. $\frac{9}{36}$ 6. $\frac{8}{12}$ 7. $\frac{9}{15}$ 8. $\frac{6}{18}$

9. $\frac{7}{21}$ 10. $\frac{32}{36}$ 11. $\frac{24}{30}$ 12. $\frac{4}{12}$ 13. $\frac{4}{18}$

14. $\frac{20}{30}$ 15. $\frac{12}{18}$ 16. $\frac{14}{42}$ 17. $\frac{20}{24}$ 18. $\frac{6}{15}$

19. $\frac{27}{45}$ **20.** $\frac{56}{64}$ **21.** $\frac{18}{30}$ **22.** $\frac{28}{36}$ **23.** $\frac{18}{63}$

24. $\frac{44}{55}$ **25.** $\frac{24}{60}$ **26.** $\frac{54}{81}$ **27.** $\frac{45}{90}$ **28.** $\frac{18}{72}$

29. $\frac{72}{108}$ **30.** $\frac{75}{100}$

Exercise 4

Cancel down or scale up the following fractions as required:

1. $\frac{6}{8} = \frac{\square}{4}$

2. $\frac{2}{6} = \frac{\square}{3}$

3. $\frac{6}{10} = \frac{\square}{5}$

4. $\frac{6}{9} = \frac{\square}{3}$

5. $\frac{9}{12} = \frac{\square}{4}$

6. $\frac{12}{15} = \frac{\square}{5}$

7. $\frac{15}{20} = \frac{\square}{4}$

8. $\frac{25}{30} = \frac{\square}{6}$

9. $\frac{2}{6} = \frac{\square}{3} = \frac{\square}{9}$

10. $\frac{3}{4} = \frac{\square}{8} = \frac{\square}{12}$

11. $\frac{8}{12} = \frac{\square}{6} = \frac{\square}{3}$

12. $\frac{1}{5} = \frac{\square}{10} = \frac{\square}{20}$

13. $\frac{7}{10} = \frac{\square}{30} = \frac{14}{\square}$

14. $\frac{1}{4} = \frac{\square}{16} = \frac{8}{\square}$

15. $\frac{7}{12} = \frac{\square}{24} = \frac{21}{\square}$

16. $\frac{6}{15} = \frac{\square}{5} = \frac{24}{\square}$

17. $\frac{\square}{10} = \frac{3}{5} = \frac{\square}{25}$

18. $\frac{\square}{21} = \frac{3}{7} = \frac{15}{\square}$

19. $\frac{\square}{3} = \frac{6}{18} = \frac{\square}{15}$

20. $\frac{21}{\square} = \frac{\square}{30} = \frac{7}{15}$

Equivalent fraction anagrams

Example: In the table given below, pick out all the letters above the fractions which are equivalent to one half ($\frac{1}{2}$).

C	Q	E	A	Y	P	R	N	H	F	letters
$\frac{5}{10}$	$\frac{3}{4}$	$\frac{2}{4}$	$\frac{21}{42}$	$\frac{1}{3}$	$\frac{3}{5}$	$\frac{6}{12}$	$\frac{3}{6}$	$\frac{4}{7}$	$\frac{5}{10}$	fractions

The letters are C, E, A, R, N, F
because ... $\frac{5}{10}, \frac{2}{4}, \frac{21}{42}, \frac{6}{12}, \frac{3}{6}, \frac{5}{10}$ are all the same as $\frac{1}{2}$.

Now rearrange the letters to make the name of a country.

C, E, A, R, N, F $\longrightarrow$ FRANCE

Exercise 5

As in the example above, find the fractions in the table which are equivalent to the given fraction. Rearrange the letters to make a word using the clue.

1. ($\frac{1}{3}$, city)

L	P	A	U	R	I	D	N	S	B
$\frac{3}{9}$	$\frac{2}{8}$	$\frac{5}{7}$	$\frac{4}{12}$	$\frac{7}{20}$	$\frac{6}{18}$	$\frac{8}{24}$	$\frac{10}{30}$	$\frac{3}{5}$	$\frac{5}{15}$

2. ($\frac{1}{4}$, fruit)

B	O	P	A	E	I	H	C	R	T
$\frac{2}{7}$	$\frac{4}{16}$	$\frac{11}{44}$	$\frac{2}{8}$	$\frac{3}{9}$	$\frac{10}{40}$	$\frac{6}{25}$	$\frac{5}{20}$	$\frac{12}{48}$	$\frac{3}{12}$

3. ($\frac{3}{4}$, sport)

R	O	F	G	A	U	B	D	Y	J
$\frac{8}{10}$	$\frac{6}{8}$	$\frac{15}{25}$	$\frac{5}{7}$	$\frac{21}{32}$	$\frac{9}{12}$	$\frac{30}{45}$	$\frac{15}{20}$	$\frac{66}{99}$	$\frac{75}{100}$

4. ($\frac{1}{10}$, drink)

R	E	F	E	F	T	O	W	C	A
$\frac{2}{20}$	$\frac{5}{60}$	$\frac{9}{108}$	$\frac{5}{50}$	$\frac{12}{96}$	$\frac{3}{30}$	$\frac{4}{20}$	$\frac{10}{100}$	$\frac{6}{50}$	$\frac{7}{70}$

5. ($\frac{2}{3}$, country)

A	N	E	R	S	B	I	Z	Q	L
$\frac{4}{6}$	$\frac{9}{12}$	$\frac{14}{22}$	$\frac{60}{90}$	$\frac{16}{25}$	$\frac{8}{12}$	$\frac{22}{33}$	$\frac{20}{30}$	$\frac{32}{49}$	$\frac{12}{18}$

6. ($\frac{1}{2}$, animal)

N	C	U	E	A	N	T	Y	R	B
$\frac{5}{10}$	$\frac{3}{18}$	$\frac{7}{14}$	$\frac{6}{9}$	$\frac{1}{3}$	$\frac{17}{34}$	$\frac{5}{12}$	$\frac{25}{50}$	$\frac{5}{15}$	$\frac{9}{18}$

7. Now make up your own question and test it on a friend.

Equivalent fraction pairs: an activity

This is an activity for 2, 3 or 4 players using the equivalent fraction cards.

How to play:

- Shuffle the cards, place them face down in a pattern of 6 rows by 4 columns.

- Decide who will go first.

- Each turn requires a player to turn over a pair of cards.

- If the pair of cards are equivalent such as $\frac{1}{5}$ and $\frac{2}{10}$ the player keeps the pair. If the cards are not equivalent turn the cards face down again.

- Try to remember which cards are where!

- If you find a pair you get another go, the player with the most pairs when no cards are left is the winner.

- Teacher's note. The fraction cards can be photocopied from the answer book. Alternatively many teachers prefer to have the cards made by pupils.

Proper and improper fractions

- A *proper* fraction is one in which the *numerator* (top number) is less than the *denominator* (bottom number).

  The fractions $\frac{1}{2}$, $\frac{2}{3}$, $\frac{3}{4}$ and $\frac{99}{100}$ are all examples of *proper* fractions.

- An *improper* fraction is one in which the *numerator* is larger than the *denominator*. They are sometimes called 'top-heavy' fractions.

  The fractions $\frac{3}{2}$, $\frac{4}{3}$, $\frac{8}{5}$ and $\frac{100}{33}$ are all examples of *improper* fractions.

- A *mixed number* is one which contains both a whole number and a fraction. *Improper* fractions can be changed into *mixed numbers* and vice versa.

(a) $\frac{3}{2} = 1\frac{1}{2}$ Step 1. 2 into 3 goes once, giving the whole number 1.
                    Step 2. The remainder is 1 which is written as $\frac{1}{2}$.

(b) $\frac{16}{3} = 5\frac{1}{3}$ Step 1. 3 into 16 goes five times, giving the whole number 5.
                    Step 2. The remainder is 1, which is written $\frac{1}{3}$.

(c) $2\frac{1}{2} = \frac{5}{2}$ Step 1. 2 times 2, gives 4 (4 halves).
                    Step 2. Add 1 from the numerator to 4 giving 5.
                    Step 3. Express 5 as a fraction of 2 which is $\frac{5}{2}$.

(d) $3\frac{5}{6} = \frac{23}{6}$ Step 1. 3 times 6 is 18 (18 sixths).
                    Step 2. There are 5 sixths to add from the numerator giving 23.
                    Step 3. Express 23 as a fraction of 6 which is $\frac{23}{6}$.

Exercise 6

Change the following improper fractions to mixed numbers or whole
numbers where applicable.

1. $\frac{7}{2}$ 2. $\frac{5}{3}$ 3. $\frac{7}{3}$ 4. $\frac{5}{4}$ 5. $\frac{8}{3}$

6. $\frac{8}{6}$ 7. $\frac{9}{3}$ 8. $\frac{9}{2}$ 9. $\frac{9}{4}$ 10. $\frac{10}{2}$

11. $\frac{10}{6}$ 12. $\frac{10}{7}$ 13. $\frac{13}{8}$ 14. $\frac{35}{15}$ 15. $\frac{42}{21}$

16. $\frac{120}{10}$ 17. $\frac{22}{7}$ 18. $\frac{15}{9}$ 19. $\frac{12}{5}$ 20. $\frac{150}{100}$

In Questions **21** to **35** change the mixed numbers to improper
fractions.

21. $1\frac{1}{4}$ 22. $1\frac{1}{3}$ 23. $2\frac{1}{4}$ 24. $2\frac{2}{3}$ 25. $1\frac{7}{8}$

26. $1\frac{2}{3}$ 27. $3\frac{1}{7}$ 28. $2\frac{1}{6}$ 29. $4\frac{3}{4}$ 30. $7\frac{1}{2}$

31. $3\frac{5}{8}$ 32. $4\frac{2}{5}$ 33. $3\frac{2}{5}$ 34. $8\frac{1}{4}$ 35. $1\frac{3}{10}$

Mixed questions

Exercise 7

1. How many halves are in: (a) $1\frac{1}{2}$,   (b) $2\frac{1}{2}$,   (c) $10\frac{1}{2}$?

2. How many thirds are in: (a) $1\frac{2}{3}$,   (b) $3\frac{1}{3}$,   (c) $5\frac{2}{6}$?

3. How many quarters are in: (a) $2\frac{1}{4}$,   (b) $3\frac{1}{2}$,   (c) $4\frac{3}{4}$?

4. Copy each sequence and write down the next four numbers

   (a) $\frac{1}{2} = \frac{2}{4} = \frac{3}{6} = \frac{4}{8} = \frac{5}{10} = \ldots\ldots$

   (b) $\frac{1}{3} = \frac{2}{6} = \frac{3}{9} = \frac{4}{12} = \frac{5}{15} = \ldots\ldots$

5. Write down the first five numbers in the sequence which starts
   $\frac{1}{5} = \frac{2}{10} = \ldots\ldots$

6. Draw these fraction charts, using squared paper.

	1		
$\frac{1}{2}$		$\frac{1}{2}$	
$\frac{1}{4}$	$\frac{1}{4}$		
$\frac{1}{8}$	$\frac{1}{8}$		

	1	
$\frac{1}{3}$		
$\frac{1}{6}$		

	1	
$\frac{1}{5}$	$\frac{1}{5}$	
$\frac{1}{10}$	$\frac{1}{10}$	

7. Use your fraction charts to answer the following:

(a) $\frac{3}{4} = \frac{?}{8}$ (b) $\frac{3}{5} = \frac{?}{10}$ (c) $\frac{1}{2} + \frac{1}{4} = \frac{?}{4}$

(d) $\frac{1}{5} + \frac{1}{10} = \frac{?}{10}$ (e) $\frac{2}{3} + \frac{1}{6} = \frac{?}{6}$ (f) $\frac{1}{4} + \frac{2}{8} = ?$

8. What fraction of the months of the year begin with the letters J, A or M?

9. What fraction of one hour is one minute?

10. What fraction of one complete turn is two right-angles?

11. What fraction of one minute is ten seconds?

12. What fraction of £1 is 60 p?

13. In a class of 30 pupils writing an essay, 23 are right-handed. What fraction are left-handed?

14. What fraction of the numbers from zero to ninety-nine contain the number 7?

15. Here are four numbers   2   4   7   11
You can use two of the numbers to make a fraction less than one (e.g. $\frac{4}{7}, \frac{2}{7} \ldots$)
(a) What is the smallest fraction you can make?
(b) What is the largest fraction you can make?

16. What number is half way between $3\frac{1}{4}$ and $3\frac{1}{2}$?

17. What fraction of the square is shaded?

18. Find six ways of adding two fractions to make one.

4.6 Angles 2

Angles on a straight line

- The angles on a straight line add up to 180°.

- Angles that add up to 180° are called supplementary.

- Angles that add up to 90° are called complementary.

Find the angles marked with letters.

(a)

D

x

A ———————— B ———— C

42°

ABC is a straight line

$\therefore \quad x + 42 = 180$

$x = 138°$

(b)

D

E

a

a

100°

A ———————— B ———— C

ABC is a straight line

$\therefore \quad a + a + 100 = 180$

$a = 40°$

Exercise 1

Find the angles marked with letters. In some questions you may
need to work out a division.

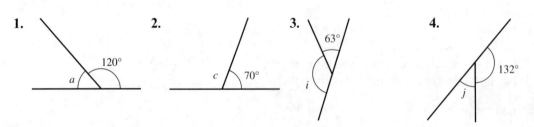

1. 120° a

2. c 70°

3. 63° i

4. 132° j

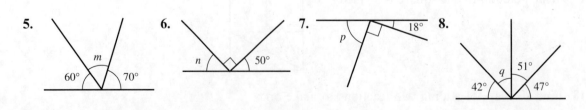

5. m 60° 70°

6. n 50°

7. p 18°

8. q 42° 51° 47°

9.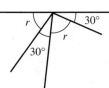

10.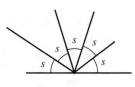

11.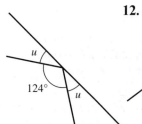

12.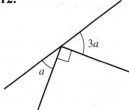

13.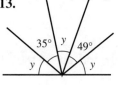

14.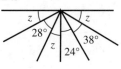

15.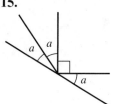

16.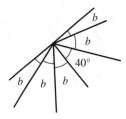

Angles at a point

The angles at a point add up to 360°

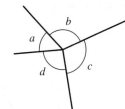

$a + b + c + d = 360°$

Exercise 2

Find the angles marked with letters.

1.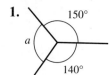

2.

3.

4.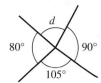

5.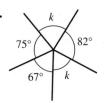

6.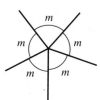

7.

8.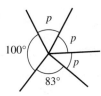

9.

10.

11.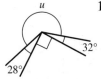

12.

Angles in a triangle

Draw a triangle of any shape on a piece of card and cut it out accurately. Now tear off the three corners as shown.

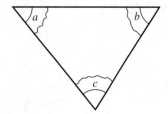

When the angles a, b and c are placed together they form a straight line.

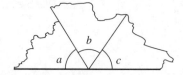

We see that:

The angles in a triangle add up to 180°

Isosceles and equilateral triangles

An *isosceles* triangle has two equal sides and two equal angles.

The sides AB and AC are equal (marked with a dash) so angles $\widehat{B}$ and $\widehat{C}$ are also equal.

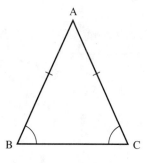

An *equilateral* triangle has three equal sides and three equal angles (all 60°).

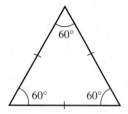

Intersecting lines

When two lines intersect, the opposite angles are equal.
In the diagram, $a = 36°$ and $b = 144°$.

The angles are called *vertically opposite* angles.

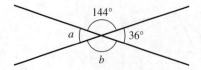

Find the angles marked with letters

(a)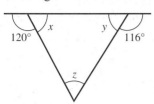

(b)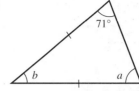

$x = 60°$ (angles on a straight line)
$y = 64°$ (angles on a straight line)
$z + 60 + 64 = 180$
$z = 56°$

$a = 71°$ (isosceles triangle)
$b + 71 + 71 = 180°$
$b = 38°$

Exercise 3

Find the angles marked with letters.

1.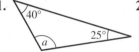

2.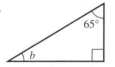

3.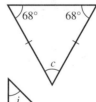

4.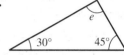

5.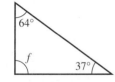

6.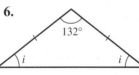

7.

8.

9.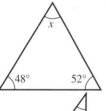

10.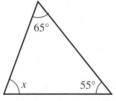

11.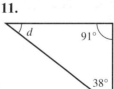

12.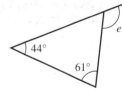

13.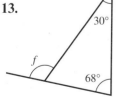

14.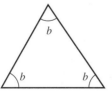

15.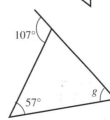

16.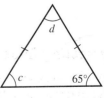

17.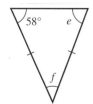

18.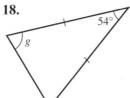

19.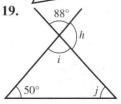

20.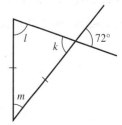

Part 5

5.1 Coordinates 2

The x axis can be extended to the left and the y axis can be extended downwards to include the negative numbers -1, -2, -3 etc.

The name 'FOXY' can be found using the letters in the following order:
$(2, 3)$, $(-2, -3)$, $(2, -2)$, $(-2, -1)$,

Similarly the coordinates of the points which spell out the word 'FOUR' are $(2, 3)$, $(-2, -3)$, $(-1, 2)$, $(3, -3)$.

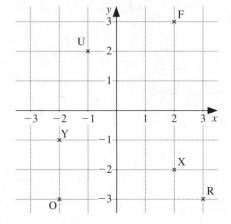

Exercise 1

The letters from A to Z are shown on the grid.
Coded messages can be sent using coordinates.

For example $(-5, -5)$ $(-4, 2)$
$\qquad$ $(2, 5)$ $(5, -2)$
$\qquad$ reads 'LOTS'.

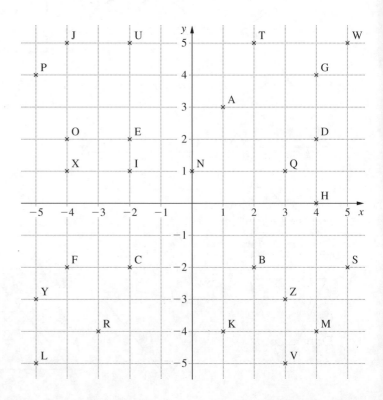

Decode the following messages:

1. (5, 5) (4, 0) (1, 3) (2, 5) # (4, 2) (−4, 2) # (−5, −3)
(−4, 2) (−2, 5) # (−2, −2) (1, 3) (−5, −5) (−5, −5) #
(1, 3) # (5, 5) (−4, 2) (4, −4) (1, 3) (0, 1) # (−2, 1) (0, 1) #
(1, 3) # (2, −2) (−4, 2) (−4, 2) (1, −4) (4, −4) (1, 3)
(1, −4) (−2, 2) (−3, −4) (5, −2) ? # (2, −2) (−2, 2) (2, 5) !

2. Change the sixth word to: (4, −4) (1, 3) (0, 1) #
Change the seventh word to: (−2, 5) (0, 1) (4, 2) (−2, 2)
(−3, −4) #
then (1, 3) # (−2, −2) (1, 3) (−3, −4) ? # (−4, 5) (1, 3)
(−2, −2) (1, −4) !

3. (5, 5) (4, 0) (1, 3) (2, 5) # (4, 2) (−4, 2) # (−5, −3)
(−4, 2) (−2, 5) # (−2, −2) (1, 3) (−5, −5) (−5, −5) #
(1, 3) # (4, 2) (−2, 2) (1, 3) (4, 2) # (−5, 4) (1, 3) (−3, −4)
(−3, −4) (−4, 2) (2, 5) ? # (−5, 4) (−4, 2) (−5, −5) (−5, −3)
(4, 4) (−4, 2) (0, 1) !

4. (5, 5) (−2, 1) (2, 5) (4, 0) # (5, 5) (4, 0) (1, 3) (2, 5) #
(4, 2) (−4, 2) # (−5, −3) (−4, 2) (−2, 5) # (5, −2) (2, 5)
(−2, 5) (−4, −2) (−4, −2) # (1, 3) # (4, 2) (−2, 2) (1, 3)
(4, 2) # (−5, 4) (1, 3) (−3, −4) (−3, −4) (−4, 2)
(2, 5) ? # (−5, 4) (−4, 2) (−5, −5) (−5, −3) (−4, −2) (−2, 1)
(−5, −5) (−5, −5) (1, 3) !

5. (5, 5) (4, 0) (1, 3) (2, 5) # (4, 2) (−4, 2) # (3, −5) (−2, 2)
(4, 4) (−2, 2) (2, 5) (1, 3) (−3, −4) (−2, 1) (1, 3) (0, 1) #
(4, −4) (−4, 2) (0, 1) (5, −2) (2, 5) (−2, 2) (−3, −4)
(5, −2) # (−2, 2) (1, 3) (2, 5) ? (5, −2) (5, 5) (−2, 2) (4, 2)
(−2, 2) (5, −2).

6. Write a message or joke of your own using coordinates. Ask a
friend to decode your words.

Coordinate pictures

These points are plotted
and then joined up in order.

(−5, −2) (−6, −3) (−4, −2) (0, −2)
(−1, −3) (1, −2) (1, −3) (2, −2)
(3, −2) (7, −1) (1, 2) (0, 2)
(1, 1) (0, 1) (−4, −1) (−6, 0)
(−5, −1) (−5, −2).

Draw a dot at (4, 0)

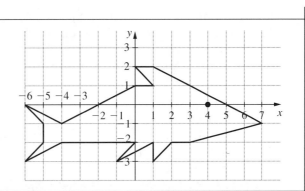

128   **Part 5**

Exercise 2

In Question **1**. Plot parts (a), (b), (c) and (d) on the same grid to show the 'sky at night'.

1. Draw x-axis from −12 to 12.
   Draw y-axis from −12 to 12.

   Plot and label each constellation.

   (a) The 'W'.

   (3, 5), (5, 6), (4, 7), (6, 7), (4, 9).

   This is called 'Cassiopeia'.

   (b) The 'Little Dipper'.

   (−3, 3), (−5, 1), (−6, 2), (−4, 4), (−3, 3), (−2, 3)
   (−1, 2), (0, 0).

   Note that (0, 0) is *Polaris* or the Pole Star.
   This constellation is called Ursa Minor.

   (c) The 'Big Dipper'.

   (−12, −2), (−9, −1), (−7, −2), (−6, −3), (−2 −3)
   (−3, −5), (−5, −5), (−6, −3).

   This is called Ursa Major.

   (d) The 'Hunter'

   (9, −10), (9, −8), (8, −9), (10, −7), (11, −5), (9, −4)
   (7, −6), (8, −9), (7, −12), (11, −11), (10, −7).

   This is called *Orion*.

Draw the following coordinate pictures in Questions **2** to **5** plotting the points and joining them up in the given order.

2. Draw x-axis from −7 to 7.
   Draw y-axis from −10 to 10.
   (0, 10), (1, 10), (4, 9), (6, 7), (7, 5), (3, 7), (1, 6) (1, −10),
   (−1, −10), (−1, 6), (−4, 7), (−5, 6), (−7, 6), (−7, 10),
   (−5, 10), (−4, 9), (−1, 10), (0, 10).

3. Draw x-axis from −10 to 8.
   Draw y-axis from −6 to 9.
   (−10, −1), (−10, 2), (−7, 3), (−6, 5), (−5, 6), (−3, 6),
   (−2, 8), (0, 7), (0, 6), (2, 5), (3, 9), (4, 7), (5, 4),
   (7, 2), (8, 0), (8, −2), (6, −6), (3, −6), (2, −5), (2, −4)
   (0, −4), (−2, −2), (−5, −4), (−8, −5), (−9, −5),
   (−10, −1).

4. Draw x-axis from −7 to 9.
   Draw y-axis from −10 to 12.
   (4, 2), (4, 4), (5, 9), (5, 12), (4, 10), (3, 12), (3, 10)
   (2, 12), (2, 10), (1, 11), (1, 9), (−1, 5), (−2, 2), (−7, 4)
   (−4, 0), (−7, −3), (−2, −1), (−1, −4), (1, −8), (1, −10)
   (2, −8), (2, −10), (3, −8), (3, −10), (4, −8), (5, −10)
   (5, −7), (4, −3), (4, −2), (7, −1), (9 −2), (7, 1), (4, 2).

5. Draw both x and y axes from -8 to 8
$(-5, -2)$, $(-5, 0)$, $(-3, 0)$, $(-3, 2)$, $(-1, 2)$, $(-1, 4)$, $(1, 4)$, $(1, 2)$, $(3, 2)$, $(3, 0)$, $(5, 0)$, $(5, -2)$, $(7, 7)$, $(0, 8)$, $(-7, 7)$, $(-5, -2)$, $(0, -7)$, $(5, -2)$, $(3, -2)$, $(3, 0)$, $(1, 0)$, $(1, 2)$, $(-1, 2)$, $(-1, 0)$, $(-3, 0)$, $(-3, -2)$, $(-5, -2)$.

You have drawn the outline for a school badge. Design a shape to complete the badge and colour in your badge.

6. Write down the coordinates of the points which will produce this picture.

   Start at $(3, 1)$ and follow the arrows.

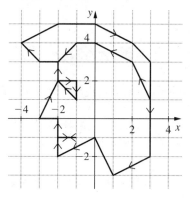

7. Design a coordinates picture of your own and write down the points needed to produce the shape.

Find the hidden treasure: an activity

This is a game for two players: one player hides the treasure and the other player tries to find it.

(a) Player A draws a grid with x and y from -6 to 6. He puts the treasure at any point with whole number coordinates. Say $(4, -2)$.

(b) Player B draws his own grid and makes his first guess. Say $(1, 1)$.

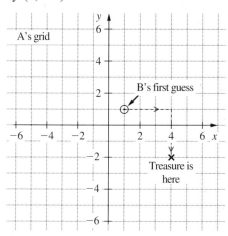

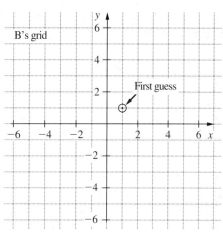

(c) Player A tells player B how far away he is by adding the *horizontal* and *vertical* distances from his guess to the treasure. So the point $(1, 1)$ is a distance 6 away.

(d) Player B has another guess and player A gives the distance from the new point to the treasure.

(e) Play continues until player B finds the treasure.

(f) Roles are then reversed so that B hides a new treasure and A tries to find it in as few goes as possible.

● After several games you may realise that you can improve your chances by using a 'mathematical strategy'.

5.2 Area and perimeter

We use area to describe how much *surface* a shape has.

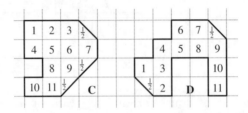

B contains 10 squares.
B has an area of 10 squares.

C has an area of $12\frac{1}{2}$ squares.
D has an area of 12 squares.

● 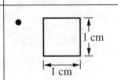 A square one centimetre by one centimetre has an area of one square centimetre. This is written $1\,cm^2$.

Exercise 1

In the diagrams below each square represents $1\,cm^2$. Copy each shape and find its area by counting squares.

1.

2.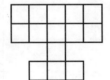

3.

4.

5.

6.

7.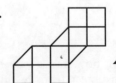

8.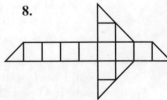

9. 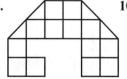   **10.** 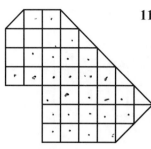   **11.** 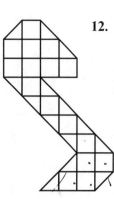   **12.**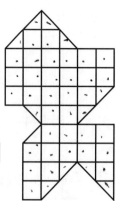

Areas of rectangles

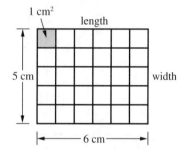

The area of a rectangle can be found by counting squares. This rectangle has an area of 30 squares.
If each square is $1\,\text{cm}^2$, this rectangle has an area of $30\,\text{cm}^2$.

It is easier to multiply the length by the width of the rectangle than to count squares.

$$\begin{aligned}\text{Area of rectangle} &= \text{length} \times \text{width}\\ &= (6 \times 5)\,\text{cm}^2\\ &= 30\,\text{cm}^2\end{aligned}$$

Area of a rectangle = length × width   Remember!

A square is a special rectangle in which the length and width are equal.

Area of a square = length × length

Exercise 2

Calculate the areas of the following rectangles. All lengths are given in centimetres.

1. 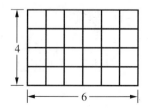   **2.** 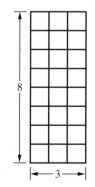   **3.**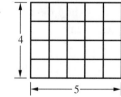

4.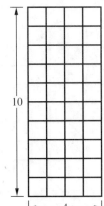

5.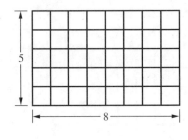

6.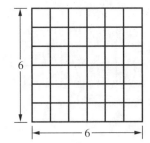

7.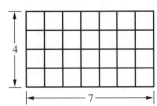

8.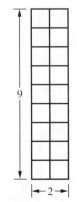

9.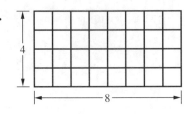

10.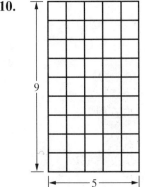

11.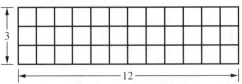

12.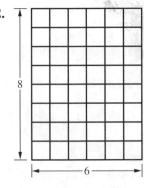

13. Find the areas of squares whose lengths are:
   (a) 3 cm   (b) 5 cm   (c) 10 cm   (d) 20 cm

14. 1 cm = 10 mm. How many square millimetres (mm^2) can fit into one square centimetre (1 cm^2)?

[not to scale]

1 cm

1 mm

15. If 1 metre (1 m) = 100 cm, how many square centimetres (cm^2) will fit into one square metre (1 m^2)?

16. If 1 kilometre (1 km) = 1000 m, how many square metres (m^2) will fit into one square kilometre (1 km^2)?

Units of area

Here are some examples of the most suitable unit for measuring the area of:

(a) a drawing pin head .... mm^2.   [square millimetres]

(b) the cover of your exercise book .... cm^2 [square centimetres]

(c) the classroom floor .... m^2 [square metres]

(d) the Atlantic Ocean .... km^2 [square kilometres]

Exercise 3

Write down the most suitable unit for measuring the area of the following:

1. A playing card   **2.** A chessboard

3. A postage stamp   **4.** A bedroom floor

5. A garden lawn   **6.** The county of Cornwall

7. A pin head   **8.** Heathrow airport

9. A classroom door   **10.** The 'on' button on your calculator

In Questions **11** to **14** write each sentence and choose the number which is the best estimate.

11. The cover of this book has an area of about [50 cm^2, 500 cm^2, 5 m^2]

12. The playground has an area of about [5 m^2, 1000 m^2, 1 km^2]

13. A postage stamp has an area of about [5 mm^2, 5 cm^2, 50 cm^2]

14. The area of the classroom floor is about [50 m^2, 500 m^2, 1000 m^2]

15. Measure the length and width of these rectangles and then work out the area of each one.

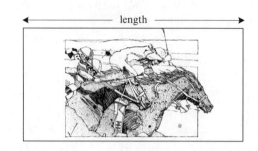

16. Find a magazine or newspaper and cut out pictures with the following areas:

(a) $12\,\text{cm}^2$ (b) $16\,\text{cm}^2$ (c) $24\,\text{cm}^2$

Stick the pictures in your book and write down the area of each one.

In Questions **17** to **20** the area is written inside the shape. Calculate the length of the side marked x.

17.

$45\,\text{cm}^2$ $\quad$ 5 cm

x

18.

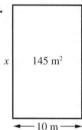

x $\quad$ $145\,\text{m}^2$

← 10 m →

19.

$72\,\text{m}^2$ $\quad$ 9 m

x

20.

$144\,\text{m}^2$ $\quad$ x

x

Areas of irregular shapes

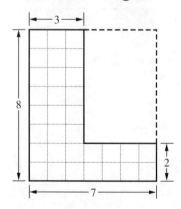

This is an irregular shape. It is possible to find its area by counting squares. A better method is to surround the irregular shape with a rectangle.

Step 1 Area of surrounding rectangle.
$$\text{Area} = \text{length} \times \text{width}$$
$$= (8 \times 7)\,\text{cm}^2$$
$$= 56\,\text{cm}^2$$

Step 2 Find the unwanted area.
$$\text{Area} = \text{length} \times \text{width}$$
$$= (8 - 2) \times (7 - 3)\,\text{cm}^2$$
$$= (6 \times 4)\,\text{cm}^2$$
$$= 24\,\text{cm}^2$$

Step 3 Required area $= (56 - 24)\,\text{cm}^2$
$$= 32\,\text{cm}^2$$

Exercise 4

Find the areas of the following irregular shapes. Each square represents $1\,\text{cm}^2$.

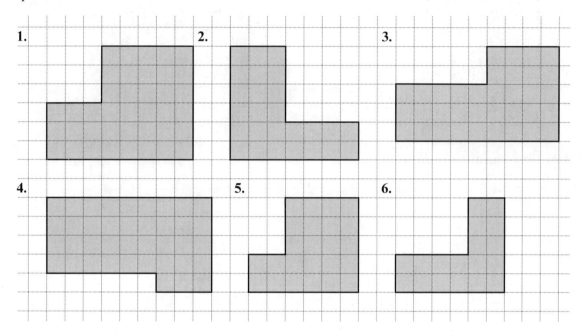

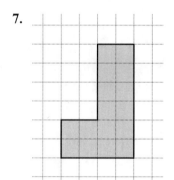

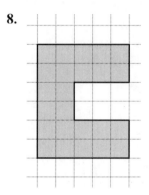

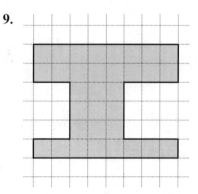

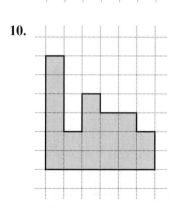

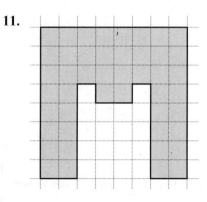

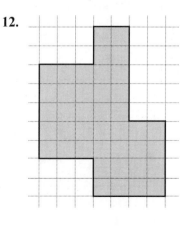

More irregular shapes

Example: Find the shaded area:

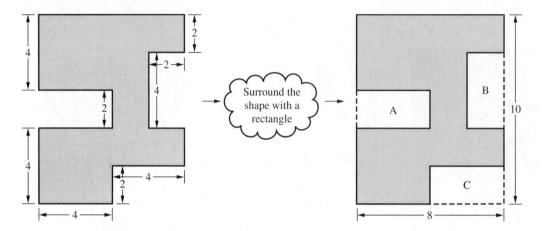

Area of surrounding rectangle $= (8 \times 10)\,cm^2$
$= 80\,cm^2$
Areas to be subtracted: $A = (4 \times 2)\,cm^2$, $B = (4 \times 2)\,cm^2$, $C = (4 \times 2)\,cm^2$
$= 8\,cm^2$ $= 8\,cm^2$ $= 8\,cm^2$
Total area to be subtracted $= (8 + 8 + 8)\,cm^2$
$= 24\,cm^2$
Required shaded area $= (80 - 24)\,cm^2$
$= 56\,cm^2$

Exercise 5

Draw each shape on squared paper and then find the area. All measurements are in centimetres.

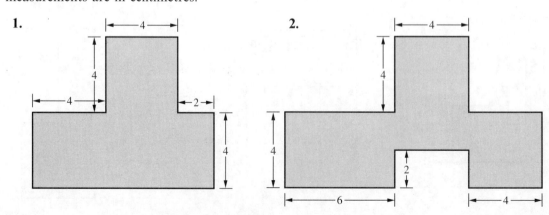

3.

4.

5.

6.

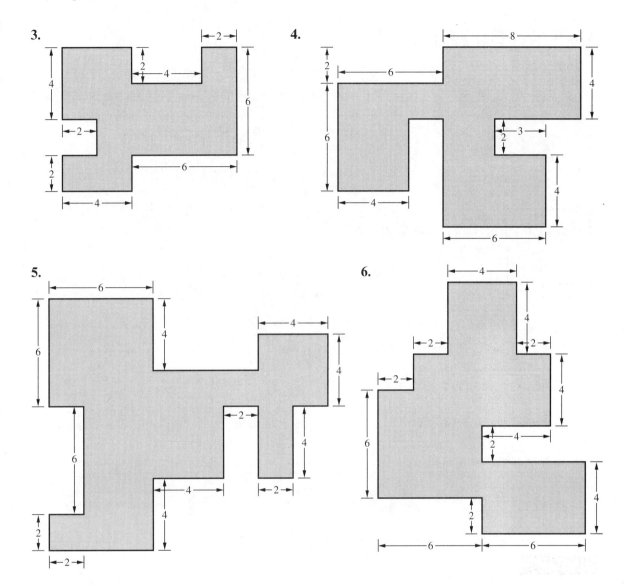

Triangles

(a) This triangle has base 6 cm, height 4 cm and a right angle at A.

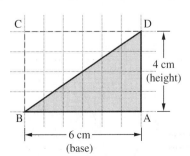

Area of rectangle ABCD $= (6 \times 4) \, cm^2$
$$= 24 \, cm^2.$$

Area of triangle ABD = area of triangle CDB.

$\therefore$ Area of triangle ABD $= 24 \div 2$
$$= 12 \, cm^2$$

(b) Here triangle PQR is drawn
    inside a rectangle.

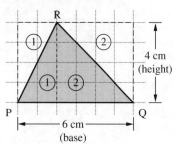

Area of triangle PQR = area ① + area ②

Area of rectangle = (2 × area ①) + (2 × area ②)

$$\therefore \text{ Area of triangle PQR} = \frac{6 \times 4}{2}$$

$$= 12 \text{ cm}^2$$

(c) In the triangle below the height
    (3 units) is measured 'outside'
    the triangle

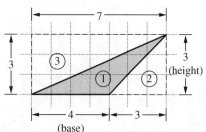

Area ① = Area of rectangle − [area ② + area ③]

$$= 21 - \left[\frac{3 \times 3}{2} + \frac{3 \times 7}{2}\right]$$

$$= 21 - [15]$$

$$= 6 \text{ square units.}$$

In each of examples (a), (b) and (c) the area of the triangle is found by multiplying the base by the height and dividing by two.

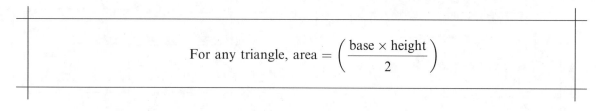

$$\text{For any triangle, area} = \left(\frac{\text{base} \times \text{height}}{2}\right)$$

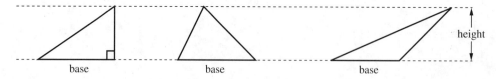

Exercise 6

Find the area of each shape.

1.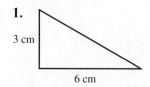

2.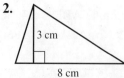

3.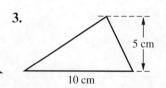

4.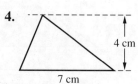

In Questions **5** to **12** the background squares are 1 cm by 1 cm.

5.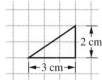

6.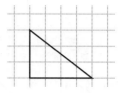

7.

8.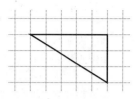

9.

10.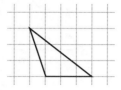

11.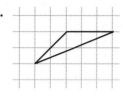

12.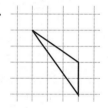

In Questions **13** to **18** the lengths are in cm.

13.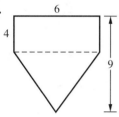

14.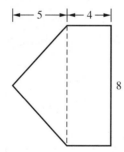

15.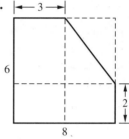

16.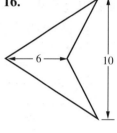

17. Find the shaded area.

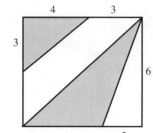

18. Find the shaded area.

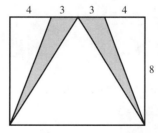

19. The triangle shown has base 10 cm and area 40 cm². Find the height of the triangle.

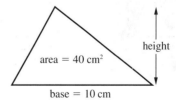

20. Find the height of each triangle below.

(a)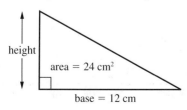

(b)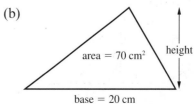

Perimeter

The perimeter of a shape is the distance around its outline.

(a) The perimeter of this rectangle
    is $4 + 10 + 4 + 10 = 28$ cm

(b) The perimeter of this triangle
    is $7 + 5 + 9 = 21$ cm.

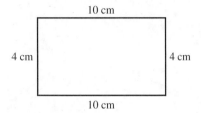

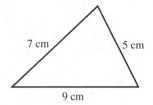

Exercise 7

1. Measure the sides of these shapes and work out the perimeter of each one.

   (a)

   (b)

   (c)

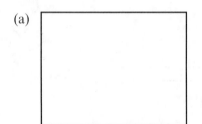

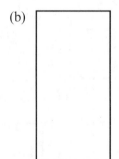

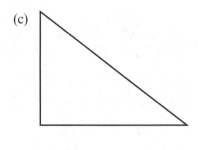

2. Find the perimeter of these pictures.

   (a)

   (b)

   (c)

3. Find the perimeters of these shapes

   (a) rectangle 7·5 cm by 4 cm   (b) square of side 6 cm

   (c) equilateral triangle of side 7 cm   (d) rectangle 3·5 cm by 2·5 cm

   (e) square of side 20 m   (f) regular hexagon of side 5 cm

The shapes in Questions **4** to **11** consist of rectangles joined together.
Find the missing lengths and then work out the perimeter of each
shape. The lengths are in cm.

4. 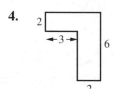 **5.** 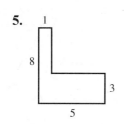 **6.** 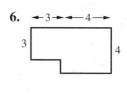 **7.**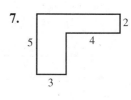

8. 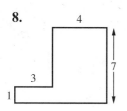 **9.** 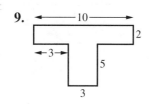 **10.** 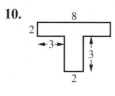 **11.**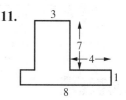

Questions **12** onwards are about perimeter *and* area.

12. Here are four shapes made with centimetre squares.

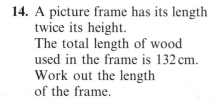

(a) Which shape has an area of $5\,cm^2$?
(b) Which two shapes have the same perimeter?

13. Each of the shapes here has an
area of $2\,cm^2$.
(a) On square dotty paper draw three
   more shapes with area $2\,cm^2$
(b) Draw three shapes with area $3\,cm^2$.
(c) Draw one shape with area $4\,cm^2$
   and perimeter $10\,cm$.

14. A picture frame has its length
twice its height.
The total length of wood
used in the frame is $132\,cm$.
Work out the length
of the frame.

height

length

15. Here are five shapes made from equilateral triangles of side 1 cm.

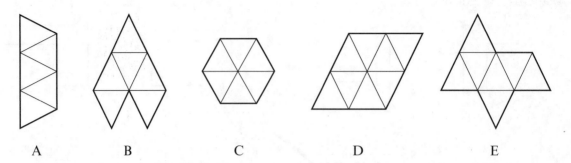

A   B   C   D   E

   (a) Which shape has the longest perimeter?
   (b) Which shape has the smallest area?
   (c) Which shape has the same perimeter as D?

16. The perimeter of a rectangular lawn is 40 m. The shortest side is 7 m. How long is the longest side?

17.* The diagram shows the areas of 3 faces of a rectangular box. What are the measurements of the box?

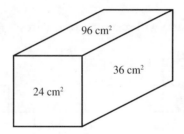

Area and perimeter: an investigation

A • Draw *four* different rectangles which all have a *perimeter* of 24 cm.

B • Draw *three* different rectangles which all have an *area* of 24 cm².

C • Draw at least four rectangles which have a perimeter of 20 cm.
    • Work out the area of each rectangle.
    • Which of your rectangles has the largest area?

D • The perimeter of a new rectangle is 32 cm.
    • Try to *predict* what the sides will be for the rectangle with the largest possible area.
    • Now check to see if your prediction was correct.

E • Try to find the rectangle with perimeter 32 cm which has the *smallest* possible area.

5.3 Mixed problems

1. Work out
   (a) 4×8 (b) $70 - 25$ (c) 8×0
   (d) $48 \div 6$ (e) $279 + 182$ (f) $314 - 276$

2. Write the number 'three thousand and fourteen' in figures.

3. (a) Copy and shade one quarter
      of this shape:
   (b) What fraction of the shape
      is left unshaded?

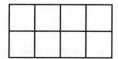

4. Steve has read 97 of the 448 pages in his book. How many more
   pages must be read to reach the middle?

5. There are 15 piles of magazines. Eight piles have 20 magazines
   each, of the other piles each have 25 magazines. How many
   magazines are there altogether?

6. There are 27 youngsters playing football.
   How many teams of five can be formed?
   How many will be left over?

7. It cost 6 children a total of £12.90 to
   watch a film. What did it cost each child?

8. Copy and complete this multiplication square

$\times$	2	5		
		40		72
			18	
7	14			
			24	36

9. Write 25555p in pounds and pence.

10. Write the number 4307 in words.

1. On average the amount of potato lost
   through peeling is 12%.
   What percentage of potato is left after
   peeling?

2. 36715 people saw Arsenal's match against Spurs. This is 2368 more than for their match against Everton. How many people saw the game against Everton?

3. Two thirds of the 246 children in a school have pets. 52 children have a rabbit and 37 have a snake. How many children have other kinds of pets?

4.

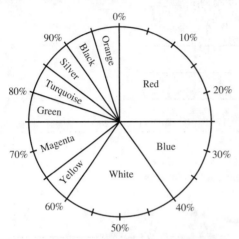

The diagram shows the distribution of colours of cars produced by the 'Cheetah' motor company.

(a) What percentage of cars produced are red, white or blue?

(b) What percentage of cars produced are green or yellow?

(c) List the four most popular colours produced and give each percentage from highest to lowest.

5. How much does *one* cost in each case?

(a) 5 for £2.65

(b) 10 for £4.50

(c) 100 for £24

6. (a) What is the length of this line in millimetres?
(b) What is this length in centimetres?

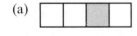

7. Work out
(a) £5 − £1·35
(b) 0·14 × 1000
(c) 4·2 ÷ 5

8. Write down what fraction of each shape is shaded.
(a)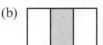
(b)
(c)

9. James is 1·31 m tall and Samita is 6 cm taller. How tall is Samita in metres?

10. A carton of 'Bisto' weighs 0·8 kg. How much would 100 cartons weigh?

11. Make up 'number stories' for the calculations below.

For example: for 7 × 55 = 385.

'7 cans of coke at 55p each will cost 385p'.

(a) 12·5 − 7 = 5·5
(b) 4·25 × 11 = 46·75
(c) 273 ÷ 6 = 45·5

Exercise 3

1. How many grams of sugar must be added to 1·3 kg to make 3 kg altogether?

2. Serena bought a packet of 100 raspberries. She ate a quarter of them on Monday. She ate a fifth of the remaining raspberries on Tuesday. How many raspberries did she have left?

3. For sports day a school has 40 litres of drink. One cup of drink is 200 ml. How many cups of drink can be provided?

4. Change this cake recipe for 4 people to a recipe for 6 people.

320 g	mixed fruit
90 g	butter
200 ml	milk
4	eggs

5. Stainless steel contains Iron, Chromium and Nickel. 74% of stainless steel is Iron, 8% is Nickel. What percentage is Chromium?

6. Work out
   (a) $114 \times 0\cdot4$ (b) $18 - 5\cdot7$ (c) $211 + 57\cdot3 + 5\cdot42$

7. Write the number 'two and a half million' in figures.

8. How many minutes are there from 08·20 to 09·15?

9. Measure the sides of the rectangle and work out
   (a) the area
   (b) the perimeter

10. Work out the missing numbers
    (a) $310 + 560 = \boxed{}$ (b) $530 + \boxed{} = 700$ (c) $734 + \boxed{} = 780$

    (d) $\boxed{} + 210 = 500$ (e) $338 + \boxed{} = 558$ (f) $\boxed{} - 420 = 535$

11. Work out the missing numbers
    (a) $5\cdot6 + \boxed{} = 6$ (b) $3\cdot7 - \boxed{} = 2$ (c) $0\cdot54 + \boxed{} = 0\cdot74$

    (d) $0\cdot4 - \boxed{} = 0\cdot15$ (e) $\boxed{} - 0\cdot7 = 1\cdot4$ (f) $0\cdot86 - \boxed{} = 0\cdot5$

12. Jesper has the same number of 20p and 50p coins. The total value is £7. How many of each coin does he have?

Exercise 4

1. There are 35 rows of chairs and there are 20 chairs in each row.
   (a) How many chairs are there altogether?
   (b) How many rows of chairs are needed for 300 people?

2. One whole number divided by another gives 0·63636363. Use a calculator to find the two numbers.

3. At the end of year 7 Mark said 'I have now lived for over one million hours'. Work out if Mark was right.

4. I think of a number, add 2·3 and then multiply by 4. The answer is 23·4. What is the number I am thinking of?

5. How many roses, costing 42p each, can be bought for £20? How much change will there be?

6. The words for the numbers from one to ten are written in a list in alphabetical order. What number will be third in the list?

7. Find two consecutive whole numbers with a product of 9506.

8. Use each of the digits 1 to 6. Put one digit in each box to make the statement true.

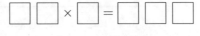

9. A restaurant has 5000 litres of milk. It sells 350 litres per day on average. How many days will the milk last?

10. Julie runs across the playground, which is 90 m wide, in 15 seconds. What was her average speed in metres per second?

Exercise 5

1. Mark is paid a basic weekly wage of £65 and then a further 30p for each item completed. How many items must be completed in a week when he earns a total of £171·50?

2. What number, when divided by 7 and then multiplied by 12, gives an answer of 144?

3. A 10p coin is 2 mm thick. Alex has a pile of 10p coins which is 16·6 cm tall. What is the value of the money in Alex's pile of coins?

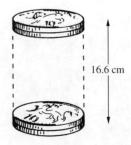

16.6 cm

2 mm

4. An Air France Concorde leaves Paris at 07 00 and arrives in New York at 10 20.
A PanAm 747 leaves Paris at 07 10 and flies at half the speed of the Concorde. When should it arrive in New York?

5. The numbers 1 to 12 are arranged on the star so that the sum of the numbers along each line is the same.

Copy and complete the star.

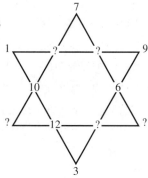

6. Find two numbers which multiply together to give 60 and which add up to 19.

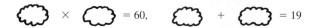

7. A shopkeeper buys coffee beans at £4·20 per kg and sells them at 95p per 100 g. How much profit does he make per kg?

8. A Jaguar XJ6 uses 8 litres of petrol for every 50 km travelled. Petrol costs 56p per litre. Calculate the cost in £'s of travelling 600 km.

9. A school play was attended by 226 adults, each paying £1·50, and 188 children, each paying 80p. How much in £'s was paid altogether by the people attending the play?

10. Arrange the following numbers in order, smallest first:
8711, 8171, 8117, 817, 8710

Exercise 6

1. A man smokes 50 cigarettes a day and a packet of 20 costs £3·08. How much does he spend on cigarettes in six days?

2. As an incentive to tidy her bedroom, a girl is given 1p on the first day, 2p on the second day, 4p on the third day and so on, doubling the amount each day.

How much has she been given after 10 days?

3. A shopkeeper has a till containing a large number of the following coins:
  £1; 50p; 20p; 10p; 5p; 2p; 1p.
  He needs to give a customer 57p in change. List all the different ways in which he can do this using no more than six coins.

4. Place the following numbers in order of size, smallest first:
  0·34; 0·334; 0·032; 0·04; 0·4.

5. A book has pages numbered 1 to 300 and the thickness of the book, without the covers, is 15 mm. How thick is each page?

6. In an election 7144 votes were cast for the two candidates. Mr Dewey won by 424 votes. How many people voted for Dewey?

7. The tenth number in the sequence 1, 4, 16, 64 . . . . . . is 262 144.
  What is (a) the ninth number,
          (b) the twelfth number?

8. Two fifths of the children in a swimming pool are boys.
  There are 72 girls in the pool.
  How many boys are there?

9. How many minutes are there between:
  (a) 09 20 and 11 10,
  (b) 07 15 and 10 00,
  (c) 14 45 and 17 15,
  (d) 02 10 and 06 10?

10. Two weights m and n are placed on scales and m is found to be more than 11 g and n is less than 7 g. Arrange the weights 8·5 g, m and n in order, lightest first.

Exercise 7

1. Lisa is 12 years old and her father is 37 years older than her. Lisa's mother is 3 years younger than her father. How old is Lisa's mother?

2. 36 small cubes are stuck together to make the block shown and the block is then painted on the outside. How many of the small cubes are painted on:
  (a) 1 face   (b) 2 faces
  (c) 3 faces   (d) 0 faces?

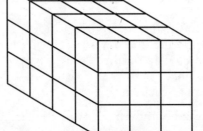

3. Find the letters in these additions.

```
(a)    8  7  A        (b)    A  2  4  5
       3  B  5               5  B  8  4
    +  C  4  2            +  1  4  C  6
    ──────────            ──────────────
    D  8  4  1            E  0  5  2  D
```

4. (a) Which four coins make a total of 77p?
   (b) Which five coins make a total of 86p?
   (c) Which five coins make a total of £1·67?

5. Work out, without a calculator
   (a) $100 \times 10\,000$ (b) $10\,000 \div 100$ (c) $0·94 + 5·6$
   (d) $4·37 \div 0·3$ (e) $246 + 33818$ (f) $4318 - 645$

6. Petrol costs 52p per litre. How many litres can be bought for £13? Give your answer to the nearest litre.

7. A flight on Concorde takes 2 h 36 min. How long would the same flight take on a plane travelling at half the speed of Concorde?

8. Seven oak trees were planted in Windsor when Queen Victoria was born. She died in 1901 aged 82. How old were the trees in 1993?

9. A mixed school has a total of 876 pupils. There are 48 more boys than girls. How many boys are there?

10. Four 4's can be used to make 12: $\dfrac{44 + 4}{4}$

   (a) Use three 6's to make 2
   (b) Use three 7's to make 7
   (c) Use three 9's to make 11
   (d) Use four 4's to make 9
   (e) Use four 4's to make 3

Exercise 8

1. Unifix cubes can be joined together to make different sized cuboids.

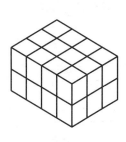
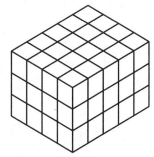

If the smaller cuboid weighs 96 g, how much does the large cuboid weigh?

2. In a 'magic' square the sum of the numbers in any row, column or main diagonal is the same. Copy and complete these magic squares.

(a)

3		
8		4
7		

(b)

14		7	2
		12	
	5	9	16
15			3

3. This table shows the approximate weights of coins

1p	2p	5p	10p	20p
3·6 g	7·2 g	3·2 g	6·5 g	5·0 g

(a) What is the lightest weight with a value of 12p made from these coins?

(b) A group of mixed coins weighs 228 g, of which 48 g is the silver coins.
What is the value of the bronze coins?

4. The test results of 50 students are shown below.

Mark	5	6	7	8	9	10
Frequency	0	2	12	17	10	9

What percentage of the students scored 8 marks or more?

5. Four and a half dozen eggs weigh 2970 g. How much would six dozen eggs weigh?

6. Which of the shapes below can be drawn without taking the pen from the paper and without going over any line twice?

(a)   (b)   (c)

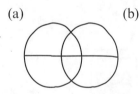 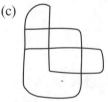

7. A satellite link between Britain and Australia can be hired at a cost of £250 per minute from 06 00 to 14 00 and at £180 per minute after 14 00.
The link is used to televise a football match which starts at 13 30 and ends at 15 22.
How much does it cost?

8. On the 30th June 1994 the day was extended by 1 second to allow for the irregularity in the speed of rotation of the Earth. A newspaper carried an article stating that people in Britain eat 54 digestive biscuits every second. How many digestive biscuits were eaten on 30th June 1994?

9. A Rover 216XL travels 7·4 miles on a litre of petrol and petrol costs 53p per litre. In six months the car is driven a total of 4750 miles. Find the cost of the petrol to the nearest pound.

10. In a code the 25 letters from A to Y are obtained from the square using a 2 digit grid reference similar to coordinates.
So letter 'U' is 42 and 'L' is 54.
The missing letter 'Z' has code 10.

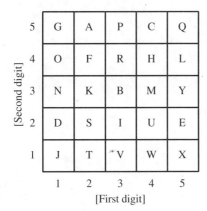

Decode the following messages:

(a) 41, 52
    13, 52, 52, 12
    43, 14, 34, 52
    22, 42, 43, 22

(b) 44, 25, 31, 52
    25
    13, 32, 45, 52
    12, 25, 53

(c) 22, 35, 42, 34, 22
    25, 34, 52
    34, 42, 33, 33, 32, 22, 44

In part (d) each pair of brackets gives one letter

(d) $\left(\frac{1}{4} \text{ of } 140\right)$, $(7^2 + 5)$, $(7 \times 8 - 4)$, $(4^2 + 3^2)$, $\left(\frac{1}{5} \text{ of } 110\right)$, $\left(26 \div \frac{1}{2}\right)$
    $(3 \times 7 + 1)$, $(83 - 31)$, $(2 \times 2 \times 2 \times 2 + 5)$
    $(100 - 57)$, $(4^2 - 2)$, (17×2), $(151 - 99)$
    $(2 \times 2 \times 2 \times 5 + 1)$, $\left(\frac{1}{4} \text{ of } 56\right)$, $(2 \times 3 \times 2 \times 3 - 2)$, $(5^2 - 2)$.

(e) Write your own message in code and ask a friend to decode it.

5.4 Number machines

- A number machine performs an *operation* on numbers.

- A simple *operation* could be   add   (+)
                                subtract (−)
                                multiply (×)
               or   divide   (÷)

- The *input* number goes into the machine.

- The *output* number comes out of the machine.

input   output

To make the number machines easier to draw we will use a box

Examples

	input	machine	output	output solution	reason
1.	5 →	+ 7	→ ?	? = 12	(5 + 7 = 12)
2.	8 →	− 3	→ ◆	◆ = 5	(8 − 3 = 5)
3.	3 →	× 6	→ ■	■ = 18	(3 × 6 = 18)
4.	20 →	÷ 4	→ ▲	▲ = 5	(20 ÷ 4 = 5)

Exercise 1

Find the outputs from these number machines.

1. 4 → | + 5 | → ☺

2. 7 → | + 11 | → ◢

3. 10 → | − 3 | → ▮

4. 14 → | − 9 | → ▬

5. 6 → | × 7 | → ▨

6. 8 → | × 2 | → ⌑

7. 25 → | ÷ 5 | → ?

8. 24 → | ÷ 4 | → ☺

9. 39 → | + 13 | → ▮

10. 7 → | × 9 | → ◣

11. 64 → | − 46 | → ⊡

12. 66 → | ÷ 6 | → 👢

13. 8 → | × 9 | → ⌑

14. 73 → | + 37 | → ✠

15. 45 → | ÷ 5 | → ◆

16. 51 → | − 15 | → ▮

17. 33 → | × 3 | → ◣

18. 8 → | × 8 | → 🎄

19. 120 → | ÷ 20 | → π

20. 52 → | ÷ 4 | → ∅

More machines

Sometimes there is more than one operation.

Here is a number machine with two operations ...

Input   Output

7 → | × 2 | → | − 5 | → 9

Exercise 2

Find the output.

1. $6 \rightarrow \boxed{+5} \rightarrow \boxed{+2} \rightarrow$ **?**

2. $3 \rightarrow \boxed{+6} \rightarrow \boxed{+8} \rightarrow$ ●

3. $13 \rightarrow \boxed{-9} \rightarrow \boxed{-3} \rightarrow$ ▲

4. $17 \rightarrow \boxed{-8} \rightarrow \boxed{-5} \rightarrow$ ◆

5. $4 \rightarrow \boxed{\times 2} \rightarrow \boxed{\times 5} \rightarrow$ π

6. $3 \rightarrow \boxed{\times 3} \rightarrow \boxed{\times 3} \rightarrow$ ⌀

7. $20 \rightarrow \boxed{\div 5} \rightarrow \boxed{\div 2} \rightarrow$ ◣

8. $48 \rightarrow \boxed{\div 4} \rightarrow \boxed{\div 6} \rightarrow$ ◢

9. $17 \rightarrow \boxed{+71} \rightarrow \boxed{-8} \rightarrow$ ▮

10. $34 \rightarrow \boxed{+43} \rightarrow \boxed{-70} \rightarrow$ 👢

11. $5 \rightarrow \boxed{+4} \rightarrow \boxed{\times 3} \rightarrow$ 🐟

12. $7 \rightarrow \boxed{+9} \rightarrow \boxed{\times 0} \rightarrow$ ☺

13. $12 \rightarrow \boxed{+6} \rightarrow \boxed{\div 6} \rightarrow$ ✦

14. $39 \rightarrow \boxed{+13} \rightarrow \boxed{\div 4} \rightarrow$ 〰

15. $89 \rightarrow \boxed{-15} \rightarrow \boxed{+4} \rightarrow$ 〰

16. $73 \rightarrow \boxed{-5} \rightarrow \boxed{+9} \rightarrow$ ▬

17. $42 \rightarrow \boxed{-38} \rightarrow \boxed{\times 7} \rightarrow$ 👢

18. $100 \rightarrow \boxed{-81} \rightarrow \boxed{\times 3} \rightarrow$ ▮

19. $85 \rightarrow \boxed{-58} \rightarrow \boxed{\div 9} \rightarrow$ 🎄

20. $76 \rightarrow \boxed{-67} \rightarrow \boxed{\div 9} \rightarrow$ 🎲

In Questions **21** to **25** there are several operations.

21. $5 \rightarrow \boxed{\times 3} \rightarrow \boxed{-10} \rightarrow \boxed{\times 2} \rightarrow \boxed{\div 10} \rightarrow$ ☂

22. $7 \rightarrow \boxed{\times 9} \rightarrow \boxed{\times 2} \rightarrow \boxed{-66} \rightarrow \boxed{\div 12} \rightarrow$ ◠

23. $50 \rightarrow \boxed{\times 10} \rightarrow \boxed{-123} \rightarrow \boxed{+13} \rightarrow \boxed{\div 10} \rightarrow \boxed{\div 13} \rightarrow$ ↑

24. $17 \rightarrow \boxed{\times 5} \rightarrow \boxed{+25} \rightarrow \boxed{\div 11} \rightarrow \boxed{\times 13} \rightarrow \boxed{\div 2} \rightarrow \boxed{+7} \rightarrow$ ⚑

25. $13 \rightarrow \boxed{+84} \rightarrow \boxed{\times 0} \rightarrow \boxed{+14} \rightarrow \boxed{\times 5} \rightarrow \boxed{-15} \rightarrow \boxed{\div 11} \rightarrow$ **!**

Inverse operations

- Using the *inverse* (or reverse) we can find the input for any machine, by using the output.

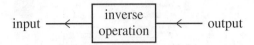

input ←─── | inverse operation | ←─── output

Operation	Inverse operation
+7	−7
−8	+8
×4	÷4
÷6	×6

- Example: Find the input.

? →─| + 9 |─→ 20

Solution: Change arrows direction and use the inverse operation

? ←─| − 9 |← 20

? = 11 since 20 − 9 = 11

Exercise 3

Find the input to these systems

1. ● →─| +6 |─→ 11

2. ▲ →─| + 4 |─→ 13

3. ⚅ →─| − 7 |─→ 2

4. ◢ →─| − 12 |─→ 24

5. ▮ →─| × 3 |─→ 18

6. ☺ →─| × 5 |─→ 45

7. $ →─| ÷ 8 |─→ 4

8. 👢 →─| ÷ 7 |─→ 8

9. 🐟 →─| + 14 |─→ 72

10. 〰 →─| + 11 |─→ 29

11. ◣ →─| − 13 |─→ 31

12. ◆ →─| − 72 |─→ 27

13. ∅ →─| × 5 |─→ 60

14. π →─| × 9 |─→ 72

15. ? →─| ÷ 4 |─→ 8

16. ◤ →─| ÷ 6 |─→ 7

17. ▬ →─| × 9 |─→ 54

18. ? →─| × 8 |─→ 56

19. ☺ →─| ÷ 7 |─→ 7

20. ◢ →─| ÷ 3 |─→ 27

Exercise 4

Find the input to these machines

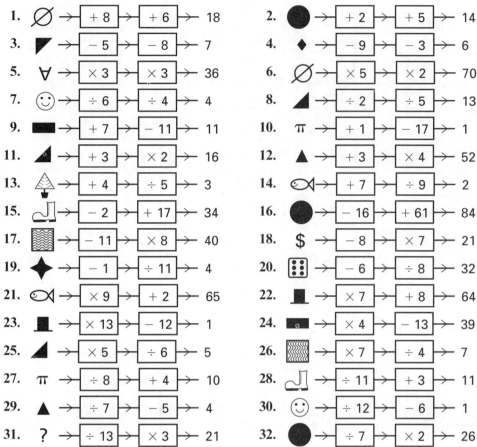

1. ∅ →→ +8 →→ +6 →→ 18
2. ● →→ +2 →→ +5 →→ 14
3. ◤ →→ −5 →→ −8 →→ 7
4. ◆ →→ −9 →→ −3 →→ 6
5. ∀ →→ ×3 →→ ×3 →→ 36
6. ∅ →→ ×5 →→ ×2 →→ 70
7. ☺ →→ ÷6 →→ ÷4 →→ 4
8. ◢ →→ ÷2 →→ ÷5 →→ 13
9. ▬ →→ +7 →→ −11 →→ 11
10. π →→ +1 →→ −17 →→ 1
11. ◢ →→ +3 →→ ×2 →→ 16
12. ▲ →→ +3 →→ ×4 →→ 52
13. ◮ →→ +4 →→ ÷5 →→ 3
14. ⋈ →→ +7 →→ ÷9 →→ 2
15. ⌐ →→ −2 →→ +17 →→ 34
16. ● →→ −16 →→ +61 →→ 84
17. ▨ →→ −11 →→ ×8 →→ 40
18. $ →→ −8 →→ ×7 →→ 21
19. ◆ →→ −1 →→ ÷11 →→ 4
20. ⊡ →→ −6 →→ ÷8 →→ 32
21. ⋈ →→ ×9 →→ +2 →→ 65
22. ▮ →→ ×7 →→ +8 →→ 64
23. ▮ →→ ×13 →→ −12 →→ 1
24. ▬ →→ ×4 →→ −13 →→ 39
25. ◢ →→ ×5 →→ ÷6 →→ 5
26. ▨ →→ ×7 →→ ÷4 →→ 7
27. π →→ ÷8 →→ +4 →→ 10
28. ⌐ →→ ÷11 →→ +3 →→ 11
29. ▲ →→ ÷7 →→ −5 →→ 4
30. ☺ →→ ÷12 →→ −6 →→ 1
31. ? →→ ÷13 →→ ×3 →→ 21
32. ● →→ ÷7 →→ ×2 →→ 26

Mystery machines

The following inputs go into a mystery machine ...

        3,   6,   27   and   0.

The diagram shows the outputs produced ...

input	machine	output
3 →	?	→→ 6
6 →	?	→→ 9
27 →	?	→→ 30
0 →	?	→→ 3

The 'mystery' machine has added three to produce the outputs because it links *all* the inputs to the outputs in the same way.

The mystery machine was ...   input →→ +3 →→ output

Exercise 5

What operation is taking place in each of these machines?

1.

input	output
1 → ? → 5	
2 → ? → 10	
3 → ? → 15	
4 → ? → 20	
5 → ? → 25	

2.

input	output
63 → ? → 7	
54 → ? → 6	
27 → ? → 3	
108 → ? → 12	
81 → ? → 9	

3.

input	output
10 → ? → 8	
9 → ? → 7	
8 → ? → 6	
7 → ? → 5	
6 → ? → 4	

4.

input	output
3 → ? → 6	
8 → ? → 11	
7 → ? → 10	
15 → ? → 18	
9 → ? → 12	

5.

input	output
12 → ? → 6	
2 → ? → 1	
50 → ? → 25	
4 → ? → 2	
34 → ? → 17	

6.

input	output
19 → ? → 57	
9 → ? → 27	
7 → ? → 21	
5 → ? → 15	
0 → ? → 0	

7.

input	output
2 → ? → 20	
5 → ? → 50	
8 → ? → 80	
0 → ? → 0	
3 → ? → 30	

8.

input	output
9 → ? → 63	
4 → ? → 28	
8 → ? → 56	
10 → ? → 70	
2 → ? → 14	

9.

input	output
8 → ? → 64	
1 → ? → 8	
3 → ? → 24	
0 → ? → 0	
$\frac{1}{2}$ → ? → 30	

For Questions **10**, **11**, **12** copy and complete the number machines

10.

input	output
5 → ÷ 5 → ?	
? → ÷ 5 → 20	
35 → ÷ 5 → ?	
75 → ÷ 5 → ?	
? → ÷ 5 → 10	

11.

input	output
9 → × 3 → ?	
? → × 3 → 21	
6 → × 3 → ?	
? → × 3 → 33	
? → × 3 → 99	

12.

input	output
9 → + 4 → ?	
? → + 4 → 7	
0 → + 4 → ?	
57 → + 4 → ?	
? → + 4 → 83	

For Questions **13** to **21** copy and complete the number machines after working out the operation for each.

13.

input	output
1 →	→ 7
7 →	→ 13
13 →	→ ?
? →	→ 26
27 →	→ ?

14.

input	output
2 →	→ 8
3 →	→ 12
4 →	→ ?
10 →	→ ?
? →	→ 48

15.

input	output
12 →	→ 5
7 →	→ 0
18 →	→ ?
? →	→ 13
? →	→ 26

16.

input	output
0 →	→ 11
3 →	→ ?
12 →	→ 23
? →	→ 31
39 →	→ ?

17.

input	output
3 →	→ 1
9 →	→ 3
? →	→ 4
15 →	→ ?
60 →	→ ?

18.

input	output
0 →	→ ?
5 →	→ 50
? →	→ 40
7 →	→ 70
? →	→ 100

19.

input	output
3 →	→ 24
4 →	→ ?
? →	→ 64
1 →	→ ?
9 →	→ 72

20.

input	output
1 →	→ ?
4 →	→ 5
? →	→ 12
16 →	→ ?
0 →	→ 1

21.

input	output
5 →	→ 18
? →	→ 30
59 →	→ ?
? →	→ 83
11 →	→ 24

Operator squares

Each empty square contains either a number or a mathematical symbol (+, −, ×, ÷). Copy each square and fill in the missing details.

1.

	×	4	→	
×		÷		
8	÷	2	→	
↓		↓		
16	÷		→	8

2.

9	×	8	→	
÷		÷		
		2	→	1
↓		↓		
3	×		→	

3.

15	÷	3	→	
+		×		
6	×		→	
↓		↓		
	−	18	→	

4.

	×	9	→	27
+		−		
	×	4	→	
↓		↓		
8	×		→	

5.

	×	5	→	
−				
7	×	6	→	
↓		↓		
3			→	90

6.

	×	10	→	100
−		÷		
3	×	5	→	
↓		↓		
	−		→	

7.

	+	69	→	
×		+		
7		15	→	105
↓		↓		
	−		→	133

8.

50	×	12	→	
+		÷		
60	÷		→	15
↓		↓		
	×		→	

9.

80	×	50	→	
÷		÷		
8	×	25	→	
↓		↓		
	÷		→	

10.

300		2	→	298
÷		×		
	+		→	25
↓		↓		
		38	→	12

11.

48	−	7.5	→	
3		2	→	1.5
↓		↓		
16	−		→	1

12.

	×	0.3	→	1.8
÷		+		
	−		→	
↓		↓		
0.6	+	1	→	

The last three are more difficult.

13.

12		10	→	1.2
+		×		
4.8	+		→	5
↓		↓		
	−		→	

14.

			→	900
×		+		
40	÷		→	0.04
↓		↓		
2000	−		→	982

15.

	÷	5	→	0.7
÷				
	+		→	10.1
↓		↓		
0.35	+	0.5	→	

Designing squares

Make up your own operator squares starting from a blank grid like the one shown. Try to make your square difficult to solve, but give enough information so that it can be done.

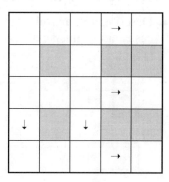

5.5 Algebra

Rod trains

● This diagram shows different colour rods.

● A green train can be made using green, red and white rods like this:

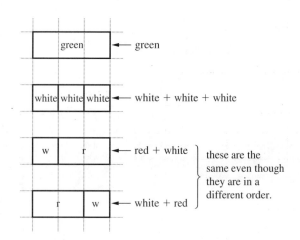

We see there are 3 ways to make a green train from the rods.

Exercise 1

Use squared paper

1. Find and draw all the different ways of making a purple train. Use purple, green, red and white rods.

2. Find and draw all the different ways of making a yellow train. Use yellow, purple, green, red and white rods.

3. Now colour your diagrams.

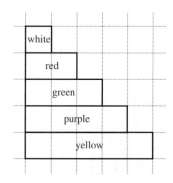

Rod trains made easier

- Describing your rod train is easier using this key ...

white = w

red = r

green = g

purple = p

yellow = y

leaf green = l

black = b

- Example: In how many ways can you make a purple train using only purple, white and green rods?

Solution: p   (purple rod)

w + w + w + w   (4 white rods)

g + w   (1 green and
                            1 white rod)

There are 3 ways to make p using p, w and g.

Exercise 2

Use the key to describe how to make the rod trains in these questions:

1. Make a purple train using only purple, red and white rods.

2. Make a yellow train using only yellow, green and red rods.

3. Make a yellow train using only yellow, green, red and white rods.

4. Make a leaf green train in as many different ways as possible.

5. Make a black train in as many different ways as possible.

Algebra as shorthand

When we let the first letter of each colour rod represent that rod, we are using *shorthand*.

Shorthand in mathematics is called *Algebra*.

Algebra is a branch of mathematics that uses letters and other symbols to represent numbers and quantities.

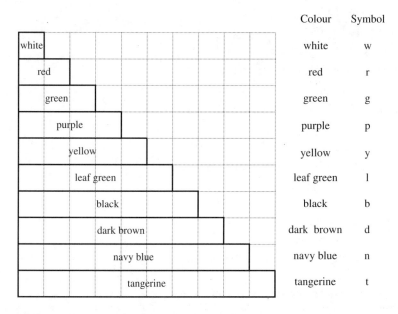

Colour	Symbol
white	w
red	r
green	g
purple	p
yellow	y
leaf green	l
black	b
dark brown	d
navy blue	n
tangerine	t

We can write a statement in words as a statement in algebra:

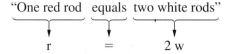

"One red rod equals two white rods"

$$r = 2w$$

Here is another statement:

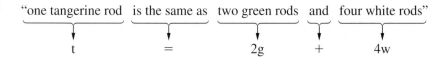

"one tangerine rod is the same as two green rods and four white rods"

$$t = 2g + 4w$$

Care needs to be taken with statements involving subtraction because the order in which you subtract is important unlike addition.

Example: 'The difference between a purple and green rod is a white rod'

$$p - g = w$$

Exercise 3

Re-write these statements using algebra as shorthand and using the given key.

1. Six white rods.
2. Three black rods.
3. Two green rods and one yellow rod.
4. Five red rods and three navy blue rods.
5. Eight purple rods plus a leaf green rod.
6. One leaf green rod equals three red rods.
7. Two yellow rods is the same as one tangerine rod.
8. One navy blue rod is equal to two purple and one white rod.
9. Three red rods and one white rod is the same as a yellow rod.
10. The difference between a tangerine rod and a navy blue rod is a white rod.
11. The difference between a yellow and a green rod is a red rod.
12. The difference between two purple rods and a green rod is a yellow rod.
13. Two dark brown rods less a navy blue rod is a black rod.
14. A white rod, a red rod and a green rod is the same as a leaf green rod.
15. Two purple rods and three navy blue rods is the same as three tangerine rods and one yellow rod.
16. Six purple rods and three green rods is the same as four black rods and a yellow rod.
17. The difference between a navy blue rod and a leaf green rod is a green rod.
18. The difference between a tangerine rod and three green rods is a white rod.
19. Five leaf green rods and six yellow rods is the same as thirty red rods.
20. It takes nine green rods to make three navy blue rods.

Roddy's custom made fishing rods

'Roddy's Rods' sells a variety of fishing rods which can either be used alone, or can be joined together so that several short rods form one longer, stronger rod, depending on the angler's needs. Below are the colours and sizes of Roddy's Rods:

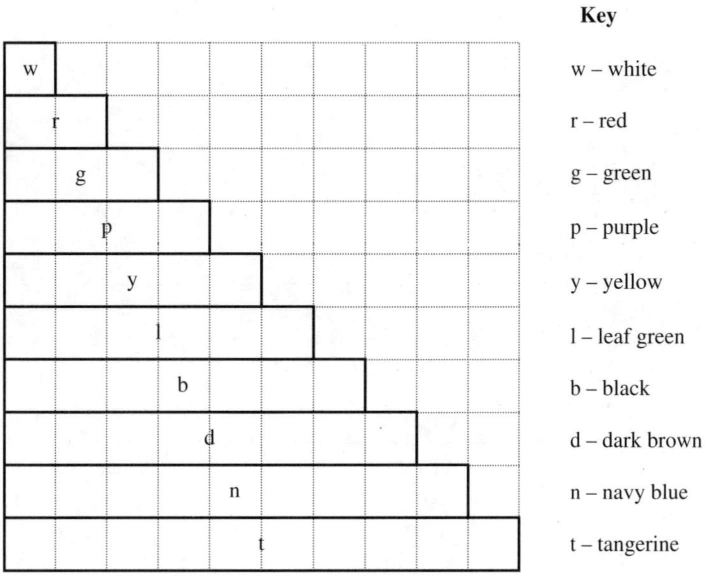

Key

w – white

r – red

g – green

p – purple

y – yellow

l – leaf green

b – black

d – dark brown

n – navy blue

t – tangerine

Roddy can combine rods like this:

one green rod + one red rod + one purple rod = one navy blue rod

In a much shorter form this can be written:

$$g + r + p = n$$

Exercise 4

Work out which single rod replaces these combinations, writing your answers in algebra.

1. white + white + white

2. green + red

3. red + purple

4. leaf green + green

5. tangerine − white

6. black + red

7. 3 greens

8. 4 reds

9. 2 purples + 1 white

10. 2 yellows − 1 red

11. 6w

12. 4r

13. b + r

14. t − l   [l = leaf green]

15. b + 3w

16. 2p − g

17. r + l − g

18. b − y + w

19. 2b − y

20. 4p − 3y

Working out costs using algebra

If a yellow rod costs £11 and a green rod costs £5, what is the cost of one yellow and two green rods?

Solution: One yellow and two greens can be rewritten as y + 2g

$$\text{The cost is } 11 + (2 \times 5)$$
$$= 11 + 10$$
$$= £21$$

Exercise 5

Rod size	Colour		Cost (£)
1	white	w	2
2	red	r	3
3	green	g	5
4	purple	p	7
5	yellow	y	11
6	leaf green	l	13
7	black	b	17
8	dark brown	d	19
9	navy blue	n	23
10	tangerine	t	29

Use the cost chart given to work out the cost of the combined rods
in the questions which follow:

1. 1 black

2. 2 whites

3. 1 red + 1 green

4. 1 yellow + 1 dark brown

5. 3 greens

6. 3 purples

7. 2 red + 1 white

8. 3 red + 1 green

9. 2 dark browns

10. 4 yellows

11. p + g

12. l + b

13. n + t

14. d + b

15. l − p

16. l − g

17. 3n

18. 4t

19. 6p − g

20. 9g − n

21. d − 2r

22. t − 2g

23. 5w + 2g

24. 3r + 2p

25. 3d − 4y

26. 2t − 5p

27. 4b + 3l − 6g

28. 8n − 9y + 2d

29. 10t − 5y

30. 6y + 5g − 10w

Algebraic Alf's price puzzles

'Algebraic Alf' sells the same type of rods as 'Roddy's Rods', except
that eccentric Alf's charges vary according to the weather, what he
had for breakfast, and so on!!

'Algebraic Alf' is selling a red rod.
He decides the cost of one red rod plus £3 equals £6 altogether.

In algebra this is written $r + 3 = 6$

Subtract 3 from both sides
to leave r, the cost of a $\left(-3\right)$ $\left(-3\right)$
red rod on its own.   r $= 3$

Exercise 6

Work out the cost of the rods in these problems using the algebraic
method in the example above.

1. 1 green rod plus £3 = £7.   **2.** 1 white rod plus £2 = £4
3. 1 yellow rod plus £5 = £16   **4.** 1 purple rod plus £4 = £12
5. 1 black rod plus £8 = £25   **6.** 1 leaf green rod plus £6 = £20
7. 1 dark brown rod plus £11 = £32 **8.** 1 navy blue rod plus £15 = £39
9. 1 tangerine rod plus £18 = £51

Algebraic Alf's prices change just as the seasons do! He now decides ...

1 red rod minus £3 = £1
                    $r - 3 = 1$

          $\left(+3\right)$ $\left(+3\right)$ add 3 to both sides to
                                          leave r, the cost of a
                r $= £4$ red rod.

Exercise 7

Work out the cost of the rods in these problems using the method in
the above example.

1. 1 green rod minus £2 = £3   **2.** 1 white rod minus £1 = £1
3. 1 yellow rod minus £5 = £6   **4.** 1 purple rod minus £4 = £3
5. 1 black rod minus £7 = £11   **6.** 1 leaf green rod minus £8 = £6
7. 1 dark brown rod minus £12 = £7 **8.** 1 navy blue rod minus £14 = £9
9. 1 tangerine rod minus £13 = £14

Alf decides to make his prices more attractive: He now decides ...

2 red rods = £8
            $2r = 8$

      $\left(\div2\right)$ $\left(\div2\right)$ divide both sides by 2 to
                                          leave r, the cost of a
            $r = £4$ red rod.

Exercise 8

Work out the cost of the rods in these problems using the method in
the last example.

1. 2 green rods = £10   **2.** 3 white rods = £6
3. 4 yellow rods = £44   **4.** 5 purple rods = £35
5. 2 black rods = £34   **6.** 3 leaf green rods = £36
7. 5 dark brown rods = £100   **8.** 4 navy blue rods = £180
9. 6 tangerine rods = £180

Alf's stocks are running low, he decides to change his prices!

One half of a red rod = £1·50
$$r \div 2 = 1·5$$

multiply both sides by 2 to
leave r, the cost of a
red rod.

$$r \qquad = 3$$

Exercise 9

Work out the cost of the rods in these problems using the method in
the last example.

1. One half of a green rod = £2·50   **2.** One third of a white rod = £1

3. One quarter of a yellow rod = £3   **4.** One fifth of a purple rod = £2

5. One third of a black rod = £6   **6.** One half of a leaf green rod = £7·50

7. One quarter of a dark brown rod = £4·50   **8.** One fifth of a navy blue rod = £5

9. One sixth of a tangerine rod = £5·50

Exercise 10

In the problems below, choose your own letters to represent the
words, then solve the problems showing your working.

Example: One banana plus 8p is equal to 24p
                    ↓
$$b \quad + \ 8 \quad = \quad 24$$
$$b \quad = \quad 16$$

1. One apple plus 13p is equal to 28p

2. Two bananas are equal to 44p

3. One pear minus 5p is equal to 13p

4. Half a coconut is equal to 46p

5. One 'burger' plus 20p is equal to £1·15

6. One 'fries' minus 18p costs 41p

7. One third of a milk shake is equal to 32p

8. Four 'bubble gums' are equal to 32p

9. One comic less 28p is equal to 79p

10. Five pens is equal to 65p

11. Three cakes is equal to 51p

12. Half of my bus-fare is equal to £2·35

13. One fifth of my maths lesson is equal to 15 minutes

14. One sixth of a T.V. programme is equal to 4 minutes

15. One third of my maths homework is the equivalent of 26 minutes

Balance puzzles

In balance puzzles the scales balance exactly.

On the balance $\bigcirc$ and $\triangle$ represent weights

Find $\bigcirc$ if $\triangle = 5$ for this balance puzzle

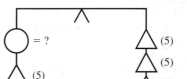

Clearly for these scales to balance exactly, then $\bigcirc = 10$

Exercise 11

Copy each diagram and find the value of the required symbol.

1. Find $\square$ if $\triangle = 4$.

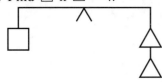

2. Find $\bigcirc$ if $\triangle = 10$.

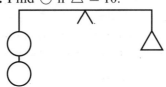

3. Find $\bigcirc$ if $\square = 4$.

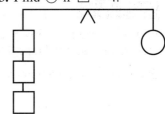

4. Find $\square$ if $\triangle = 12$.

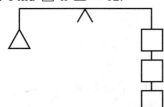

5. Find $\triangle$ if $\square = 2$.

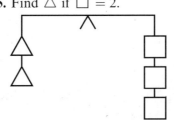

6. Find $\triangle$ if $\bigcirc = 6$.

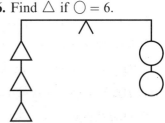

7. Find □ if ○ = 8.

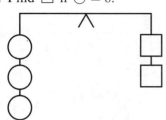

8. Find △ if □ = 15.

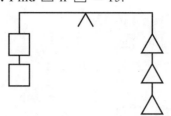

9. Find △ if ○ = 14.

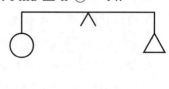

10. Find △ if □ = 7.

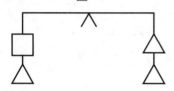

11. Find □ if △ = 8.

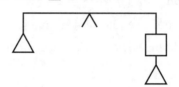

12. Find □ if ○ = 13.

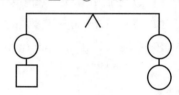

13. Find △ if □ = 14.

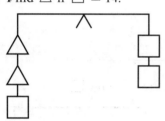

14. Find ○ if △ = 10.

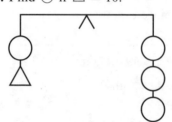

15. Find ○ if □ = 9.

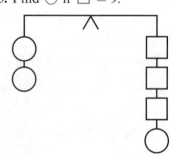

16. Find △ if □ = 11.

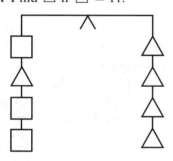

17. Find ○ if □ = 21.

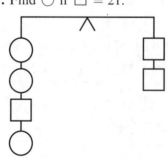

18. Find □ if ○ = 8.

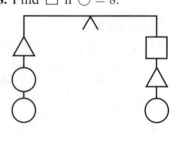

19. Find ○ if △ = 6.

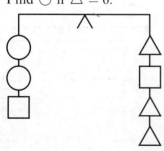

20. Find ○ if □ = 5.

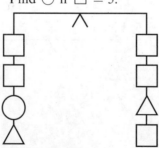

Bigger balance puzzles

In the diagram below, $\triangle = 4$
Find the value of   (a) $\bigcirc$ (b) $\square$

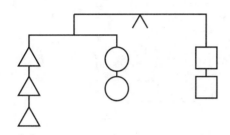

Solution: (a) $3\triangle = 2\bigcirc$
                    $12 = 2\bigcirc$
                     $6 = \bigcirc$

             (b) $3\triangle + 2\bigcirc = 2\square$
                    $12 + 12 = 2\square$
                        $24 = 2\square$
                        $12 = \square$

Exercise 12

Copy each diagram and find the value of the unknown symbols.

1. $\bigcirc = 10$, find $\triangle$ and $\square$.

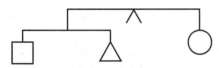

2. $\triangle = 8$, find $\bigcirc$ and $\square$.

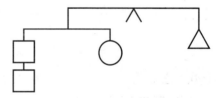

3. $\square = 14$, find $\bigcirc$ and $\triangle$.

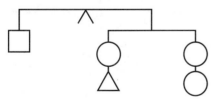

4. $\square = 6$, find $\bigcirc$ and $\triangle$.

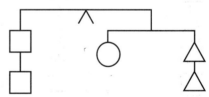

5. $\bigcirc = 8$, find $\square$ and $\triangle$.

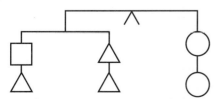

6. $\square = 4$, find $\bigcirc$ and $\triangle$.

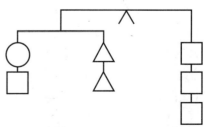

7. $\triangle = 4$, find $\bigcirc$ and $\square$.

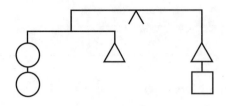

8. $\bigcirc = 10$, find $\triangle$ and $\square$.

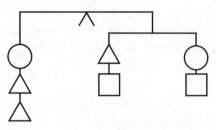

9. $\triangle = 5$, find $\bigcirc$ and $\square$.

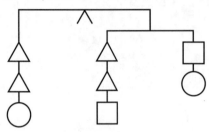

10. $\square = 3$, find $\bigcirc$ and $\triangle$.

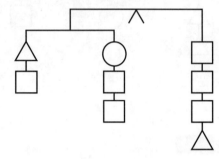

11. $\square = 6$, find $\triangle$ and $\bigcirc$.

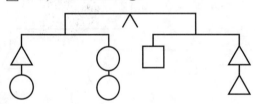

12. $\bigcirc = 5$, find $\square$ and $\triangle$.

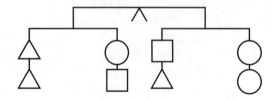

13. $\triangle = 4$, find $\bigcirc$ and $\square$.

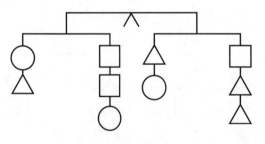

14. $\bigcirc = 8$, find $\square$ and $\triangle$.

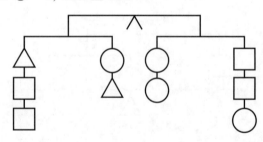

15. $\square = 4$, find $\bigcirc$ and $\triangle$.

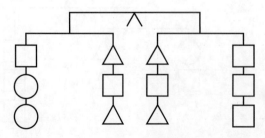

Part 6

6.1 Fractions 2

- If a prize of £50 is shared equally between two people, each person receives $\frac{1}{2}$ of £50.

  This is £50 ÷ 2 = £25 each

  > To find one *half* of a quantity, divide the quantity by *two*

- 'Nutty', 'Bushy' and 'Bobtail' are a family of three squirrels with a bag of peanuts. The bag contains 216 nuts. How many nuts does each squirrel get if they are shared out equally?

  We need to find $\frac{1}{3}$ of 216

  This is 216 ÷ 3 = 72 nuts each

  > To find $\frac{1}{3}$ of a quantity, divide the quantity by 3

Exercise 1

1. Copy and complete this table.

No.	Fraction of quantity required	Divide the quantity by ...
(a)	$\frac{1}{2}$	2
(b)	$\frac{1}{3}$	
(c)	one quarter	
(d)		10
(e)	$\frac{1}{5}$	
(f)	$\frac{1}{8}$	
(g)		16
(h)	one twelfth	
(i)		100

In Question **2** to **19** copy and complete.

2. $\frac{1}{2}$ of £8 = ? **3.** $\frac{1}{4}$ of 28 litres = ? **4.** $\frac{1}{3}$ of 60 kg = ?

5. $\frac{1}{4}$ of 20 kg = ? **6.** $\frac{1}{2}$ of 16 kg = ? **7.** $\frac{1}{3}$ of 60 kg = ?

8. $\frac{1}{2}$ of 150 cm = ? **9.** $\frac{1}{3}$ of 27 cm = ? **10.** $\frac{1}{4}$ of 280 cm = ?

11. $\frac{1}{5}$ of £10 = ? **12.** $\frac{1}{10}$ of £100 = ? **13.** $\frac{1}{5}$ of 45 litres = ?

14. $\frac{1}{10}$ of 250 cm = ? **15.** $\frac{1}{8}$ of £72 = ? **16.** $\frac{1}{20}$ of 300 cm = ?

17. $\frac{1}{12}$ of 288 m = ? **18.** $\frac{1}{9}$ of 729 kg = ? **19.** $\frac{1}{100}$ of £5000 = ?

20. We can write $\frac{1}{5}$ of 70 = 70 ÷ 5 = $\frac{70}{5}$

Copy the following and fill in the missing numbers.

(a) $\frac{1}{4}$ of 28 = $\boxed{}$ ÷ $\boxed{}$ = $\dfrac{\boxed{}}{\boxed{}}$

(b) $\boxed{}$ of $\boxed{}$ = 45 ÷ 9 = $\dfrac{\boxed{}}{\boxed{}}$

(c) $\boxed{}$ of $\boxed{}$ = $\boxed{}$ ÷ $\boxed{}$ = $\dfrac{54}{6}$

(d) $\frac{1}{5}$ of 4 = $\boxed{}$ ÷ $\boxed{}$ = $\dfrac{\boxed{}}{\boxed{}}$

Fraction of a number

(a) In a mixed school with 364 pupils, $\frac{3}{7}$ of the pupils are girls.
How many girls are there?

We need to work out $\frac{3}{7}$ of 364.

$\frac{1}{7}$ of 364 = 364 ÷ 7
= 52

$\left[\text{Working:} \quad 7\overline{)3\,6\,{}^14} \quad \begin{array}{c} 5\,2 \end{array}\right]$

So $\frac{3}{7}$ of 364 = 52 × 3
= 156

$\left[\text{Because } \frac{3}{7} \text{ of 364 is 3 times as many as } \frac{1}{7} \text{ of 364.}\right]$

There are 156 girls in the school.

(b) Work out $\frac{2}{5}$ of £560

$\frac{1}{5}$ of 560 = 560 ÷ 5
= 112

$5\overline{)5\,6\,{}^10} \quad \begin{array}{c} 1\,1\,2 \end{array}$

So $\frac{2}{5}$ of 560 = 112 × 2
= 224

Answer: £224.

Exercise 2

Copy and complete these problems. (Use a calculator if needed)

1. $\frac{3}{8}$ of £24 = ?   2. $\frac{2}{5}$ of £15 = ?   3. $\frac{3}{4}$ of £36 = ?

4. $\frac{4}{7}$ of £84 = ?   5. $\frac{5}{9}$ of £108 = ?   6. $\frac{2}{3}$ of £216 = ?

7. $\frac{3}{4}$ of 20 kg = ?   8. $\frac{2}{3}$ of 30 kg = ?   9. $\frac{7}{10}$ of 30 g = ?

10. $\frac{5}{8}$ of 480 cm = ?   11. $\frac{4}{5}$ of 80 cm = ?   12. $\frac{2}{3}$ of 120 cm = ?

13. $\frac{2}{5}$ of 30 p = ?   14. $\frac{5}{8}$ of 64 p = ?   15. $\frac{3}{10}$ of 150 p = ?

16. $\frac{2}{7}$ of 140 m = ?   17. $\frac{5}{12}$ of 60 km = ?   18. $\frac{8}{9}$ of 72 litres = ?

19. In a maths test full marks were 120. How many marks did Ben get if he got $\frac{7}{10}$ of full marks?

20. A petrol tank in a car holds 56 litres when full. How much petrol is in the tank when it is $\frac{3}{4}$ full?

21. Sally has driven around $\frac{2}{5}$ of the motorcycle circuit. If the circuit is 1750 metres, how far has she travelled?

22. Mario has an order for 600 pizzas. If $\frac{5}{12}$ of his pizzas must be vegetarian, how many will be non-vegetarian?

23. If a book has 440 pages and you have read $\frac{3}{8}$ so far, how many more pages do you still have to read?

24. Which is larger $\frac{5}{9}$ of £27 or $\frac{4}{7}$ of £28?

25. 'Tommy' the Toucan's beak is $\frac{7}{10}$ his height. If Tommy stands 210 mm high, how long is his beak?

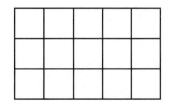

26. Sumitra's fishtank contained 140 fish. If $\frac{3}{5}$ of the fish were females, how many of the fish were males?

27. Which is smaller $\frac{7}{12}$ of £60 or $\frac{5}{8}$ of £64?

28. A television is bought for £287 and sold at a car bootsale for $\frac{3}{7}$ of the original price. What was the selling price?

29. Draw a copy of the rectangle.
    (a) Shade in $\frac{1}{3}$ of the squares.
    (b) Draw crosses in $\frac{1}{5}$ of the unshaded squares.
    (c) How many squares are neither shaded nor have crosses in them?

30. Richard has a packet of 32 Polos.

For some unknown reason Richard gives $\frac{3}{8}$ of his Polos to his sister Jane.

Generous Jane then gives $\frac{1}{4}$ of her share to a friend and eats the rest.

Richard meanwhile eats $\frac{2}{5}$ of his remaining Polos.

(a) How many Polos does Richard have left at the end?

(b) How many Polos does Jane eat?

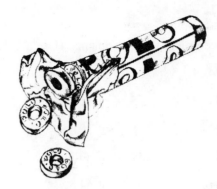

6.2 Probability

In probability we ask questions like ...

'How likely is it?'

'What are the chances of ... ?'

Here are some questions where we do not know the answer ..

'Will I grow up to be famous?'

'Will I live to be over 100 years old?'

'Who will win the F.A. cup?'

Some events are certain. Some events are impossible.

Some events are in between certain and impossible.

The probability of an event is a measure of the chance of it happening.

The probability (or chance) of an event occurring is measured on a scale like this ...

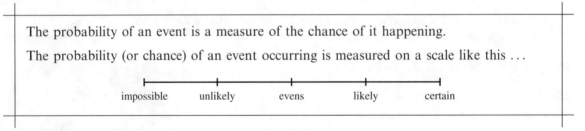

impossible   unlikely   evens   likely   certain

Exercise 1

Draw a probability scale like this ...

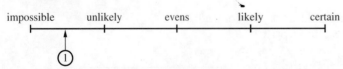

impossible   unlikely   evens   likely   certain

Draw an arrow to show the chance of the events below happening.

The arrow for question ① has been done for you.

1. When a card is selected from a pack it will be an 'ace'.

2. When a coin is tossed it will show a 'head'.

3. Your local vicar will win the national lottery next week.

4. The day after Monday will be Tuesday.

5. There will be a burst pipe in the school heating system next week and the school will have to close for 3 days.

6. You will blink your eyes in the next minute.

7. You will be asked to tidy your room this week.

8. When a slice of toast is dropped, it will land on the floor buttered side down.

9. You will get maths homework this week.

10. England will win the World Cup in 2006.

11. Your maths teacher has a black belt in Judo.

12. You will be captured by aliens tonight.

Probability as a number

Different countries have different words for saying how likely or unlikely any particular event is.
All over the world people use probability as a way of doing this, using numbers on a scale instead of words.
The scale looks like this ...

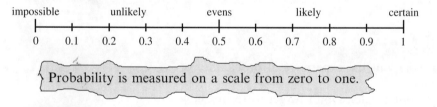

Probability is measured on a scale from zero to one.

Exercise 2

Look at the events in the last exercise and for each one estimate the probability of it occurring using a probability from 0 to 1.

As an example in question ① you might write 'about 0·1'. Copy each question and write your estimate of its probability at the end.

Experimental probability

The chance of certain events occurring can easily be predicted. For example the chance of tossing a head with an ordinary coin. Many events, however, cannot be so easily predicted.

Experiment: To find the experimental probability that the third word in the third line on any page in this book contains the letter 'a' (You could use a non-mathematical book if you prefer)

Step 1. We will do 50 *trials*. Write down at
random 50 page numbers between 1 and
180 (say 3, 15, 16, 21, 27, etc.).

Step 2. For each page look at the third word in
the third line. This is a *trial*.
If there is not a third word on the third
line it still counts as a trial. (The third line
might be all numbers.)

Step 3. If the word contains the letter 'a' this is a
success.

Step 4. Make a tally chart like this ...

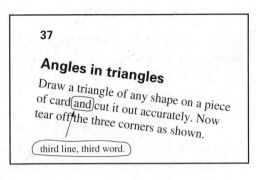

Number of trials	Number of successes
JHT JHT II	JHT II

$$\text{Experimental probability} = \frac{\text{Number of trials in which a success occurs}}{\text{Total number of trials made}}$$

Exercise 3

Carry out experiments to work out the experimental probability of
some of the following events.
Use a tally chart to record your results. Don't forget to record how
many times you do the experiment (the number of 'trials').

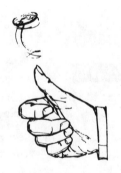

1. Roll a dice. What is the chance of rolling a six? Perform 100 trials.

2. Toss two coins. What is the chance of tossing two tails? Perform
100 trials.

3. Pick a counter from a bag containing counters of different
colours. What is the chance of picking a red counter? Perform
100 trials.

4. Roll a pair of dice. What is the chance of rolling a double?
Perform 100 trials.

5. Butter a piece of toast and drop it on the floor. What is the
chance of it landing buttered side down? Would you expect to
get the same result with margarine? How about butter and jam?
Suppose you don't toast the bread?
If you run into difficulties at home, blame your maths teacher,
not the authors of this book.

Expected probability

For simple events, like throwing a dice or tossing a coin, we can work out the expected probability of an event occurring.
For a fair dice the *expected probability* of throwing a '3' is $\frac{1}{6}$.
For a normal coin the expected probability of tossing a 'head' is $\frac{1}{2}$

$$\text{Expected probability} = \frac{\text{the number of ways the event can happen}}{\text{the number of possible outcomes}}$$

Random choice: If a card is chosen at random from a pack it means that every card has an equal chance of being chosen.

Nine identical discs numbered 1, 2, 3, 4, 5, 6, 7, 8, 9 are put into a bag. One disc is selected at random.

In this example there are 9 possible equally likely outcomes of a trial.

(a) The probability of selecting a '4' $= \frac{1}{9}$

This may be written p (selecting a '4') $= \frac{1}{9}$

(b) p (selecting an odd number) $= \frac{5}{9}$

(c) p (selecting a number greater than 5) $= \frac{4}{9}$

Exercise 4

1. A bag contains a red ball, a blue ball and a yellow ball. One ball is chosen at random. Copy and complete these sentences.

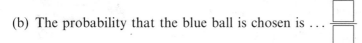

(a) The probability that the red ball is chosen is ... $\dfrac{\Box}{3}$

(b) The probability that the blue ball is chosen is ... $\dfrac{\Box}{\Box}$

(c) The probability that the yellow ball is chosen is ... $\dfrac{\Box}{\Box}$

2. One ball is chosen at random from a bag which contains a red ball, a blue ball, a yellow ball and a white ball. Write down the probability that the chosen ball will be

(a) red   (b) blue   (c) yellow.

3. One ball is chosen at random from a box which contains 2 red balls and 2 blue balls. Write down the probability that the chosen ball will be
   (a) red.
   (b) blue.
   (c) yellow.

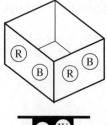

4. A hat contains 2 white balls and 1 black ball. One ball is chosen at random. Find the probability that it is
   (a) white.
   (b) black.

5. A pencil case contains pencils of the following colours:- 6 red, 3 black, 1 green and 1 blue. One pencil is selected without looking. Find the probability that the pencil is
   (a) red.
   (b) black.
   (c) green.

6. I roll an ordinary dice.
   Find the probability that I score
   (a) 3
   (b) 1
   (c) less than 5

7. Eight identical discs numbered 1, 2, 3, 4, 5, 6, 7, 8 are put into a bag. One disc is selected at random. Find the probability of selecting
   (a) a '5'.   (b) an odd number.   (c) a number less than 6.

8. Nine identical discs numbered 1, 3, 4, 5, 7, 8, 10, 11, 15 are put into a bag. One disc is selected at random. Find the probability of selecting.
   (a) a '10'.   (b) an even number.   (c) a number more than 6.

9. A bag contains 4 red balls and 7 white balls. One ball is selected at random. Find the probability that it is
   (a) red.   (b) white.

10. One card is selected at random from the ten cards shown ...
    Find the probability of selecting
    (a) the King of spades   (b) a heart
    (c) a diamond   (d) a 3

11. A bag contains 2 red balls, 4 white balls and 5 blue balls. One ball is selected at random. Find the probability of selecting.
    (a) a red ball   (b) a white ball   (c) a blue ball

12. I buy a fish at random from a pond containing 3 piranhas, 2 baby sharks and 7 goldfish. Find the probability that the fish I choose is
    (a) a goldfish.   (b) a baby shark
    (c) dangerous   (d) glad I rescued it!
    (e) able to play the piano.

Probability Problems

A pack of playing cards, without Jokers, contains 52 cards.
There is Ace, King, Queen, Jack, 10, 9, 8, 7, 6, 5, 4, 3, 2 of four suits.
The suits are . . .

spades	hearts	diamonds	clubs

A pack of cards is shuffled and then one card is chosen at random.
(a) The probability that it is a King of hearts is $\frac{1}{52}$
(b) The probability that it is an ace is $\frac{4}{52}\left(=\frac{1}{13}\right)$
(c) The probability that it is a spade is $\frac{13}{52}\left(=\frac{1}{4}\right)$

Exercise 5

1. One card is picked at random from a pack of 52.
   Find the probability that it is
   (a) a Queen
   (b) the King of diamonds
   (c) a spade

2. One card is selected at random from a full pack of 52 playing cards. Find the probability of selecting
   (a) a heart
   (b) a red card
   (c) a '2'
   (d) any King, Queen or Jack
   (e) the ace of spades

3. A small pack of twenty cards consists of the Ace, King, Queen, Jack and 10 of spades, hearts, diamonds and clubs. One card is selected at random. Find the probability of selecting
   (a) the ace of hearts
   (b) a King
   (c) a '10'
   (d) a black card
   (e) a heart

4. A bag contains 3 black balls, 2 green balls, 1 white ball and 5 orange balls. Find the probability of selecting
   (a) a black ball
   (b) an orange ball
   (c) a white ball

5. A bag contains the balls shown. One ball is taken out at random. Find the probability that it is

(a) yellow   (b) blue   (c) red

One more blue ball and one more red ball are added to the bag.

(d) Find the new probability of selecting a yellow ball from the bag.

Y = yellow
B = blue
R = Red

6. If Jake throws a 1 or a 4 on his next throw of a dice when playing 'Snakes and Ladders' he will climb up a ladder on the board. What is the probability that he will *miss* a ladder on his next throw?

7. A box contains 11 balls: 3 green, 2 white, 4 red and 2 blue
  (a) Find the probability of selecting
     (i) a blue ball
     (ii) a green ball
  (b) The 3 green balls are replaced by 3 blue balls. Find the probability of selecting
     (i) a blue ball
     (ii) a white ball.

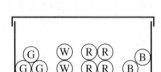

8. Here are two spinners.
Say whether the following statements are true or false. Explain why in each case.
  (a) 'Sarah is more likely to spin a 6 than Ben'.
  (b) 'Sarah and Ben are equally likely to spin an even number.'
  (c) 'If Sarah spins her spinner six times, she is bound to get at least one 6.'

Sarah's spinner   Ben's spinner

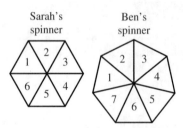

In Questions **9**, **10**, **11**, **12** a bag contains a certain number of red balls and a certain number of white balls. The tally charts show the number of times a ball was selected from the bag and then replaced. Look at the results and say what you think was in the bag each time.

9. 2 balls ⟶

red	ЖЖ ЖЖ	10
white	ЖЖ ЖЖ	10

10. 3 balls ⟶

red	ЖЖ	5
white	ЖЖ IIII	10

11. 3 balls ⟶

red	ЖЖ ЖЖ ЖЖ ЖЖ I	21
white	ЖЖ ЖЖ	9

12. 4 balls ⟶

red	ЖЖ IIII	9
white	ЖЖ ЖЖ ЖЖ ЖЖ ЖЖ ЖЖ I	31

13. A bag contains 9 balls, all of which are black or white. Jane selects a ball and then replaces it. She repeats this several times. Here are her results (B = black, W = white):

B W B W B B B W B B W B B W B
B B W W B B B B W B W B B W B

How many balls of each colour do you think there were in the bag?

14. Cards with numbers 1, 2, 3, 4, 5, 6, 7, 8, 9, 10 are shuffled and then placed face down in a line. The cards are then turned over one at a time from the left. In this example the first card is a '4'.

Find the probability that the next card turned over will be
(a) 7
(b) a number higher than 4.

15. Suppose the second card is a 1

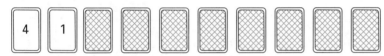

Find the probability that the next card will be
(a) the 6
(b) an even number
(c) higher than 1.

16. Suppose the first three cards are   4 1 8   ...

Find the probability that the next card will be
(a) less than 8
(b) the 4
(c) an odd number.

17. Melissa, who is 8 years old, plays two games with her mother, 'Snakes and Ladders' and then 'Monopoly'. Comment on the following statements:
(a) Melissa has an evens chance of winning at 'Snakes and Ladders'.
(b) Melissa has an evens chance of winning at 'Monopoly'.

18. Three friends Aljit, Ben and Curtis sit next to each other on a bench.
(a) Make a list of all the different ways in which they can sit. (Use A = Aljit, B = Ben and C = Curtis).
Find the probability that
(b) Aljit sits in the middle.
(c) Aljit sits next to Curtis.
(d) Ben sits at one end of the bench.

6.3 Percentages

Percentages are fractions with denominator (bottom number) equal to 100.
So 25% means $\frac{25}{100}$, 67% means $\frac{67}{100}$ and so on.

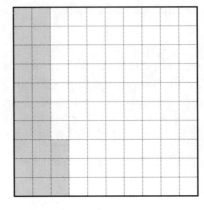

The square contains
100 squares and 23
squares are shaded

Fraction shaded $= \frac{23}{100}$

Percentage shaded $= 23\%$

Exercise 1

1. Draw each square and write underneath it

   (a) what fraction is shaded   (b) what percentage is shaded

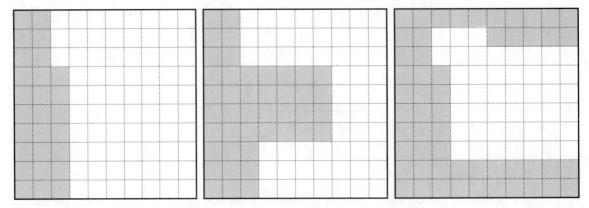

2. If 40% of a square is shaded, what percentage of the square is not shaded?

3. If 73% of a square is shaded, what percentage of the square is not shaded?

4. Approximately 67% of the earth's surface is covered with water. What percentage of the earth's surface is land?

5. In this square, 25 out of 100 squares are
shaded to show 25%.
Draw your own numbers (like 17, 21 or 33)
and shade in the correct number of squares to
show the percentage. Try to draw the
numbers the same size.

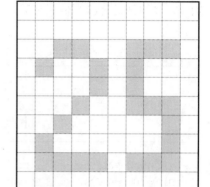

6. Write the following as percentages.

(a) $\frac{7}{100}$ (b) $\frac{15}{100}$

(c) $\frac{99}{100}$ (d) $\frac{3}{100}$

(e) $\frac{100}{100}$ (f) $\frac{130}{100}$

7. Jacques is scuba diving and has used 64%
of his oxygen supply. What percentage of
his oxygen does he still have?

8. On a coach trip 35% of the passengers were
adults and the rest were children. What
percentage of the passengers were children?

9. Goldylocks decided to make porridge for the
3 bears. Father bear got 43% of the porridge
and mother bear got 38% of the porridge.
What percentage of the porridge did baby
bear receive?

10. (a) What percentage of the 100 squares contain
(i) ticks?
(ii) crosses?
(iii) circles?

(b) What percentage of the 100 squares are blank?

11.

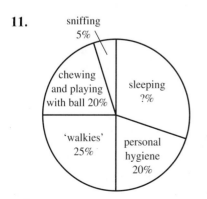

This chart shows how
'Bonzo' the dog spends his
day. What percentage of the
day does Bonzo spend
sleeping?

12. This diagram shows the percentage of 'ingredients' in making concrete patio blocks.

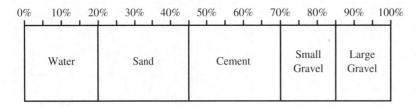

(a) What percentage is sand and cement?
(b) What percentage is gravel?
(c) What percentage is non-liquid?

13. The diagram shows the percentage of people who took part in activities offered at a sports centre on a Friday night.

(a) What percentage went swimming?
(b) What percentage played squash?
(c) What percentage played a racket sport?
(d) What percentage did not play football?
(e) What percentage played activities involving a ball?

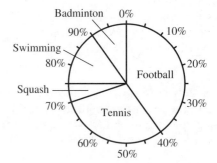

Common percentages

• Some percentages are used a lot and you should learn them.

$$10\% = \frac{10}{100} = \frac{1}{10}, \qquad 30\% = \frac{30}{100} = \frac{3}{10}, \qquad 70\% = \frac{7}{10}, \qquad 90\% = \frac{9}{10}, \qquad 20\% = \frac{20}{100} = \frac{1}{5},$$

$$40\% = \frac{40}{100} = \frac{2}{5}, \qquad 60\% = \frac{3}{5}, \qquad 80\% = \frac{4}{5}, \qquad 25\% = \frac{1}{4}, \qquad 50\% = \frac{1}{2},$$

$$75\% = \frac{3}{4}, \qquad 33\frac{1}{3}\% = \frac{1}{3}, \qquad 66\frac{2}{3}\% = \frac{2}{3}$$

$$\frac{1}{4} = 25\%$$

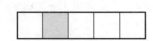

$$\frac{1}{5} = 20\%$$

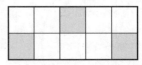

$$\frac{3}{10} = 30\%$$

Exercise 2

1. For each shape write
   (a) what fraction is shaded
   (b) what percentage is shaded.

A B 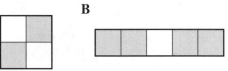 C 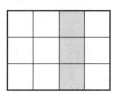 D

E 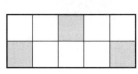 F 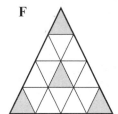 G 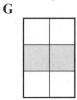 H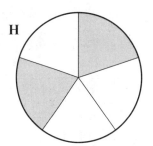

2. Copy these and fill in the spaces.
   (a) $30\% = \frac{}{10}$
   (b) $\frac{3}{4} = \quad \%$
   (c) $\frac{1}{3} = \quad \%$
   (d) $1\% = \frac{}{100}$
   (e) $80\% = -$
   (f) $\frac{1}{10} = \quad \%$

3. These pictures show how much petrol is in a car. E is Empty and F is Full.
   What percentage of a full tank is in each car?

   (a)
   (b)
   (c)
   (d)
   (e)

4. What percentage could be used in each sentence?
   (a) Three quarters of the pupils at a school had school dinners.
   (b) Three out of five workers voted for a strike.
   (c) Nicki got 15 out of 20 in the spelling test.
   (d) One in three cats prefer 'Whiskas'.
   (e) Half of the customers at a supermarket thought that prices were too high.
   (f) One in four mothers think children are too tidy at home.

5. Draw three diagrams of your own design, like those in Question **1** and shade in:
   (a) 30%
   (b) 75%
   (c) $66\frac{2}{3}\%$

Percentage of a number

(a) Work out 25% of £60.
25% is the same as $\frac{1}{4}$, $\frac{1}{4}$ of £60 is £15.

(b) In a sale, prices are reduced by 20%. Find the 'sale price' of the dress shown.

20% is the same as $\frac{1}{5}$

$\frac{1}{5}$ of £40 = £8.

Sale price = £40 − £8
            = £32.

£40

Exercise 3

1. Work out
   (a) 20% of £50   (b) 75% of £12   (c) 10% of £90
   (d) 25% of £4000   (e) $33\frac{1}{3}$% of £90   (f) 30% of £40

2. Now do these
   (a) 90% of £100   (b) 40% of $30   (c) $66\frac{2}{3}$% of £12
   (d) 50% of $1200   (e) 1% of £300   (f) 5% of £100

3. Kate earns £15 for doing a paper round. How much *extra* does she earn when she gets a 20% rise?

4. Full marks in a maths test is 60. How many marks did Tim get if he got 60%?

5. Of the 240 children at a school, 75% walk to school. How many children walk to school?

6. Find the actual cost of the following items in a sale. The normal prices are shown.

(a) £60

25% off
marked price

(b)

£15

50% off!

(c) £24

$33\frac{1}{3}$% off
normal
price

(d)

£40

10%
discount
off price

(e)

£80

75% off!

(f) £25

40%
discount
off price

7. In many countries Value Added Tax [V.A.T.] is charged at $17\frac{1}{2}\%$. Here is a method for finding $17\frac{1}{2}\%$ of £4000 without a calculator.

$$17\frac{1}{2}\% \text{ of £4000:} \qquad 10\% = \text{£400}$$
$$5\% = \text{£200}$$
$$2\frac{1}{2}\% = \text{£100}$$
$$\overline{17\frac{1}{2}\% = \text{£700}}$$

Use this method to work out:

(a) $17\frac{1}{2}\%$ of £6000   (b) $17\frac{1}{2}\%$ of £440   (c) $17\frac{1}{2}\%$ of £86

8. The price of a car was £6600 but it is increased by $17\frac{1}{2}\%$. What is the new price?

9. The price of a boat was £36 000 but it is increased by 5%. What is the new price?

10. In a sale the price of a shirt costing £12 is reduced by 25%. Find the reduced price of the shirt.

11. A car is worth £3400. After an accident its value falls by 30%. How much is it worth now?

12. On the first of March a shopkeeper puts all his prices up by 5%. Find the new prices of the following.
(a) a scarf at £10.
(b) a pair of gloves at £12
(c) a coat at £40.

13. A lizard weighs 500 g. While escaping from a predator it loses its tail and its weight is reduced by 1%. How much does it weigh now?

14. Find the odd one out
(a) 50% of £30   (b) 20% of £50   (c) 25% of £60

15. Find the odd one out
(a) 10% of £70   (b) 25% of £60   (c) 5% of £140

16. A hen weighs 3 kg. After laying an egg her weight is reduced by 2%. How much does she weigh now?

17. A marathon runner weighs 60 kg at the start of a race. During the race his weight is reduced by 5%. How much does he weigh at the end of the race?

6.4 Line symmetry

Paper folding activities

1. Take a piece of paper, fold it once and then
cut out a shape across the fold.
This will produce a shape with   cut along
one line of symmetry.   the broken line →

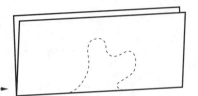

2. Fold another piece of paper twice so that the
second fold is at right angles to the first fold.
Again cut along the fold to see what shapes
you can make.
This will produce a shape with two lines of
symmetry.

3. Fold the paper three times and cut.

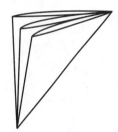 

This will produce a shape with four lines of symmetry.

Below are three shapes obtained by folding and cutting as above.
Try to make similar shapes yourself.
Stick the best shapes into your exercise book.

1.   **2.**   **3.**

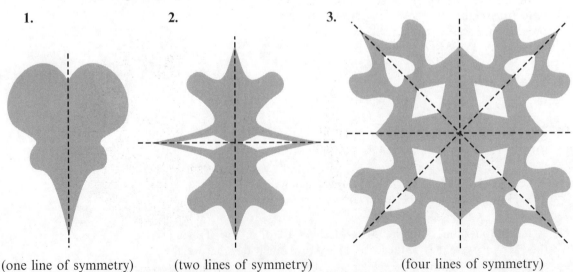

(one line of symmetry)   (two lines of symmetry)   (four lines of symmetry)

4. More interesting shapes can be obtained as follows:
   (a) Cut out a circle and fold it in half.

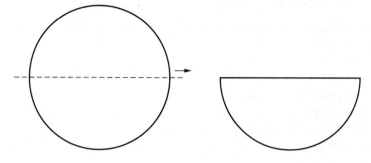

   (b) Fold about the broken line so
       that sectors A and B are equal.

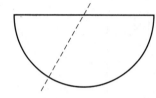 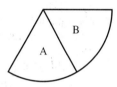

   (c) Fold sector B behind sector A. Now cut
       out a section and see what you obtain.

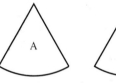

   (d) Even more complicated shapes can be
       obtained by folding once again down the
       middle of the sector.

Here are two shapes obtained by this method of folding.

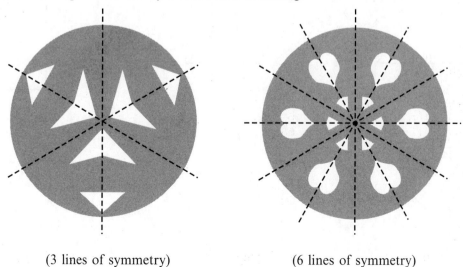

   (3 lines of symmetry)   (6 lines of symmetry)

Line symmetry

An object has line symmetry if we can draw a straight line through it
(usually dotted) so that it balances perfectly.

To check if a line of symmetry
balances perfectly you can:-

(a) Trace over the shape on
     tracing paper and fold it
     along the line of symmetry.
     If the two sections either
     side of the symmetry line fit
     onto each other exactly,
     then it really is a line of
     symmetry.

(b) Put a small mirror onto the
    line of symmetry. Look into
    the mirror and remove it
    quickly. If there was no
    difference in what you saw
    then it must be a line of
    symmetry.

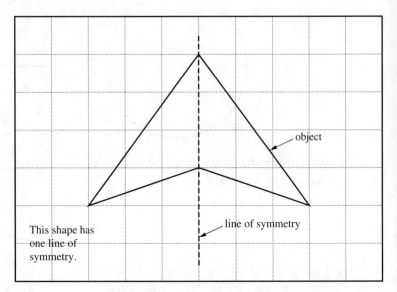

object

This shape has
one line of
symmetry.

line of symmetry

Exercise 1

Copy each of the following shapes and mark on the diagram all lines of symmetry.

1.

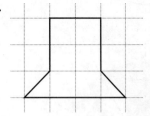

2.

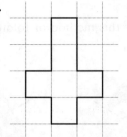

3.

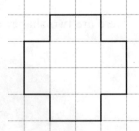

4.

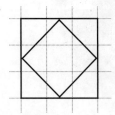

5.

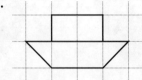

6.

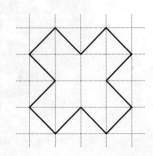

7. 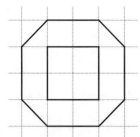   **8.** 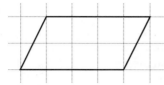   **9.**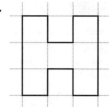

10. 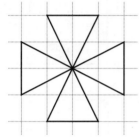   **11.** 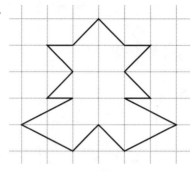   **12.**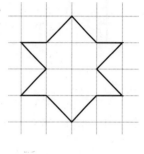

13. Design your own pictures with line symmetry.

Line symmetry puzzles

Shade in as many squares as necessary so that the final pattern has lines of symmetry shown by the broken lines.

(a)

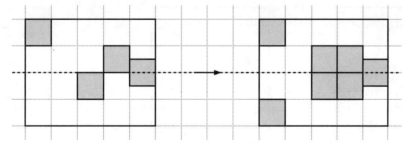

3 squares have been added

(b)

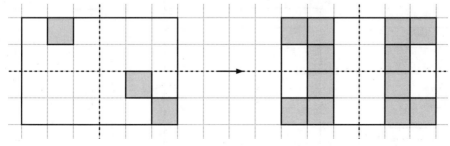

9 squares have been added

Exercise 2

Copy each diagram and, using a different colour, shade in as many squares as necessary so that the final pattern has lines of symmetry shown by the broken lines. For each question write down how many new squares were shaded in.

1.
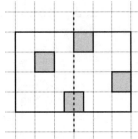

2.
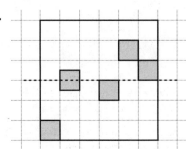

3.
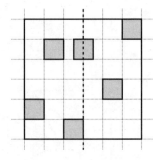

4.
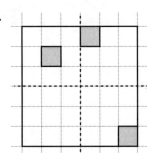

5.
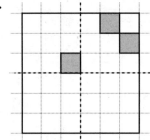

6.
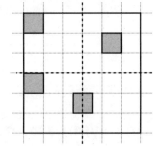

Be careful when the line of symmetry is a diagonal line. You can check your diagram by folding along the line of symmetry.

7.
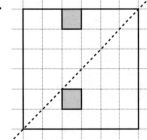

8.
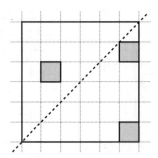

9.
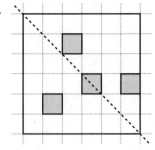

10.
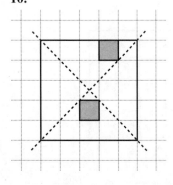

11.
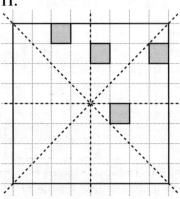

12.
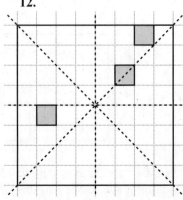

Investigating line symmetry

Exercise 3

1. You have 3 square black tiles and 2 square white tiles, which can be joined together along whole sides.

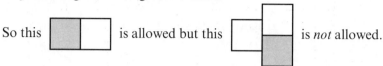

So this [ ] is allowed but this [ ] is *not* allowed.

Draw as many diagrams as possible with the 5 tiles joined together so that the diagram has line symmetry.

For example fig. 1 and fig. 2 have line symmetry but fig. 3 does not have line symmetry so fig. 3 is not acceptable.

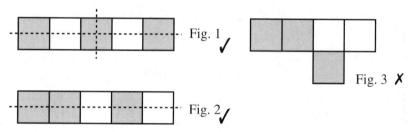

2. Now you have 2 black tiles and 2 white tiles. Draw as many diagrams as possible with these tiles joined together so that the diagram has line symmetry.

3. Finally with 3 black tiles and 3 white tiles draw as many diagrams as possible which have line symmetry.

Here is one diagram which has line symmetry

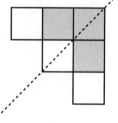

4. Shape A is a single square. 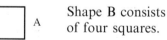 Shape B consists of four squares.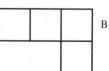

Draw three diagrams in which shapes A and B are joined together along a whole edge so that the final shape has line symmetry.

5. Shape C is a single square. Shape D consists of five squares.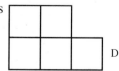

Draw four diagrams in which shapes C and D are joined together along a whole edge so that the final shape has line symmetry.

The tile factory: an activity

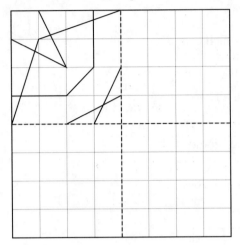

1. Copy this square and pattern onto the top left hand corner of a piece of A4 centimetre squared paper.

2. Lightly mark the reflection lines on the diagram as shown.

3 Use these lines to help you reflect the pattern across ...

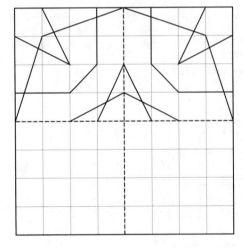

... and then down.

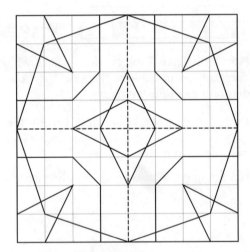

4. Repeat the process with the same tile so that your tile neatly covers the piece of paper →.

5. Now colour or shade in your work as neatly and symmetrically as you can.

6.5 Handling data

Bar charts and bar-line graphs

When you do a survey the information you collect is called *data*.
This data is usually easier for someone else to understand if you
display it in some sort of chart or graph.

(a) The scores of 35 golfers competing
in a tournament were

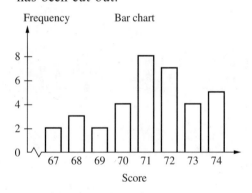

68	74	71	72	71	68	70
74	69	71	70	67	73	71
70	74	69	72	73	74	71
72	74	71	72	72	70	73
67	68	72	73	72	71	71

(b) A tally chart/frequency table is
made for the scores.

score	tally	frequency
67	||	2
68	|||	3
69	||	2
70	||||	4
71	ЖЖ |||	8
72	ЖЖ ||	7
73	||||	4
74	ЖЖ	5

(c) This data can be displayed on either a bar chart or on a bar-line
graph. The '⌐⌐⌐' shows that a section on the horizontal axis
has been cut out.

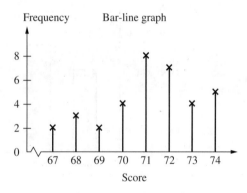

Exercise 1

1. In a survey children were asked to name their
favourite sport.
   (a) What was the most popular sport?
   (b) How many children chose Athletics?
   (c) How many children took part in the survey?

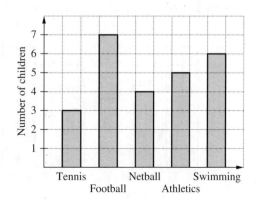

2. Here is a *bar-line graph* showing the number of children in the families of children in a school.
   (a) How many families had three children?
   (b) How many families were there altogether?

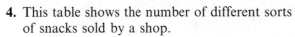

3. Collect your own data for a bar line graph like the one in Question **2**. Ask lots of people to state the number of children in their families.
   Draw a graph of the results and use colour to make it more attractive.

4. This table shows the number of different sorts of snacks sold by a shop.
   (a) How many snacks were sold on Thursday?
   (b) Each Aero costs 22 p. How much was spent on Aeros in the whole week?
   (c) Draw a bar chart to show the number of each kind of snack sold in a week.

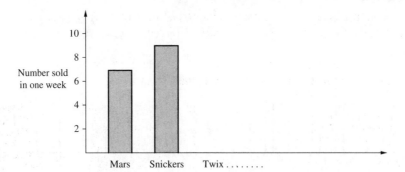

Nestlé®	Mon	Tu	Wed	Th	Fri
Mars	3	1	0	0	3
Snickers	0	4	1	2	2
Twix	2	2	1	3	4
Aero	5	0	0	1	4
Crunchie	2	3	4	1	1
Kit Kat	5	0	2	1	1

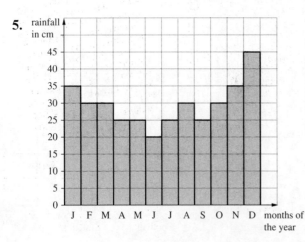

5. The monthly rainfall in the Lake District is shown left.
   (a) How much rain fell in August?
   (b) Which was the driest month in the year?
   (c) Which was the wettest month in the year?
   (d) In which months did 25 cm of rain fall?
   (e) In which months did 30 cm of rain fall?

6. Some children were asked to state which was their favourite T.V. programme from the list below.

Eastenders	E
Top of the Pops	T
Animal Hospital	A
Neighbours	N
Sister Sister	S

The replies were:

```
S N S A N E T T N A E T A E N
A S N A T E S E N S E N N E N
N A E N N E A A N S E A N A N
```

Make a tally chart and then draw a bar chart to show the results

		Tally	Total
EastEnders	E		
ToTP	T		
Animal Hospital	A		
Neighbours	N		
Sister Sister	S		

Frequency

7. In English some letters occur more frequently than others [e.g. there are more 'a's than 'z's]. In French different letters are more common.

Here are two paragraphs: one in English and one in French. There is the same number of letters in each paragraph.

The England football captain Alan Shearer walks up an ordinary suburban garden path in full kit. He rings the doorbell and asks, "Is Daniel in?", Daniel's mum shouts, "It's Alan", but Daniel is lying on the floor watching Dennis the Menace on the TCC (The Children's Channel) network. "I'm busy," he shouts and his mum shuts the door. Shearer rings the bell again. "He promised he'd come out," he complains, only to have the door shut on him again.

Eurogoals Magazine Les plus beaux buts des championnats européens de football Ce magazine hebdomadaire de cinquante-deux minutes présente une sélection des meilleures rencontres du Championnat espagnol, portugais, belge, néerlandais ou français. L'acent est mis sur les buts, et les matchs se soldant par un 0–0 sont systématiquement écartés. Les grandes équipes telles que l'Ajax d'Amsterdam ou le Real

(a) For each paragraph make a tally chart to record how many times the letters k, i, u appear.

(b) Draw a bar chart for each language and write a sentence about the main differences in the two charts.

Letter	Tally

Data in groups and line graphs

- Here are the ages of the people at a wedding.

33 11 45 22 50 38 23 54 18 72   5   58
37   3 61 51   7 62 24 57 31 27 66   29
25 39 48 15 52 25 35 18 49 63 13   74

With so many different numbers over a wide range it is helpful to put the ages into *groups*.

- Here is the start of a tally chart

Ages	Tally	Total (Frequency)
0–9	|||	3
10–19	⊪	5
20–29	⊪ ||	7
30–39		
40–49		
50–59		
60–69		
70–79		

- Here is the start of a frequency chart

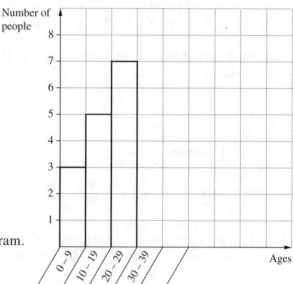

- Finish the tally chart and the frequency diagram. Notice that when the data is in groups the bars are touching.

Exercise 2

1. Shruti started with one frog but it laid eggs and now she has lots! One day she measures all her little pets. Here are the lengths in mm.

82 63 91 78 27 93 87   48 22 15
42 28 84 65 87 55 79   66 85 38

(a) Make a tally chart and then draw the frequency diagram.

Length (mm)	Tally	Frequency
0–20		
21–40		
41–60		
61–80		
81–100		

(b) How many frogs were more than 60 mm long?

2. Tom has lots of snakes and he likes to weigh them every week. The weights are shown.
   (a) How many snakes weigh between 61 and 80 grams?
   (b) How many snakes weigh less than 41 grams?
   (c) How many snakes does he have altogether?

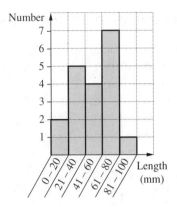

3.  Farmer Gray rears pigs. As an experiment, he decided to feed half of his pigs with their normal diet and the other half on a new high fibre diet. The diagrams shows the weight of the pigs in the two groups.

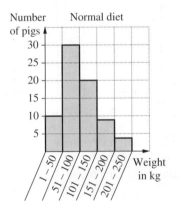 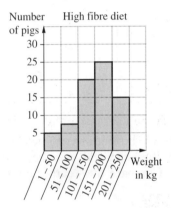

In one sentence describe what effect the new diet had.

4. Here is some information about fireworks.

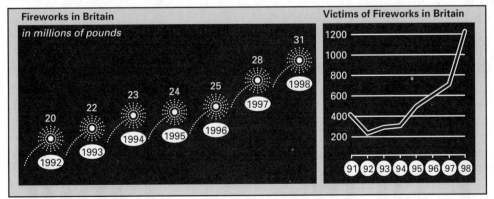

In which year were the lowest number of people injured by fireworks?

5. This diagram shows the temperature and rainfall readings in one week.

The rainfall is shown as the bar chart.

The temperature is shown as the line graph.

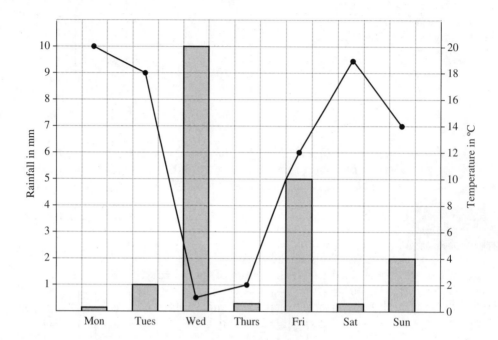

(a) Use both graphs to describe the weather on Monday.

(b) On which day was the weather cold and wet?

(c) Compare the weather on Thursday and Saturday.

6. The bar charts show the sale of different things over a year but the labels on the charts have been lost. Decide which of the charts A, B, C or D shows sales of:

(a) Christmas trees

(b) Crisps

(c) Flower seeds

(d) Greetings cards [including Christmas, Valentine's Day, etc.]

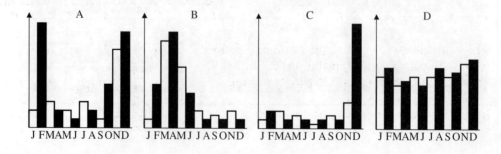

7. A car went on a five hour journey starting at 12 00 with a full tank of petrol. The volume of petrol in the tank was measured after every hour; the results are shown below.

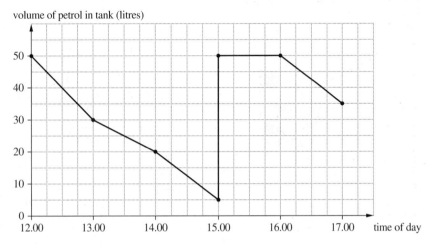

volume of petrol in tank (litres)

(a) How much petrol was in the tank at 13 00?
(b) At what time was there 5 litres in the tank?
(c) How much petrol was used in the first hour of the journey?
(d) What happened at 15 00?
(e) What do you think happened between 15 00 and 16 00?
(f) How much petrol was used between 12 00 and 17 00?

8. The number of people staying in two different hotels in each month of the year is shown below.

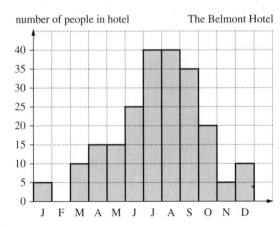

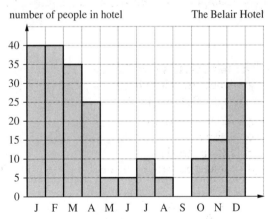

(a) How many people stayed in the 'Belmont' in July?
(b) How many people stayed in the 'Belair' in July?
(c) What was the total number of people staying in the two hotels in April?
(d) One hotel is in a ski resort and the other is by the seaside. Which hotel is in the ski resort?

Pie charts

In a pie chart a circle is divided into sectors to display information.
Pie charts are often used to show the results of a survey. The
sectors of the circle show what *fraction* of the total is in each group.
Here are two pie charts.

- How children go to a school in the Alps.

- People in a Spanish jail.

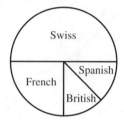

$\frac{1}{2}$ of the children walk to school

$\frac{1}{4}$ of the children swim to school

$\frac{1}{4}$ of the children hang glide to school

$\frac{1}{8}$ of the people were Spanish

$\frac{1}{8}$ of the people were British

$\frac{1}{4}$ of the people were French

$\frac{1}{2}$ of the people were Swiss

Exercise 3

1.

The pie chart shows the contents of a bar
of chocolate.
(a) What fraction of the contents is chocolate?
(b) What fraction of the contents is toffee?
(c) If the total weight of the packet is 400 g,
what is the weight of nuts?

2. In a survey children said what pets they
had at home.
(a) What fraction of the children had a hamster?
(b) What fraction of the children had a dog?
(c) 40 children took part in the survey.
How many of these children had a pet spider?

3. In another survey children were asked what *pests* they had at
home. $\frac{1}{3}$ of the children said, 'my sister'.
What angle would you draw for the 'my sister' sector on a pie
chart?

4. The pie chart shows the results of a survey in which 80 people were
asked how they travelled to work. Copy this table and fill it in.

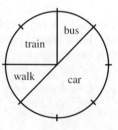

Method	car	walk	train	bus
Number of people				

5. In 1997 and 1998 children were asked in a survey to say which country they would most like to go to for a holiday. The pie charts show the results.

100 children answered in each year

Countries in the 'others' section had only one or two votes each.

1997

1998

(a) Which was the most popular country in the 1997 survey?
(b) Which country was less popular in 1998 than in 1997?
(c) *Roughly* how many children said 'Jamaica' in the 1997 survey?

6. A hidden observer watched Philip in a 40 minute maths lesson.

He spent: 20 minutes talking to a friend,

10 minutes getting ready to work,

5 minutes working,

5 minutes packing up.

Draw and label a pie chart to show Philip's lesson.

7.
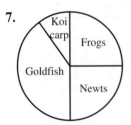

Jodie counted the different animals in her pond. Altogether there were 200 animals or fish.
(a) *About* how many frogs were there?
(b) *About* how many goldfish were there?

8. The children at a school were asked to state their favourite colour. Here are the results.

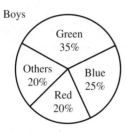

There were 40 boys   There were 25 girls

John says 'The same number of boys and girls chose red.'
Tara says 'More boys than girls chose blue.'
(a) Use both charts to explain whether or not John is right.
(b) Use both charts to explain whether or not Tara is right.

Michael Adman and the 'Vibe-Master 2000™'

PROFESSOR M. ADMAN

Professor M. Adman of the University of Central Barking, won this year's **P.I.O.G.C.V.** prize by inventing the fabulous 'Vibemaster 2000™'. This machine enables anyone to judge their own mood at any time of the day or night, and even to keep a record of what their day was like in the form of a graph.

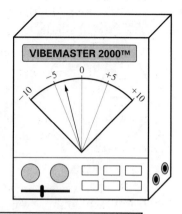

P – Pointless
I – Inventions
O – Of
G – Great
C – Commercial
V – Value

Prize Winner

VIBEMASTER™ mood scale Analyser		
	+ 10	Totally mega-cool, Hyper good vibes.
	+ 5	Fairly groovy, good karma, life's on the up and up …
	0	O.K., Fine, not bad, mellow.
	− 5	Could be better, some heavy vibes going on though.
	− 10	Real bad vibes, dull, unhappy miserable dude.

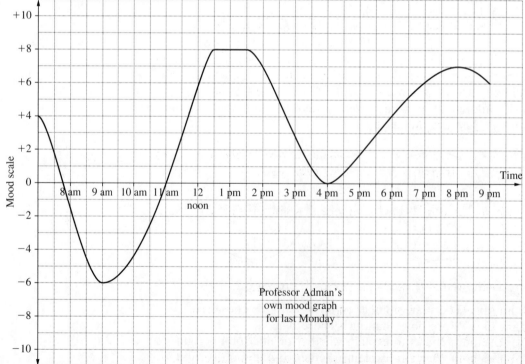

Professor Adman's own mood graph for last Monday

Exercise 4

Make a copy of Professor Adman's graph for last Monday. Use it to help you complete each of these sentences using the most appropriate option from the brackets to describe how he felt on each occasion.

1. 'I woke up in a (good/bad) mood'
2. 'I (was/was not) looking forward to work'
3. 'Work (was/was not) as bad as I had expected that morning'
4. 'The best thing about last Monday was (breakfast/lunch)'
5. 'After lunch everything seemed to go (right/wrong)'
6. 'The afternoon was full of really (good/bad) vibes, man'
7. 'By the time I left at about 5:30 p.m. things were getting much (better/worse)'
8. 'There were some really (groovy/dull) tunes on the radio which helped me chill out for the rest of the evening.'

Exercise 5

1. Draw a mood graph to describe what last Monday was like for you. Make a list of at least 5 sentences describing what happened during the day.

2. Draw a mood graph for each school day. Include registration, break, lunch, assemblies and the name of each lesson.
   By looking at the graphs Monday→Friday you have a record of the whole school week!

6.6 Mathematical reasoning

This section contains a wide variety of activities. There is no standard method for most of these problems. You need to think logically and should avoid guessing.

General statements

In each question below there is a *general statement* about numbers. Think of two examples which illustrate each statement.

For example, here is a general statement:
'The sum of three consecutive numbers is three times the middle number.'
A. $4 + 5 + 6 = 15$; $3 \times 5 = 15$
B. $7 + 8 + 9 = 24$; $3 \times 8 = 24$

1. Any odd number is double a number plus one.

2. A multiple of 9 is also a multiple of 3.

3. The product of two consecutive numbers is even.

4. A multiple of 12 is both a multiple of 3 and a multiple of 4.

5. Dividing a number by 0·1 makes the answer ten times as big.

6. The product of three consecutive numbers is a multiple of 6.

7. To multiply by 25, multiply by 100 and divide by 4.

8. The product of four consecutive numbers is 1 less than a square number.

Cross numbers without clues

Here are cross number puzzles with a difference. There are no clues, only answers, and you have to find where the answers go.
(a) Copy out the cross number pattern.
(b) Fit all the given numbers into the correct spaces. Work logically and tick off the numbers from lists as you write them in the squares.

1. Ask your teacher if you do not know how to start.

2 digits	3 digits	4 digits	5 digits	6 digits
18	375	1274	37 125	308 513
37	692	1625		
53	828	3742		
74		5181		
87				

2.

2 digits	3 digits	4 digits	5 digits	6 digits
13	382	2630	12 785	375 041
21	582	2725		
45	178	5104		
47		7963		
72				

3.

2 digits	3 digits	4 digits	6 digits
53	182	4483	375 615
63	324	4488	
64	327	6515	*7 digits*
	337		3 745 124
	436		4 253 464
	573		8 253 364
	683		8 764 364
	875		

4.

2 digits	3 digits	4 digits	5 digits	6 digits
27	161	1127	34 462	455 185
36	285	2024	74 562	
54	297	3473	81 072	
63	311	5304	84 762	
64	412	5360		
69	483	5370		
	535	5380		
	536			
	636			
	714			

5.

2 digits	3 digits	4 digits	5 digits	6 digits
21	121	1349	24 561	215 613
22	136	2457	24 681	246 391
22	146	2458	34 581	246 813
23	165	3864		
36	216	4351		
53	217	4462		
55	285	5321		
56	335	5351		
58	473	5557		
61	563	8241		
82	917	8251		
83		9512		
91				

6. *This one is more difficult.*

2 digits	3 digits	4 digits	5 digits	6 digits
16	288	2831	47 185	321 802
37	322	2846	52 314	
56	607	2856	56 324	
69	627	2873	56 337	
72	761	4359		
98	762	5647		
	768	7441		
	769			
	902			
	952			

Diagonals

Look at the squares below.

(a) Draw a similar diagram for a 7 × 7 square and count the squares along the two diagonals.
(b) How many squares are there along the diagonals of
    (i) a 10 × 10 square?   (ii) a 15 × 15 square?
(c) A square wall is covered with square tiles. There are 33 tiles altogether along the two diagonals. How many tiles are there on the whole wall?
(d) Another square wall has 40 tiles altogether along the two diagonals. How many tiles are there on the whole wall?
(e) A square wall is covered by 900 square tiles. How many tiles are there along the two diagonals?

Dominoes: an investigation

● A **domino** consists of two squares joined along an edge. There is only one shape a domino can be:-

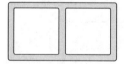

The above domino is 'double blank'. This is the basic domino, but there's only one in the set. This does not make for much of a game!
You can increase the number of dominoes in a set by using spots as well as blanks.

● Using 'blanks' and 'one spot' I can have this set of dominoes ...

(double blank)   (blank, one or   (double one)
                   one, blank)

There are 3 dominoes in this set.

Investigate:-

1. How many dominoes are there in a set using blank, one and two spots?

2. How many dominoes are there in a set using blank, one, two and three spots?

3. Continue this process until you can find how many dominoes make up a complete set containing blank, one, two, three, four, five and six spots.

4. How many spots are there altogether on a full set of dominoes?

Puzzles 1

1. The totals for the rows and columns are given. Unfortunately some of the totals are hidden by ink blots. Find the values of the letters.

(a)

A	A	A	A	28
A	B	C	A	27
A	C	D	B	30
D	B	B	B	
	25	30	24	

(b)

A	B	A	B	B	18
B	B	E	C	D	21
A	B	B	A	B	18
C	B	C	B	C	19
E	B	D	E	D	26
27	10	25	23	17	

This one is more difficult

(c)

A	A	A	A	24
C	A	C	D	13
A	B	B	A	18
B	B	D	C	12
16	18	15	18	

(d)

A	B	B	A	22
A	A	B	B	22
A	B	A	B	22
B	B	A	B	17
27	17	22	17	

2. Here are some black and white beads in a pattern

(a) What colour is the 20th bead?
(b) What colour is the 71st bead?
(c) What position in the line is the 12th black bead?
(d) What position in the line is the 12th white bead?

3. In these triangle puzzles the numbers
a, b, c, d are connected as follows:

$a \times b = c$
$c \times b = d$

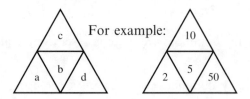

For example:

Copy and complete the following triangles:

(a)

(b)

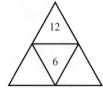

(c)

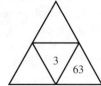

(d)

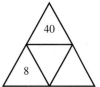

(e)

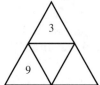

(f)

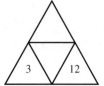

Puzzles 2

1. What is the largest possible number of people in a room if no
two people have a birthday in the same month?

2. The letters A, B, C, D, E appear once in every
row, every column and each main diagonal of
the square. Copy the square and fill in the
missing letters

				B
D				
				E
	A	D		

3. Two different numbers on this section of a till receipt are
obscured by food stains. What are the two numbers?

tapes at £ ●.99 :£87.89

4. Draw four straight lines which pass through
all 9 points, without taking your pen from the
paper and without going over any line twice.
[Hint: Lines can extend beyond the square].

5. Draw six straight lines to pass through all 16 points, subject to the same conditions as in question 4.

6. King Henry has 9 coins which look identical but in fact one of them is an underweight fake. Describe how he could discover the fake using just *two* weighings on an ordinary balance.

7. Write the digits 1 to 9 so that all the answers are correct.

6.7 Mathematical games

Biggest number: a game for the whole class

(a) Draw a rectangle like this with 4 boxes

(b) Your teacher will throw a dice and call out the number which is showing. (eg 'four')

(c) Write this number in one of the boxes.

| | 4 | | |

(d) Your teacher will throw the dice again. (eg 'two') Write the number in another box.

| | 4 | | 2 |

(e) Your teacher will throw the dice two more times (eg 'three' and then 'two') and again you write the numbers in the boxes.

| 2 | 4 | 3 | 2 |

(f) The object of the game is to get the biggest possible four figure number. The skill (or luck!) is in deciding which box to use for each number.

You score one point if you have written down the largest four digit number which can be made from the digits thrown on the dice. In the example above you score a point if you have 4322 and no points for any other number.

The game can also be played with 5 boxes or 6 boxes for variety.

Wordsearch

The wordsearch below contains keywords associated with Addition, Subtraction, Multiplication and Division.

Your targets are ... 15 words – Good
                  20 words – Very Good
                  30 words – Excellent.

D	N	O	I	S	I	V	I	D	E	X	B	H	E	A
I	P	Q	M	U	W	X	L	J	P	K	S	L	N	L
F	M	R	U	M	P	G	O	E	S	I	A	O	R	T
F	Y	C	L	S	H	A	R	E	D	N	I	T	R	O
E	B	U	T	J	U	B	L	E	F	T	J	S	K	G
R	D	F	I	O	K	B	H	Y	A	O	D	O	R	E
E	E	D	P	M	X	R	T	C	P	T	R	F	A	T
N	D	H	L	E	S	S	I	R	L	G	E	P	D	H
C	I	T	Y	N	P	L	U	S	A	Z	M	R	D	E
E	V	O	J	T	P	R	O	D	U	C	T	X	I	R
J	I	T	L	I	R	C	F	R	O	M	T	C	T	G
D	D	A	T	M	O	R	E	T	H	A	N	I	I	Z
S	Z	L	D	E	F	E	W	E	R	K	U	V	O	W
U	U	G	T	S	H	X	E	T	Y	E	M	C	N	N
M	I	N	U	S	J	K	R	X	W	T	X	O	P	Z

Boxes: a game for two players

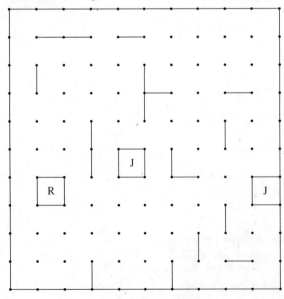

- Draw around the border of a 10 × 10 square on dotty paper (you can also use squared paper).
- Two players take turns to draw horizontal or vertical lines between any two dots on the grid.
- A player wins a square (and writes his initial inside the square) when he draws the fourth side of a square.
- After winning a square a player has one extra turn.
- The winner is the player who has most squares at the end.

In the game above J has two squares so far and R has one square.

'Lines': a game for two players

- Mark several points on a piece of paper (say 13 points).

- Players take turns to join two of the points with a straight line.

- It is not allowed to draw a line which crosses another line or to draw two lines from one point.

- The winner is the last player to draw a line.

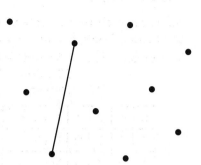

Polyominoes

- The *domino* has only one shape:-

- The *triomino* consists of 3 squares joined along complete edges. Here are both types of triominoes:-

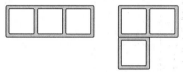

- The *tetromino* consists of 4 squares joined along complete edges

Task 1 Draw the five possible shapes for tetrominoes.

- The *pentomino* consists of 5 squares joined along complete edges.

Task 2 Draw the twelve different pentominoes.
*Note:- Shapes that can be fitted on top of each other are the same (congruent)

Here are some examples of Pentominoes ...

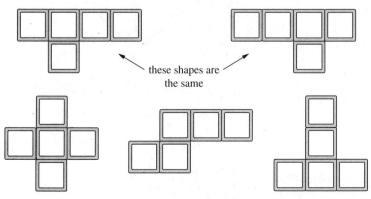

... which leaves you just 8 more to find!

Task 3
Here is a 6 × 5 rectangle which we have started to fill with *different* pentominoes.
Draw your own 6 × 5 rectangle and try to fill it with six different pentominoes.
Colour your design.

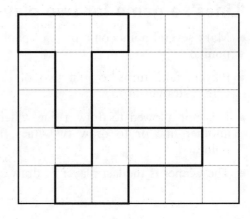

 Task 4
Draw an 8 × 8 square. Fill up the square with as many *different* pentominoes as you can. You will need a 2 × 2 'filler' somewhere in your design.

It is possible to make a design with all 12 different pentominoes.

 Task 5
[For enthusiasts!] Try to fit 12 pentominoes into a 12 × 5 rectangle. It is easier if you can draw your pentominoes on cardboard so that you can move them around. Good luck!

Radar battleships

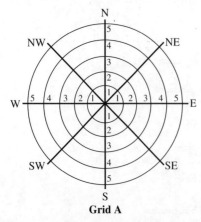

Grid A

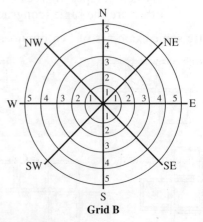

Grid B

Step 1. The two grids above are photocopiable from the teacher's answer book. Ask your teacher for two photocopies as the game is for 2 players.

Step 2. Mark your fleet on Grid A making sure you mark your
       ships and submarines where lines cross circles.

Example:-

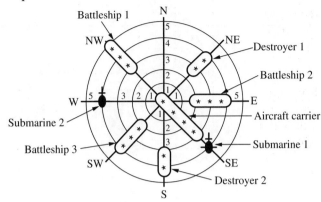

You are allowed:-

   3 battleships.
     (3 points in a line for each).

   2 destroyers.
     (2 points in a line for each).

   2 submarines.
     (a single point for each).

   1 aircraft carrier
     (4 points in a line).

Step 3. Decide who will go first

Step 4. Take it in turns to shoot at your opponents fleet. Record
       your shots on Grid B.

Step 5. After a shot your opponent must say 'hit', 'miss' or 'hit and
       sunk'!

- To sink one of your opponents fleet it must 'hit' in all places.

- You have to sink all of your opponents fleet to win.

- You describe a position by giving the circle number and compass
  direction:-

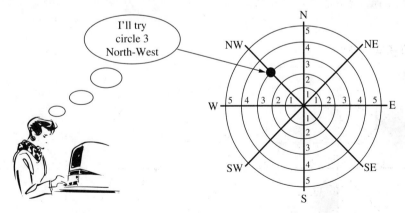

Don't forget to record your shots on Grid B ... good shooting!

Part 7

7.1 Numeracy tests

This section contains two numeracy tests each with fifty questions. A calculator is not allowed with either test.

Numeracy test 1

1. Write 87 in words

2. Write seventy-five in figures.

3. What is the value of the underlined digit in this number: 3<u>6</u>7?

4. What is $7 + 8 + 9$?

5. What is the sum of 5, 6 and 7?

6. What is 13 subtract 7?

7. What is 39 take away 17?

8. What is 7×8?

9. What are nine elevens?

10. What fraction of this shape is shaded?

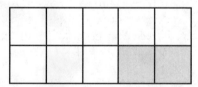

11. What is $24 + 19 - 11$?

12. What number divides 32 into 8 equal parts?

13. Work out $9 + 7 - 5$.

14. Write down the next number in this sequence: 5, 11, 17, 23, ☐

15. Write down the missing number in this sequence: 30, 23, 16, ☐, 2.

16. What fraction of the whole line is AB?

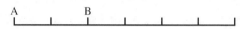

17. What is 50% as a fraction?

18. A pie is cut into four equal parts. What fraction of the whole pie is each piece?

19. Work out $24 \div 3$.

20. Fifty-five per cent of pupils in a school are girls. What percentage are boys?

21. What fraction of this circle is shaded?

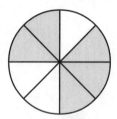

22. What is $2·2 + 3·6$?

23. What is $1·2 + 3·5 + 2·1$?

24. What is $\frac{3}{10}$ as a decimal?

25. What is the value of the underlined digit in this decimal: $0·1\underline{2}$?

26. What is the speed in km/hr shown by the pointer?

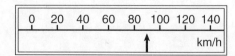

27. What is the reading on this scale indicated by the arrow?

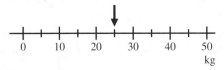

28. Estimate the length of this line in centimetres:

29. How much money is here?

30. What is the cost of 8 pencils at 9 pence each?

31. If I buy 5 cakes for 40 pence, how much does each cake cost?

32. If I buy a portion of chips for 57 pence, how much change will I receive from one pound?

33. How many 50 pence coins should I receive in exchange for 12 one pound coins?

34. A compact disc system costs £320. I am given a discount of £80. What price do I have to pay?

35. Four sisters share 72 pence equally between them. How much does each receive?

36. Each side of a square is 7 cm. What is the area of the square in cm^2?

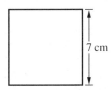

37. How many grams are there in 5 kilograms? (1 kg = 1000 g)

38. If 8 pints = 1 gallon, how many gallons is 24 pints?

39. Jean-Paul skis 7000 metres. How far is this in kilometres? (1000 m = 1 km).

40. How many litres is 3000 millilitres? (1 l = 1000 ml)

41. A piece of wood is 3 metres long. Thirty centimetres is cut off. How much, in centimetres, is left? (1 m = 100 cm).

42. What is the area of this rectangle in m^2?

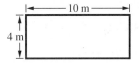

43. If 8 km is about 5 miles, how many miles is 48 km?

44. If there are 60 minutes in an hour, how many minutes is 4 hours?

45. A television programme starts at 18 30 and ends at 19 05. How long is the programme?

46. A 'CD' takes 45 minutes to play. I start the 'CD' at 12 35. At what time does it finish?

47. If I record a 35 minute TV programme on a 2 hour recording tape, how many minutes recording time do I still have on the tape?

48. What is the perimeter of this rectangle?

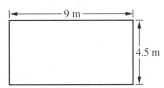

49. If a dog walks an average speed of 4 miles per hour, how far will the dog walk in 3 hours?

50. What is the average of 6 and 10?

Numeracy test 2

1. Write the number six hundred and fifty-seven in figures.

2. Write the number 703 in words.

3. What is the value of the underlined figure in this number: 9_8_13?

4. What is $537 + 246$?

5. What is $16 + 27 + 48$?

6. What is $78 - 19$?

7. What is $453 - 371$?

8. What is 9×6?

9. Work out 16×8.

10. What is $56 \div 7$?

11. Work out $725 \div 5$.

12. What fraction of the whole figure is shaded in this diagram?

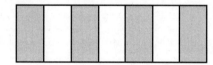

13. Write the next number in this sequence: 1, 3, 6, 10, 15, ☐.

14. Write the missing number in this sequence: 7, 18, ☐, 40.

15. Find the missing number: $36 - ☐ = 17$.

16. Find the missing number: $29 + ☐ = 44$.

17. Find the missing number: $☐ - 7 = 61$.

18. If 84% of people wear a wristwatch, what percentage does not?

19. What is 70% as a fraction?

20. What is $36 + 42 - 17$?

21. In which of the following diagrams is $\frac{5}{8}$ of the shape shaded?

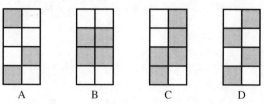

22. Write the fraction $\frac{6}{8}$ in its simplest form.

23. What fraction of the whole line is AB?

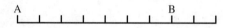

24. What fraction is 0·75?

25. What is $12·37 + 31·98$?

26. What is $3·14 + 2·52 + 1·31$?

27. What is the reading in kilograms shown in this scale?

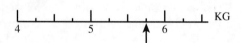

28. Estimate the length of this line:

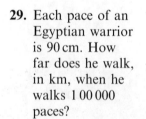

29. Each pace of an Egyptian warrior is 90 cm. How far does he walk, in km, when he walks 1 00 000 paces?

30. What is the cost of 5 chocolate bars at 32 pence each?

31. If you buy 3 tins of cat food for £2·16, how much did each tin cost?

32. If Ben spends £1·47 on his lunch, how much change will he receive from £2?

33. How many 20 pence coins can I exchange for £3·60?

34. A mountain bicycle  costs £500 plus 10% charge. much extra you pay for delivery charge?

35. A personal computer costs £350. In a sale it is reduced by 20%. What is the reduction in the original price?

36. Trisha, Stella and Vikky have lunch together and agree to share the cost equally. If lunch costs £24.99, how much should each pay?

37. A metal rod is 12 cm long. A piece 1 cm 2 mm is cut off. What length of rod is left in centimetres?

38. What is 4500 grams in kilograms?

39. A cross-country course is 5 km. How far is this in metres?

40. Over a month a man drank 36 pints of beer. How many gallons is this? (1 gallon = 8 pints)

41. What is the area of this square in square metres?

|←—30 m—→|

42. A rectangular bowling green is 15 metres long and 12 metres wide. What is its area in square metres?

43. What is the perimeter of this shape?

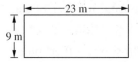

44. A train leaves St Pancras London at 13 20 and arrives in Sheffield at 15 35. How many minutes did the journey take?

45. A journey by bus takes 35 minutes. If Judith got on the bus at 14 45, at what time does she arrive?

46. A car travels at 60 miles per hour on a motorway. How far has it travelled after $2\frac{1}{2}$ hours?

47. A train covers a journey of 395 miles in 5 hours. What is its average speed in m.p.h?

48. A two hour cassette tape is used to record a radio programme. If the programme lasts 40 minutes, how much recording time is left on the cassette tape?

49. A marathon runner runs on average at 10 m.p.h. How many hours will she take to run 25 miles?

50. Three people are aged 12, 20 and 28. What is their average age?

7.2 End of book review

Review exercise 1   Number and algebra

1. In a 'magic square' all rows (◀——▶) columns $\left(\begin{smallmatrix}\uparrow\\\downarrow\end{smallmatrix}\right)$ and diagonals $\left(\begin{smallmatrix}\diagdown\diagup\\\diagup\diagdown\end{smallmatrix}\right)$ add up to the same 'magic number'. Copy and complete this magic square.

6		12	7
	4		
	16	13	2
10			11

2. Harminder has to visit a relative who lives 196 miles away. He stops for lunch after driving 117 miles. How much further does he still have to go?

3. In a new airport terminal, 25 new doors are required.

    (a) If each door is fastened by 3 hinges, how many hinges are needed altogether?

    (b) If each hinge requires 6 screws, what is the total number of screws required to fit all the doors?

4. A multi-storey office block has 104 offices altogether. If there are 8 offices on each floor, how many storeys does the building have?

5. Numbers are missing on four of these calculator buttons. Copy the diagram and write in numbers to make the answer 28.

$$\boxed{2}\boxed{8}\boxed{+}\boxed{}\boxed{}\boxed{-}\boxed{}\boxed{}\boxed{=}\boxed{2}\boxed{8}$$

6. Here are some number cards. $\boxed{3}\quad\boxed{4}\quad\boxed{7}\quad\boxed{2}\quad\boxed{9}$

    (a) Use two cards to make a fraction which is equal to $\frac{1}{2}$. $\dfrac{\square}{\square}$

    (b) Use three of the cards to make the smallest possible fraction. $\dfrac{\square}{\square\,\square}$

7. (a) How many 12 centimetre pieces of string can be cut from a piece of string which is 1 metre in length?

    (b) How much string is left over?

8. Look at this group of numbers ...

$$15,\ 9,\ 27,\ 24,\ 7$$

    (a) Which of the numbers is a multiple of both 3 and 4?

    (b) Which of the numbers is a prime number?

    (c) Which of the numbers is a square number?

9. Write down these calculations and find the missing digits.

  (a)   3 □ 4   (b)   5 □ 9   (c)   □ 2 □
       + 2 6 □   + 3 8 □   + 3 □ 4
        6 3 9   □ 2 5   8 0 0

10. The rule for the number sequences below is '*double and add 2*'. Write down each sequence and fill in the missing numbers.

    (a) $1 \rightarrow 4 \rightarrow 10 \rightarrow 22 \rightarrow \square$

    (b) $\square \rightarrow 6 \rightarrow 14 \rightarrow 30$

    (c) $\square \rightarrow 8 \rightarrow \square \rightarrow \square$

11. Charlie likes to use number patterns when he
   selects his lottery numbers.
   (a) Write down the next two numbers in
      Charlie's pattern:

   1, 3, 6, 10, <u>?</u>, <u>?</u>,

   (b) Charlie won £10 with this pattern

   1, 4, 9, <u>?</u>, 25, 36

   What was the missing number?

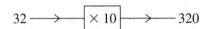

12. The numbers on the left have been multiplied either by 10, 100
   or 1000. Write the correct number in the boxes. The first one
   has been done for you. Copy and complete.

   32 ⟶ ☐× 10☐ ⟶ 320

   (a) 20 ⟶ ☐× ☐ ⟶ 2000

   (b) 1.1 ⟶ ☐× ☐ ⟶ 110

   (c) 25 ⟶ ☐× ☐ ⟶ 25000

13. This shape has $\frac{1}{3}$ shaded.

   Copy each diagram and shade the given fraction.

   (a)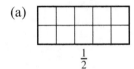

   $\frac{1}{2}$

   (b)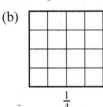

   $\frac{1}{4}$

   (c)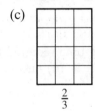

   $\frac{2}{3}$

14. Look at the following numbers …

   −9,   4,   0,   −2,   +5

   (a) Write down the positive numbers.
   (b) Write down the negative numbers.
   (c) Write the numbers in order, lowest to highest,
   (d) Write down the difference between the highest and lowest
      numbers.

15. Copy and complete this table showing equivalent fractions,
   decimals and percentages:

Fraction	Decimal	Percentage
	0·5	
$\frac{1}{4}$		
		75%

16. Look at the following input/output machine ...

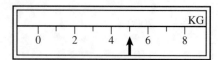

input ⟶ — ×10 ⟩ ⟶ — −2 ⟩ ⟶ output

Copy and complete this table using the machine above:

	Input	Output
	3	28
(a)	4	
(b)	7	
(c)	10	
(d)		108
(e)		148

17. Bob the butcher was weighing a turkey ...

KG

0   2   4 ↑ 6   8

(a) Write down the weight in kilograms of the turkey.
(b) Bob is selling his turkeys at £1·35 a kilogram. What price ticket would Bob put on this turkey?

Bob tells his customers that the cooking time for the turkey is 20 minutes per kilogram plus 20 minutes.

(c) For how long will the turkey on the scales above have to be cooked?
(d) What is the cooking time required for an 8 kg turkey?
(e) Convert your answer to (d) into hours.

18. Here is a sequence of diagrams showing an arrangement of counters ...

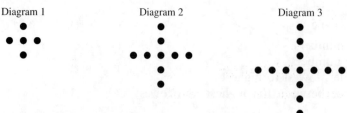

Diagram 1   Diagram 2   Diagram 3

(a) Draw diagram number 4.
(b) Copy and complete this table for the diagrams so far.

Diagram Number	Counters used
1	5
2	
3	
4	

(c) Without drawing, how many counters will be needed for diagram number 5?

(d) Write in words how you found your answer without drawing.

19. The diagrams below show three test tubes containing a liquid.

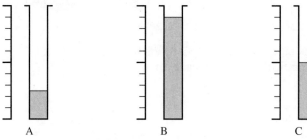

(a) Which of the test tubes above is 0·9 full?
(b) Which of the test tubes is $\frac{1}{4}$ full?
(c) Which of the test tubes is 50% full?

20. Which is larger ...
   (a) $\frac{3}{10}$ of £50   or   (b) 25% of £40?

21. An ice cream and a can of drink together cost 85p.

Two ice creams and a can of drink together cost £1·40.

(a) How much does one ice cream cost?
(b) How much would you pay for three ice creams and two cans of drink?

22. Find the number I am thinking of in each part:
   (a) If I take away 13 from it, I get 44.
   (b) If I double it, I get 350.
   (c) If I divide it by 10, I get 3·2.

Review exercise 2   Shape and space

1. Tara and Quentin had these shapes and they were asked to sort the shapes into two groups.

Tara chose shapes A, C and E. She gave Quentin shapes B, D and F.
(a) Who should have this shape, Tara or Quentin?
(b) Give a reason.

2. (a) Sort the shapes below into two groups and label them Group A and Group B.

 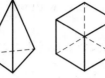

    Shape 1   Shape 2   Shape 3   Shape 4   Shape 5   Shape 6

(b) Give a reason why you put your shapes into groups 'A' and 'B'.

(c) Write down the correct mathematical name for each of the six shapes.

3. Listed below are various items that can be measured. Copy the list and insert next to each item the most suitable unit of measurement.

(a) The fuel tank of an aircraft.

(b) The mass of a packet of crisps.

(c) The height of your bedroom.

(d) The distance from London to Edinburgh.

(e) The amount of cough mixture on a teaspoon.

(f) The width of a postage stamp.

Units
1. centimetres
2. millilitres
3. grams
4. kilometres
5. litres
6. metres

4. Draw a grid like this ...

(a) Plot these points on the grid and join them up in the order given:
(2, 2), (3, 3), (3, 4), (2, 5), (5, 5), (4, 4), (4, 3), (5, 2), (2, 2)

(b) How many lines of symmetry does the shape have?

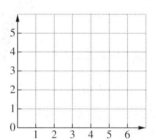

5. The diagram shows a logo for the 'Ace' sports company. It represents the letter A in 'Ace'. If each square is one square centimetre, work out the area of the logo in centimetre squares.

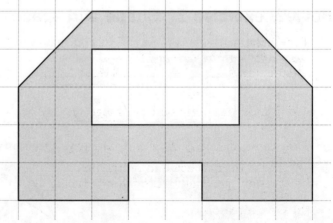

6. Calculate the area of each shape.

(a)

5 cm

9 cm

(b)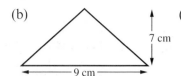

7 cm

9 cm

(c)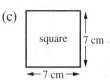

square

7 cm

7 cm

7. On squared paper draw these shapes:
(a) a quadrilateral with just one right angle
(b) an isosceles triangle
(c) a quadrilateral with no right angles and no parallel sides.

8. A piece of A4 size paper measures 297 mm by 210 mm.
(a) A money spider starts at a corner and decides to walk around all sides of the paper.
How far will the spider walk in millimetres?
(b) Change your answer in part (a) into centimetres.
(c) Has the spider travelled more or less than one metre?

297 mm

210 mm

9. A birthday card rests on a horizontal table.
Copy these sentences and fill the space with one of the words:

'vertical;   horizontal;   parallel;   perpendicular'

(a) The edge BC is _____ .

(b) The edge AB is _____ to edge AD.

(c) Edges DE and DC are _____ .

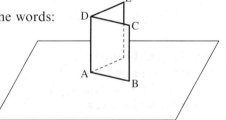

10. In each of the following diagrams, mirror lines are shown as broken lines. Copy each diagram and complete the reflections.

(a)   (b)   (c)

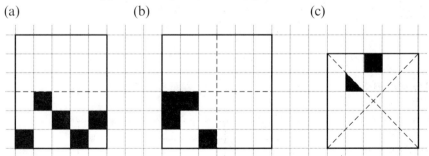

11. Here is a diagram of a designer's logo for 'speedo' training shoes:

(a) Make an accurate drawing of the logo using a ruler, pencil and protractor.
(b) Measure the length AB on your drawing.

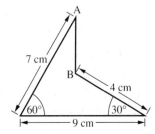

A

7 cm

B

4 cm

60°   30°

9 cm

12. Draw the shape on squared paper.
Draw the new position after it is
turned clockwise through one right
angle around the point A.

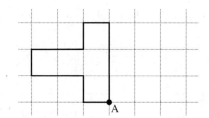

13. (a) Points A, D and E are three vertices of a
square. Write down the coordinates of the
other vertex.

(b) A, B and C are three vertices of a square.
Write down the coordinates of the other
vertex.

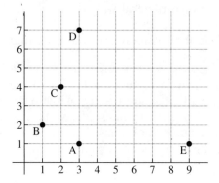

14.

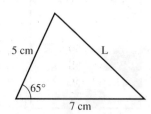

A ship is sailing around an island.
Copy and complete the missing compass
directions of the ship's journey.

East | then ⬜ then ⬜ then ⬜ then ⬜ then ⬜

15. On squared paper draw a four-sided shape which has one pair of
parallel sides.

16. Draw, as accurately as you can,
the triangle shown.
Measure the length marked L.

5 cm   L

65°

7 cm

17. ABCD is a rectangle.

(a) Write down the coordinates of A.

(b) M is mid-way between A and B.
What are the coordinates of M?

(c) N is in the middle of the rectangle.
What are the coordinates of N?

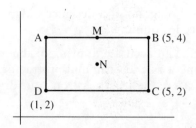

Review exercise 3   Handling data and probability

1. Here is a table showing the percentage of votes for the main political parties in the 1997 General Election predicted by various polling organisations:

Organisation	Labour vote (%)	Conservative vote (%)	Lib Dem vote (%)	Others (%)	Labour lead over Conservative (%)
Harris	48	31	15	6	17
NOP	50	28	14	8	22
ICM	43	33	18	6	10
Gallup	46	33	16	5	13
MORI	47	29	19	5	18
Poll of polls	47	31	16	6	16
Actual result	44	31	17	8	13

(a) Which organisations correctly predicted the Conservative vote?

(b) Which organisation was closest to predicting the Labour vote?

(c) Which organisation correctly predicted the Labour lead over the Conservatives?

(d) Represent the actual result of the election on a bar chart.

2. Eggs are sorted into size by weight. The weight is then converted into an egg size. The sizes range from 1 to 7.
Here are the weights of eggs produced by a farmer's chickens:

65, 56, 62, 69, 64, 51, 53, 57, 60, 59,
45, 59, 50, 57, 54, 58, 53, 59, 55, 58,
56, 46, 55, 44, 61, 55, 52, 70, 60, 56,
70, 66, 62, 42, 49, 63, 50, 57, 64, 72.

Copy and complete this table:

Weight (grams)	Size	Tally	Frequency
Under 45 g	7		
45–49	6		
50–54	5		
55–59	4		
60–64	3		
65–69	2		
70 g or over	1		

3. This chart shows the number of packets of different flavours of crisps sold by a shop.

	M	Tu	W	Th	F
Ready Salted	3	1	2	4	0
Salt 'n Vinegar	4	2	5	3	1
Cheese 'n Onion	5	1	3	1	4
Roast Beef	3	2	6	4	1
Prawn	1	1	2	4	4

(a) How many packets of crisps were sold on Wednesday?

(b) Each packet of Ready Salted crisps costs 15p. How much was spent on Ready Salted crisps in the whole week?

(c) This is a graph of one flavour of crisps.
Which flavour is it?

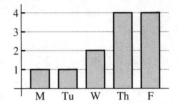

4. In a survey the children at a school were asked to state their favourite sport in the Olympics.
(a) Estimate what fraction of the children chose gymnastics.
(b) There are 120 children in the school. Estimate the number of children who chose athletics.

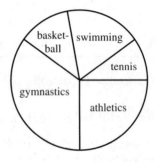

5. This bar line graph shows the number of bedrooms in the houses in one road.
(a) How many houses had 4 bedrooms?
(b) How many houses are in the road?
(c) Why would it not be sensible to join the tops of the bars to make a line graph?

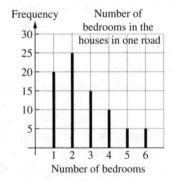

6. Some keen gardeners collect rain water from the roofs of their homes into rain barrels. They use the water from the barrel when the ground is dry to save using tap water.
Look at this graph and write down what you think is happening. Use the labels A, B, C ...

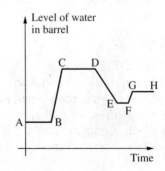

7. This scale shows the probability of events occurring:

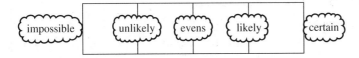

Here are four events:

A. You will have contact with water today.
B. You will not see a red car tomorrow.
C. A coin is tossed and it comes down tails.
D. You will be kidnapped by aliens going home from school in 10 years time.

Copy the scale and mark 4 arrows on it indicating where you would expect A, B, C, and D to be.

8. Here are two spinners
Say whether the following
statements are true or false.
Explain why.

Gill's spinner   Nick's spinner

(a) 'Gill is more likely than Nick to spin a 4.'
(b) 'Gill and Nick are equally likely to spin an even number.'
(c) 'If Nick spins his spinner eight times he is bound to get at least one 8.

9. A bag contains 1 blue ball, 3 red balls and 7 white balls.

(a) If I select a ball at random from the bag without looking, what colour ball am I most likely to select?
(b) What is the probability I select:
  (i) a white ball?
  (ii) a red ball?
  (iii) a green ball?
  (iv) a blue ball?

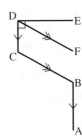

(c) After ten selections from a different bag, with the balls replaced after each selection, Tony has picked white 8 times and red twice. He says 'There are only balls of two different colours in this bag, red and white and there are more whites than red!'
What would you suggest to Tony to help him check his conclusions?

Practice test A

1. Look at the diagram opposite . . .
  (a) Name one pair of parallel lines.
  (b) Which pair of lines are perpendicular?
  (c) Write down an acute angle.
  (d) Write down an obtuse angle.
  (e) Write down a right angle.

2. Work out

(a)   139   (b)   592   (c)   53   (d) 4)68
    + 406   − 156   ×   9

    _____   _____   _____

3. Write down the names of the following two dimensional shapes:

(a) 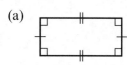   (b)    (c) 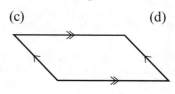   (d)

(e)   (f) 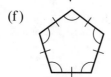   (g)    (h)

4. In the following diagrams write down the value of the angles marked with letters.

(a) 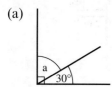   (b) 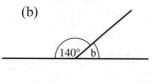   (c) 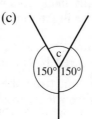   (d)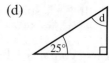

5. Find the area of the following triangles ...

(a) 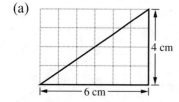   (b)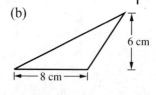

6. Find the value of each letter in the following equations ...
   (a) g −4 = 6, g = ?
   (b) n + 3 = 7, n = ?
   (c) 2p = 16, p = ?
   (d) r ÷ 3 = 21, r = ?

7. Solve the following balance puzzle, writing your answer x = ...

8. What six coins make eighty-eight pence?

9. What fraction of one complete turn is one right angle?

10. If 10% of pupils in a class are left-handed, what percentage are right-handed?

11. Change the following 12 hour clock times into 24 hour clock times
  (a) eight o' clock in the morning
  (b) four o'clock in the afternoon

12. Change the following 24 hour clock times into 12 hour clock times
  (a) 07·15   (b) 20·45

13. Round the following numbers as indicated
  (a) 56 to the nearest 10
  (b) 723 to the nearest hundred
  (c) 21,590 to the nearest thousand

14. Give the metric unit you would use to measure the following
  (a) The area of this piece of paper
  (b) The length of a double-decker bus
  (c) The mass of a hen's egg

15. The diagram opposite shows a room which is to be carpeted.
  (a) Find the area of carpet required to cover the floor.
  (b) What is the perimeter of the room?

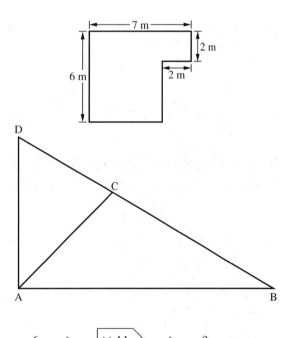

16. In the diagram opposite ...   ⟶
  (a) Measure angle AB̂D using a protractor.
  (b) Measure angle AĈB using a protractor.
  (c) What is the length of the line DB in centimetres?
  (d) What is the length of the line AB in millimetres?
  (e) What type of triangle is △ABC?
  (f) How many triangles can you see in the diagram?
  (g) What do all the angles in any triangle add up to?

17. (a) What is the output for this number machine ...

  (b) What is the input for this machine ...

  (c) What is the rule for this machine ...

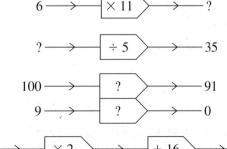

  (d) What was the input into this chain of machines ...

18. If ⬜ represents one square centimetre,
what is the area of this shape ...? ... ⟶

19. A recipe uses 3 eggs and 2 apples for every cake.
A chef has an order for several cakes.
He uses 24 eggs. How many apples does he use?

20. What is the area of a square of side 5 metres?

Practice test B

1. Give the value of the underlined digits in the following decimals
   (a) 3·1̲4   (b) 5·7̲2̲

2. Arrange the following decimals in order of size, smallest to largest
   1·37,   1·1.   1·172,   1·05

3. Work out:
   (a)   £3·87   (b)   £5·00   (c)   £3·75   (d) 4)£2·16
       + £2·43   − £1·67   ×   3
       ‾‾‾‾‾‾   ‾‾‾‾‾‾   ‾‾‾‾‾‾

4. Look at the following numbers ...   2,   3,   8,   9,   11,   15
   (a) How many numbers are odd?
   (b) How many numbers are even?
   (c) Write down the prime numbers.
   (d) Write down the number that is a multiple of five.
   (e) Write down the numbers that are factors of twenty-four.
   (f) Write down the number that is a square number.

5. In how many ways can you join the square X to shape Y along
an edge so that the final shape has line symmetry?

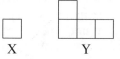

X   Y

6. Using the coordinate grid opposite   ⟶
write down the coordinates of
the following points ...
   (a) I
   (b) K
   (c) C
   (d) W
   (e) D
   (f) E

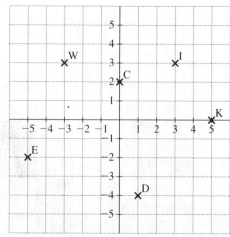

7. Copy and complete the compass directions for the compass below ...

8. Draw a factor tree to find the prime factors of sixty.

9. Write the missing numbers in the following sequences ...

(a) 1, 8, 15, 22, ☐, ☐ ...

(b) 1, 3, 7, 15, ☐, ☐ ...

(c) Write down the rule you used to find your answer in (a).

(d) Write down the rule you used to find your answer in (b).

10. Write each of the following in the units shown, using decimals when needed.

(a) 2 m 35 cm = ☐ m   (b) 350 g = ☐ kg

(c) 0·62 m = ☐ cm   (d) 3·3 kg = ☐ g

(e) 44 cm = ☐ m   (f) 27 mm = ☐ cm

11. Which of these shapes is split into quarters?

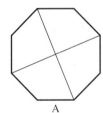   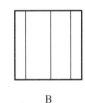

A   B   C   D

12. Write down what fraction of each of the following shapes is shaded.

(a)   (b) 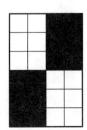   (c)

13. Draw the two patterns on the right
and shade in one more square so that
the final patterns have reflective
symmetry.

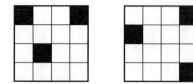

14. In a survey children were
asked to name their
favourite sport ...
   (a) What was the most
   popular sport?
   (b) How many children
   chose cricket?
   (c) How many children
   took part in the survey?

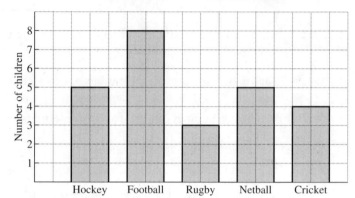

15. Twenty children were asked to estimate the number of 'Smarties'
in a tube. Here are their guesses ...

35, 50, 47, 30, 43, 45, 32, 35, 40, 35, 40, 36, 48, 32, 46, 43,
38, 37, 50, 39

Complete the following tally/frequency chart

Number of Smarties	Tally	Frequency
30–34		
35–39		
40–44		
45–49		
50–54		

16. Write down the probability of the following events occurring ...
   (a) When a fair coin is tossed it will come down 'heads'
   (b) You will roll a 'six' on a fair dice.
   (c) From a bag containing six red balls and one yellow ball you
   select a red ball

17. The diagram shows a spinner.
The letters on the probability scale below
(x, y and z) correspond to the chance
of getting blue, red or white on the
spinner. State which colours x, y and z
relate to.

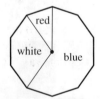

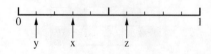

18. What fraction of the area of the rectangle is the area of the triangle?

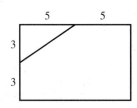

19. Here is a table of temperatures at 06·00 on the same day.
   (a) What is the difference in temperature between Rome and London?
   (b) At 12·00 the temperature in New York has risen by 5°C. What is the temperature in New York at 12·00?

London	−5°C
Paris	−3°C
Rome	+1°C
Melbourne	+11°C
New York	−8°C

20. The pie chart shows the most popular colours of cars after a survey.
There were 80 cars in the survey.
   (a) How many cars were red?
   (b) How many cars were blue or white?
   (c) How many cars were not red, white or blue?

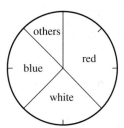

21. The line graph below shows the fuel gauge reading of a car at different times throughout a day ...

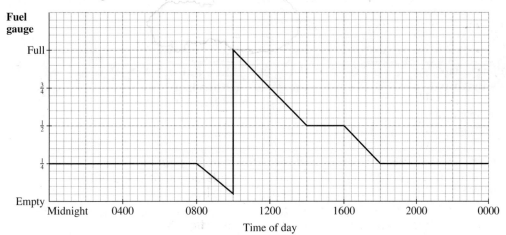

Time of day

   (a) Was the car moving or stationary between midnight and 8·00 am?
   (b) What happened to the car at 10·00 a.m.
   (c) How much petrol was used between 10·00 am and 2·00 pm?
   (d) At what time in the evening was the car put in the garage?

22. Work out
   (a) $\frac{1}{4}$ of £24 = ? (b) $\frac{1}{2}$ of £36 = ? (c) 25% of £48 = ?
   (d) $\frac{3}{4}$ of £80 = ? (e) 25% of £96 = ? (f) 75% of £1000 = ?

INDEX